Immigrant America

Immigrant America

European Ethnicity in the United States

Edited by
Timothy Walch

Garland Publishing, Inc.
New York & London / 1994

Copyright © 1994 by Timothy Walch
All rights reserved

Library of Congress Cataloging-in-Publication Data

Immigrant America : European ethnicity in the United States / edited by
  Timothy Walch.
      p.   cm.
    Includes bibliographical references and index.
    ISBN 0–8153–1609–7. — ISBN 0–8153–1665–8 (pbk.)
    1. European Americans—Ethnic identity.   2. European Americans—
Cultural assimilation.   3. European Americans—History.   4. Ethnicity—
United States.   5. Immigrants—United States—History.   6. United States—
Emigration and immigration—History.   I. Walch, Timothy, 1947–   .
E184.E95I46   1994
305.84—dc20
                                                                94–9522
                                                                CIP

Cover design by Patti Hefner
Cover photo credit: Eric Meola / The Image Bank

Printed on acid-free, 250-year-life paper
Manufactured in the United States of America

For Mary Winslow Irons,
descendant of the first English immigrants to America,
in gratitude for all that she has done
for her Irish-American son-in-law

Contents

Introduction

"Remember," said Franklin D. Roosevelt in a 1938 speech to the Daughters of the American Revolution, "remember always that all of us, and you and I especially, are descended from immigrants." The president was making an important point. From its first permanent European settlement in 1565 at St. Augustine in Florida, the United States has been a nation of immigrants. To be sure, time, distance, culture, religion, and language all had an impact on the nature of the immigration experience. But at the most basic level, the vast majority of Americans are descendants of immigrants.

Yet in spite of this common heritage, Americans have had an ambivalent attitude toward succeeding generations of immigrants. The Founding Fathers had frequently referred to the new nation as an asylum for anyone seeking equality of opportunity and freedom from tyranny. Yet none of these White Anglo-Saxon Protestant men ever envisioned a nation of multiple cultures and religions. It was assumed that every immigrant would, in the words of John Quincy Adams, "cast off the European skin" and become American.

Such was an erroneous assumption on the part of the Founding Fathers and their descendants. Millions of immigrants were attracted to the United States, but shedding their "European skin" was not among their highest priorities. They came to America for more fundamental reasons. They were fleeing political and religious oppression. They were escaping the ravages of poverty and famine. They simply were looking for work to support their families. The arduous and melancholic process of abandoning a European past and embracing an American future would take time, far more time than the American-born populace ever imagined.

These descendants of the first immigrants were not very patient, however. In fact, throughout the great century of European immigration from 1830 to 1930, native-born Americans pushed and prodded the nation's newest arrivals to become Americans or return to Europe. This campaigning was a mixture of optimism and despair punctuated with periods of violence. It was a long and arduous process for both the immigrants and the native-born population.

Yet in spite of the hostility and the violence, wave after wave of immigrants rolled into American ports during the nineteenth century. The decision to leave Europe for this new land had not been easy to make, and many family members argued that it was not a rational or wise decision. "For most immigrants," notes historian Philip Perlmutter, "optimism outweighed the pragmatic difficulties of moving, which were considerable, especially for adults who had to forfeit the security of friends and familiar places, overcome guilt feelings about having left aged parents, learn a new language, and cope with the uncertainty of living in a strange new land." Freedom and economic security were powerful incentives.

Like the process of immigration itself, the history of immigration has been written in several waves. The immigrants and their children established ethnic historical societies and published books brimming with pride and filio-pietism. For the most part, the function of these books was to chronicle past achievements and stimulate ethnic pride. More important, these books shared a single theme—that immigrants were an integral but often unappreciated part of the American experience.

The first scholarly history of immigration came from the pen of Marcus Lee Hansen in the late 1930s. A student of Frederick Jackson Turner, Hansen wrote of the immigrant as an individual pitted against the elements, not unlike the frontiersmen who so dominated Turner's work. "Hansen dismissed the role of government, ignored the family, and paid scant attention to ethnic differences," notes the historian John Higham. "Describing the myriad circumstances of the immigrants' departures and the varied origins from which they sprang, Hansen sought not to distinguish one strain from another, not to compare classes or nationalities, but rather to convey a common process."

Hansen was followed by Oscar Handlin, who published his extraordinary doctoral dissertation on Boston's immigrants in 1941. But it was *The Uprooted*, published a decade later, that made Handlin the foremost historian of immigration for the next twenty years. Even though he stressed the commonalities of the immigrant experience as Hansen had done, Handlin also put the immigrant into a broader social context. The immigrant was not a lone individual; he had a home and a family, friends and a religion, a neighborhood and a job. *The Uprooted* is an evocative, even passionate account of both the agony and the opportunity of the process of immigration and assimilation.

Hansen and Handlin shared a perspective on immigration, in the words of John Higham, "as an accumulation of responses that individuals made, bit by bit, to new conditions." Both historians wrote of the immigrant experience using the narrative form and their work remains valuable because of its ability to capture the drama and pathos of these great migrations.

But Hansen and Handlin only skimmed the surface of the immigrant experience. They described action and activity without fully exploring the subtleties of what happened or the motivation of the protagonists. A new generation of social historians emerged in the late 1960s intent on an in-depth investigation of immigrant culture on both sides of the Atlantic.

The end result has been a marked shift away from Hansen and Handlin in both form and focus. "Rebelling against narrative," adds Higham, "most social historians since the 1960s have sought meaning outside the old framework of incremental progressive change. In place of direction, the new social history fixes attention on constraint and resistance." Rather than the flow of experience, the new social historians focus on slices of time in specific places and study those moments intensely.

The work that has most directly benefitted from the work of the new social history has been John Bodnar's *The Transplanted*, published in 1985. Rather than focus on immigrants as individuals as Hansen did, Bodnar concentrated on the immigrant working class in all its manifestations, linking the world of work with home, family, and faith. "In Bodnar's telling," notes Higham, "the immigrant working class deserves our respect not for the heroic initiatives of its venture into a new world, or the embattled pride of its struggle there, but rather for its stubbornly conservative adaptation to forces it could not control."

To Bodnar's thinking, therefore, the European immigrant did not so much change as move in place. Ethnic culture was used as a shield against the relentless onslaught of change that was the American experience. To be sure, succeeding generations became increasingly American, but much of their experience was filtered through a prism of ethnicity. In fact, ethnicity has been and continues to be a permanent element of American culture. Millions of Americans continue to identify with their ethnic heritage many generations after their ancestors arrived in this country.

This collection of essays expands upon the themes developed by Bodnar and the current generation of immigration historians and much of their work is listed in the guide to further reading at the end of the volume. In many ways, this book mirrors the state of ethnic and immigration scholarship today. These are essays that explore neglected topics such as immigrant family life as well as essays that provide a new perspective on familiar subjects such as immigrants in the workplace. There are essays that utilize quantitative techniques as well as essays that offer a personal perspective. Taken together, the various chapters of *Immigrant America* provide additional evidence of the rich mosaic of experiences that constitutes the European ethnic heritage of the United States.

Immigrant America is divided into four parts, each one addressing a fundamental aspect of European ethnic life in this country. Part one is entitled "A Clash of Cultures" and addresses the fundamental conflict between the predominantly Anglo-Saxon culture of the landed generations and the diverse European cultures of the newly arrived immigrants. The clash precipitated confrontation and violence, but eventually led to compromise and assimilation by both the American-born and the foreign-born.

Part two, "Haven in a Strange New Land," is an effort to look into one of the most neglected sub-topics in American ethnic history—the immigrant home and family. The societal pressure to become American was filtered through the home and family. In fact, immigrant homes were laboratories that mixed together varying amounts of the ethnic heritage so important to the parents with liberal doses of the American ideas and values brought home by the children. The result was an amalgamation process that continued from one generation to the next.

"Agents of Acculturation," the third part of the book, focuses on three major institutions in the immigration process. Few people—immigrants or historians—would dispute the claim that religion, education, and employment were effective agents of assimilation. Religion offered consolation to those immigrants troubled by the loss of their past. Education provided direction and instruction to those immigrants looking toward their future in the new land. Employment offered the means to support a family and buy a home to those immigrants shut out of the European economy. Certainly religion, education, and employment were not the only institutions that promoted assimilation, but they were among the most powerful.

The last part of the book concentrates on the ever-changing contours of ethnic community in this country. Immigrant community life was rich and diverse and varied from region to region and from decade to decade. The image of immigrants as prisoners of slum tenements is a pervasive but inaccurate generalization. To be sure, many immigrants lived in ghettos, but millions of others owned homes and farms, held public office, and ran companies. They were all part of the definition of "ethnic community."

As is evident in the table of contents, *Immigrant America* is a collaborative effort by a diverse group of scholars from colleges and universities across the country. I am grateful for the willingness of these men and women to share their ideas on European immigration and ethnicity. I am particularly grateful for the continuing advice and support of Edward Kantowicz, who has guided my thinking on this topic. The value of this book is a reflection of their hard work and effort.

At its core, *Immigrant America* is an effort to add a few more pieces to the mosaic that is the history of American immigrant culture. Each of the essays that follows provides new ideas and information to students and scholars alike. Just as important, *Immigrant America* is a reprise of Franklin Roosevelt's admonition more than forty-five years ago: "Remember always that all of us are descended from immigrants."

Timothy Walch
Iowa City, Iowa
Constitution Day, 1993

Immigrant
America

PART I

A Clash of Cultures

Introduction

What does it mean to be "an American"? This has been a fundamental question in the United States for more than two centuries. During the first half century after the Revolution, American identity was closely linked to British social and cultural values. To be sure, the colonies had rejected the oppression of the British political system, but the new nation remained something of a cultural child of the British empire. The United States of America was largely white, Anglo-Saxon, and Protestant. Africans, Catholics, Jews, and other minorities had little impact on American culture during those years.

But in establishing a political system based on the principle of individual liberty, and in opening its borders to all who would risk a perilous ocean voyage, the American people laid the foundation for a new society that would become increasingly diverse. Evidence of this transformation was in every port by the 1830s with the arrival of tens of thousands of immigrants from Ireland and Germany. For the next century, America conducted a raucous and sometimes violent debate over the definition of "American."

In the years before the Civil War, the conflict was something of a moral crusade. Millions of Irish and German Catholics poured into emerging American communities in the Northeast and Midwest between 1830 and 1860. They were poor, illiterate, and many did not understand the English language. Even worse, they were followers of a foreign religion controlled by a pope in Rome. Could these new arrivals somehow be transformed into American patriots?

Many Americans had their doubts. Attacks on immigrant Catholics were common between 1830 and 1860. A convent was burned in Boston in 1836 and churches were attacked in Philadelphia in 1844. Protestant clergymen preached that the pope and the Jesuits were plotting to seize control of the country. These and many other incidents convinced Irish and German Catholics to build high the ghetto walls and prepare for a siege.

As Dale Knobel points out in the first essay in this section, the anti-foreign and anti-Catholic backlash against immigration reached its zenith in the nativist movements of the 1850s. Yet these nativists were more than reactionaries. They had their own ideology and their own political and social aspirations. As Knobel points out, nativists were ambitious in their effort to define the meaning of Americanism through the politics of exclusion.

But the nativist movement was highly unstable and organizations such as Thomas Whitney's Order of United Americans fragmented by the 1860s. Yet nativism as a reaction to immigration did not die. In the decades from 1860 to 1890, antagonism toward the foreign-born shifted from anti-Catholicism to racism. Many Americans agreed with a popular 1881 comment that "the best remedy for whatever is amiss in America would be if every Irishman should kill a Negro and be hanged for it."

The general animosity toward immigrant culture in the late nineteenth century was the result of several factors. Foremost, perhaps, was the rise in the number of immigrants from eastern and southern Europe. Many Americans believed that these Italians, Greeks, Poles, Jews, and other nationalities were little more than mongrels unfit for American society. It was racism pure and simple, but a racism that had a popular appeal among the native-born majority.

General animosity toward these new immigrants, as well as specific antagonism toward the German American population, became intense in the years from 1914 to 1924. With war on the horizon, America united against all things foreign. Immigrants were pressured to abandon their ethnic customs and language and even their names. "Americans All" became a national slogan.

The end of the war did little to diminish anti-foreign feelings. The federal government conducted a massive campaign against "subversives" in American society, most of whom were identified as immigrants or foreigners. State legislatures passed laws against the use of foreign languages in schools and Oregon went so far as to outlaw private schools as uncivic if not altogether un-American. It is not surprising, therefore, that Congress passed the Immigration Act of 1924. The golden door to America, wide open for more than a century, was virtually closed.

The unrelieved hostility toward the immigrants and their culture during that century generated a wide variety of responses. As David Salvaterra notes in his essay below, the debate over assimilation, pluralism, and ethnic identity continues to the present day. Some immigrants attempted to allay the fears of the majority by arguing that ethnic culture was fully compatible with American citizenship. The key word in the immigrant defense was freedom. Assimilation would come, they argued, but not at the price of personal freedom. One could be fully ethnic and still be fully American. Ethnic writers like Mary Antin and Louis Adamic explained this concept of dual loyalties in almost mystical terms.

But mysticism did not ameliorate the arduous process of assimilation, especially during the second and third decades of the twentieth century. This intense period of Americanization had its costs. As Betty Burch suggests in her essay, immigrants may have accepted the outward signs of Americanization, but they still felt alienated from American values. As Burch notes, they were marginalized—caught between two cultures. They captured their feelings of marginality in novels, short stories, and in other creative outlets.

The arduous process of assimilation and Americanization that began in the 1830s continues to the present day. At its foundation, the process is a clash of cultures. The three essays in this section outline the parameters and the price of the conflict.

CHAPTER 1

Beyond "America for Americans"
Inside the Movement Culture of Antebellum Nativism

Dale T. Knobel

> At the head of the procession was a cavalcade of about
> fifty horsemen, wearing the Continental hat and regalia of
> the Order, each carrying a baton; these were followed by
> the Grand Marshal and his special Aides, all mounted;
> next came the Chancery of New-York, preceded by
> Willis's magnificent band; and following the Chancery, the
> several Chapters of the Order, in five divisions, each
> escorted by a military corps, with bands of music.
> Washington Chapter made a magnificent display, having
> a car drawn by eight white horses, elegantly caparisoned;
> on the car was a massive temple, occupied by three young
> ladies, representing, in costume, Liberty, Justice, and
> Plenty, guarded by thirteen youths in naval uniforms,
> representing, with banners, each of the original States.[1]

This was the report of New York City's 1852 Washington's
Birthday parade orchestrated by a nativist fraternity, the Order
of United Americans. It is not too hard to make fun of this
colorful account and tempting to write off the OUA and other
organizations of its kind as havens for cranks and dreamers.
Almost any list of the nativist societies of the mid-nineteenth
century sounds odd to modern ears: "Brotherhood of the
Union," "United Sons of America," "Order of the American
Star." These are names that conjure up images of flatulent
rituals, whispered passwords, and comic-opera regalia.

Undeniably, the so-called "American" orders had all that, but amusement should not get in the way of our critical faculties.

Some assert that American nativism was an emotion, not an ideology, and Washington Chapter's "elegantly caparisoned" white horses and sailor boys make that easy enough to believe. Of course, we take seriously the sheer size and political potency of organized nativism during the decades preceding the Civil War, but this has not required paying much attention to nativist ideas. In fact, doubting the cohesive strength of nativist ideology, historians tend to focus on what pulled the movement apart from the outside: slavery, sectionalism, the temperance controversy.

But the movement had both ideology and ideologists—or, more accurately, its constituent organizations did. For these— like the Order of United Americans—ideology was more than self-justification but a whole way of looking at the world. As such, ideology was empowering, and those nativist organizations that devoted attention to the development of ideology attracted and retained many adherents thereby. But any full-fledged ideology also imposes demands, particularly the need to seem intellectually consistent, and consistency limits what an organization can say and how it can please members and prospects. Accordingly, even as ideology strengthens organization-based mass movements, it weakens them. This was demonstrably the case for the Order of United Americans and more typical of nativistic organizations generally than historians usually concede.

There has not been much encouragement to think of American nativism as a social movement possessed of a movement "culture" and suspended upon a framework of formal organizations. The Nazi era in Europe and the Civil Rights years in America taught historians and social scientists to trace racial, ethnic, and nationalist prejudices to societal rather than interest group conditions. Gunnar Myrdal, for example, termed white racism an "American dilemma" rather than a Southern dilemma or a Klan dilemma—and the idea stuck.[2] In turn, the tendency to view nativism in terms of "big" societal pressures rather than "small" organizational interests focuses attention exclusively upon its rhetorical identity and ignores all the little things that brought activists into nativist organizations, distinguished true believers from hangers-on, held constituencies together, and—ultimately—allowed adherents to fall away. American nativism is best remembered as an "anti" movement: against unregulated immigration, against the enfranchisement of the foreign-born through uniform naturalization procedures, and against the allegedly malign "foreign influence" in American life. "America for Americans" is its most early-recalled rallying cry. Yet a host of interests and issues brought nativists together, held them in organizations, and frequently drove them apart.

In 1907, when Albert C. Stevens prepared the second edition of his (still very useful) reference book, *The Cyclopedia of Fraternities*, he catalogued nearly seventy different organizations much like the Order of United Americans strewn across the preceding century. He discovered fully thirty-eight of these still active—some, in fact, newly formed. They actually represented one-tenth of all of the "friendly" societies in the United States' history (a broad array from the Masons to B'nai B'rith to the Grange) that Stevens was able to identify. Stevens called them "Patriotic and Political Orders."[3] Despite variations in specific aims and structure, they all shared this basic principle: that persons and things "native" demanded precedence over persons and things "foreign." They constituted, in fact, the organizational skeleton of the American nativist movement.

Lest we smirk at these organizations (and it is not hard to smile at the Order of the Little Red Schoolhouse, the Order of the Mystic Brotherhood, or the American Knights), be reminded that at the very time that Albert Stevens was compiling his institutional census, pressure was mounting in the United States for the imposition of a literacy test upon immigrants seeking to pass through the "golden door" and, beyond that, to place severe limits upon the admissibility of the foreign-born altogether. Was it only coincidental that membership in the "patriotic orders" peaked just before federal immigration restriction was instituted in the early 1920s or, for that matter, that the most serious efforts to suspend the routine naturalization of European immigrants accompanied the rise of the Order of United Americans and its sister societies seventy-five years earlier? To assume so would be to deny the signs of fire posed by the smoke. Close examination of one highly visible mid-nineteenth-century nativist fraternity and its most commanding leader may help us better understand the nativist "movement culture" which educated, emboldened, and sustained the enthusiasm of individual participants. At the same time, it may give us a better idea of the movement's weaknesses and the sources of its political failure (despite its ability to mobilize large numbers of adherents) in the late antebellum period.

No one may have worked harder at forging a systematic nativist ideology and applying it to organization-building than Thomas Richard Whitney of the Order of United Americans (OUA), a society he twice led as "Grand Sachem." To Whitney, the OUA was native Americanism's "Old Guard," the description he gave it in an 1855 Washington's Birthday address to draw attention less to its longevity than to what he believed were its uncompromised ideals.[4] By 1855, of course, the Order was being publicly overshadowed by the American, or Know–Nothing, political party. Leaving aside the hoary debate over the OUA's role in the rise of the new party (a debate in which Whitney himself played a conspicuous early part), it is useful enough for our purposes to accept Whitney's description of the Order as "a politico-benevolent institution [with] a beneficiary feature, something on the nature of Odd Fellowship."[5] It was organized in New York City in December 1844 as the American Brotherhood, following the demonstrated incohesiveness of supposed nativist voting strength at the polls the month before. Among the reported thirteen founders were such well-known and prosperous New Yorkers as James Harper and Simeon Baldwin but also a young engraver in his mid-thirties, Thomas Whitney. Renamed the Order of United Americans within a month of its founding, the organization grew rapidly. In less than a year, there were enough chapters in the metropolis and its suburbs to justify the creation of a state-wide executive agency. In 1846 it added its first Massachusetts offspring and in 1848 and 1849 spawned chapters in Pennsylvania, New Jersey, and Connecticut, necessitating a national leadership. Although local clubs could be counted in sixteen states by the mid-1850s, its strength always remained in New York State, particularly in the

City and the Hudson River Valley. There were some ninety
chapters state-wide in 1851. Whitney once put 30,000 as the total
number of New York State adherents, and if we are not too
particular about the depth of involvement by individual
members this represented, we may take it as not wildly
inaccurate.[6]

Among the most distinctive cosmetic features of the Order
were its faux-American Indian nomenclature (e.g., Sachems,
Wigwams, and Council Fires) and its filiopietism, especially with
respect to the American Revolution generation. The latter was
represented not only by the Order's emphasis upon its founding
by a sacred Revolutionary thirteen but by the names of the
chapters themselves. Of 45 New York chapters identified in 1851,
all but six were named for Founding Fathers, Revolutionary
battles, heroes of the Revolution and the War of 1812, or other
patriotic icons.[7]

Thomas R. Whitney flourished with the OUA itself. Born
in Norwalk, Connecticut, to a silversmith and watchmaker, he
moved with his family to New York City as a five-year-old in
1812. His father had not been nearly so prosperous or notable as
his grandfather and great-grandfather, both of whom had been
ship masters and local Revolutionary heroes. But for Whitney,
eventually, it was perhaps enough that his father had been
born—providentially—only six weeks after the Declaration of
Independence and died in 1812 just after the second war for
independence had broken out. This was little consolation for a
boy of five, however, and was made worse within a year by the
death of his mother, who followed four of her seven children to
the grave. Thomas Whitney may have been raised by relatives in
Connecticut or, perhaps, by an older brother, just a teenager
himself, who succeeded his father as a jeweller. In any event,
Whitney was out on his own at an early date, trained by
apprenticeship in the art of engraving. In 1830, at just 23 years of
age, he published a book on the subject, *The Young Draftsman's
Companion*. By that time, he had already been married three
years and had commenced on a family of five children, only
three of whom survived to adulthood. His wife died young, too,
and, turning pain into verse, in 1844 he published a collection of
exceedingly melancholy poems, *Evening Hours*.[8]

It was in 1844–1845, the period in which he participated in founding the OUA, that Whitney's prospects began—more than coincidentally—looking up. He became connected with New York newspaperman Mordecai Noah (a Zionist who propounded a theory that the native inhabitants of North America were the twelfth and lost tribe of Israel) in a new venture, the *New York Sunday Times*. He published an epic historical poem about the Seminole of Florida, *The Ambuscade*. And he represented the OUA at the grand nativist "unity" convention in Philadelphia in July. Better things happened in rapid succession. He was elected third Grand Sachem of the OUA (standing out a bit from the famous publisher and the wealthy businessman who preceded him but quite in line with the rice broker, ship grocer, auctioneer, tailor, sashmaker, truss seller, clerk, upholsterer, and picture frame gilder who succeeded him up to the Civil War). During the following year, 1847, he became editor and proprietor of his own newspaper, the *Sunday Morning News,* was elected to the Common Council of New York City, and shortly thereafter formed a new union with a second wife and severed an old one by leaving the OUA's Alpha Chapter to found his own Franklin #9, named for the patron of American printers. Somewhere in the next couple of years he picked up the courtesy title of "Colonel," apparently in connection with the recruitment of native-born-members-only militia companies, and in 1851 launched an ambitious monthly magazine, *The Republic*.[9]

In 1853 Whitney reprised his role as OUA Grand Sachem and, in 1854, was elected state Senator, salving the disappointment of a loss two years earlier in a race for Assemblyman (to, significantly, a German American Democrat). In November 1855, he was elected to the United States House of Representatives from New York City's Fifth Congressional District. During his first year in Congress, he published amidst considerable fanfare his *Defense of the American Policy*, at once a nativist manifesto and a promotional tract for the OUA. Falling seriously ill, he served out his term a near invalid and died just a few months out of office in early 1858. In twenty years, he had listed seven New York City addresses, each one just a little better than the last, finally ending his days on fashionable Broadway.[10]

My identification of Whitney as chief OUA ideologist rests especially upon his two-year tenure as editor and proprietor of *The Republic: A Monthly Magazine of American Literature, Politics, and Art*, which functioned as the Order's official organ until January 1853, when Whitney gave it up to press on with plans for a nativist weekly newspaper that ultimately never got off the ground. Based on Whitney's repeated complaints to subscribers about how many paying customers it took to support the journal, we can estimate that the magazine was delivered to between three and six thousand addresses nationwide, a modest publishing success. More than a one-man operation, *The Republic* was nonetheless undeniably Whitney's. He wrote regular feature articles, poems, and occasional fiction. The lengthy editorial section was his alone, apart from readers' correspondence. And on behalf of the OUA, he devoted the whole back part of each issue to organizational matters, discussing rules and regulations, chapter news, and ideology. In fact, almost all of the ideas he assembled in *Defense of the American Policy* he tried out here first. Even the magazine's cover page, which featured an aboriginal American and a Continental soldier gazing upon a prosperous nineteenth century American urban landscape, was Whitney's own artwork.[11]

But it was not only in print that Whitney functioned as ideologist. Throughout the early 1850s he kept up a relentless pace of weekly visits to OUA chapters throughout the northeast, answering their organizational questions and repeating lecture after lecture on "the principles and objects of the Order." The extent of Whitney's personal identification with the native American movement is perhaps best illustrated by one of his first and one of his last actions in Congress. As the House was organizing in the spring of 1856, a hostile lawmaker read off the names of putative nativist legislators. Thinking he had been omitted, Whitney called for the floor and demanded, "Have you read my name there . . . I was afraid my name was not on the list, and I wanted to have it set in." The next year, in the aftermath of Millard Fillmore's disappointing American party Presidential race, Whitney cut a lonely figure in the House trying futile stalling stratagems to prevent Congress's inevitable final reading and certification of the election results.[12]

Having access to the full run of *The Republic*, a number of Whitney's published speeches, scattered correspondence, and the relevant legislative journals, we can follow the workings of this ideologist and organizer. Looking closely, we can observe the centrifugal forces that Whitney's quest for ideological consistency unleashed within the OUA's rank and file, the strains placed on nativist organization by organizational imperatives themselves, and the efforts of the OUA not to be what historians are prone to tag nineteenth-century nativism—a one issue movement. In fact, Whitney's paramount concern seems to have been for his movement to have a stand on all the issues of the day—but always in consistency with the movement's particular world view. Such an examination will suggest some useful new lines of inquiry about antebellum nativism's rise and fall.

The editorial in the March 1852 number of *The Republic* listed the key goals and understandings of the Order of United Americans:

1. no State should have the ability to enfranchise immigrants
2. Congress should amend or abolish "wholesale naturalization" of the foreign-born
3. all levels of government should participate in the "rigid practice of economy in public expenditures"
4. the "public domain should be held as a sacred legacy to the people"
5. domestic "manufactures and the arts should be encouraged"
6. "a large army and navy are not needed"
7. the pay of public officials should be reduced.[13]

This is a rather more elaborate list than the usual nativist slogan, "Americans should rule America," would imply. Yet, for a serious ideologist like Whitney, it was essential that the movement follow the logic of its central ideas to stake out positions on a variety of mutually supporting issues. To Whitney's sorrow, they could also be mutually eroding.

Historians know quite well that nativism meant different things to different people—this, in fact, provided much of its appeal. It could equally serve private grievance, community frustration, and selfless patriotic anxiety. And—miraculously—it offered the same simple answer to each: that salvation would arrive when political power rested exclusively in the hands of "true Americans." Moreover, the movement line went, "true Americanism" was most easily identified in those of native birth. Birth on republican soil putatively promoted brotherly common interest, independence of character, loyalty to motherland, and other vaguely-defined attributes gained by imbibing the New World's ether of liberty. Accordingly, prominent among nativist objects was usually the reformation of the laws relating to franchise and citizenship so that the first could not come without the second and the second require a nationwide twenty-one-year waiting period for naturalization, mimicking the maturation of native-born youth.

Even on nativist terms, though, this formulation had problems. After all, the nativist interpretation of what constituted "true Americanism" was actually a cultural definition, and there was plenty of evidence that even native birth—much less twenty-one years probation—did not necessarily guarantee the religious, associational, and personal behaviors that nativists regarded as "native." Conversely, there were immigrants of less than twenty-one years' standing and natives with certain "foreign" taints whom nativists regarded as culturally and politically sound. Nativists usually finessed these logical problems by arguing that, on the one hand, you could be "in" but not "of" the republic if you were insulated by nativity and nurture in an immigrant neighborhood but, on the other, you could be acceptably American if you subscribed to the "foreign" Roman Catholic "religion" but resisted the demands of the "political church." Of course, there was plenty of illogic to this and it invited attack.

Recognizing the weaknesses in this line of argumentation, Thomas Whitney sent the Order of United Americans off in a different direction and tried, by sheer force of personality, to hold it there. The OUA called for no naturalization of the foreign-born—and thus no franchise rights as citizens—ever. "Naturalization," Whitney asserted, "may be appropriately called a misnomer, because the process of naturalization is one of the most unnatural of all proceedings," a mere contract "of a mercenary character" which could invest the recipient with legal "rights and privileges" but not "home sentiment," the key to authentic nationality.[14] "Sentiment" was important to Whitney, and he made it central to OUA ideology. He was mightily offended by what a later generation would call "hyphenization," repeatedly attacking anyone native or naturalized who would call himself "Irish-American" or "German-American" for lacking a truly American "heart." This sentimental element to nationality was also captured in the OUA's—and Whitney's—reverence for the heroes and icons of the American Revolution. Unwilling—as were most other nativist ideologues—to take the position that immigration itself should be entirely suspended, Whitney unflinchingly followed the logic of his position and propounded, in place of naturalization, a system of "denizenship" for the foreign-born that would confer what he called "social rights" (what we might term "civil rights") but not the vote. This, he argued, would allow immigrants to take advantage of America's personal liberty and economic opportunity without permitting them to corrupt the franchise or become captives of wily native politicians.[15]

To advocate creation of a class of permanent noncitizens was an innovation in a nation which had, often despite itself, gradually moved in the direction of more democracy rather than less, and Whitney faced up squarely to its implications. "I am no democrat . . . if democrat implies universal suffrage," Whitney boldly announced in *Defense of the American Policy*. That he was not. In fact, he took great pains to show that the United States was not and should not be a democracy but was rather a "republic" ruled on a representational basis by those with appropriate "intelligence . . . morals . . . and principles." Laying out a theory of human inequality closely modeled on Edmund Burke, Whitney averred that men might be "created" equal but that they did not develop the capacities for republican citizenship equally.[16] If the nation was to be composed of politically capable governors and politically incapable denizens, then it was necessary to argue the virtues of a "virtual" representation, which Whitney did with an enthusiasm that would have done credit to George III and Lord North. In this, he was advantaged by traditional republican rhetoric that forecast the degeneration of democracy into anarchy and despotism. But he paid relatively more attention to contemporary events in France, where what he called "universal suffrage" had lately been implicated in the "election" of a dictator—Napoleon III.[17]

Possessed of a certain internal logic, this was still awfully dangerous stuff for a movement trying to build a popular base. But Whitney drove the OUA line out even further onto thin ice. If native birth, love of country, and the New World's heady atmosphere were so irreproducible as to prohibit naturalization, what could be said about the large population of native-born black Americans, especially free blacks, and the real, aboriginal "native Americans"? Whitney dove right in, using *The Republic* to address the status of both in early 1852. Whitney's key editorial in the January issue denounced the "pseudo-philanthropists" of the African colonization movement: "We are utterly opposed to the proposition of a wholesale expatriation of the colored race. . . . We question very much the assumed right to remove them, or the policy of encouraging them to emigrate." Further, the native-born and bred black man was inherently more "American" than any European immigrant.[18] Remarkably, Whitney successfully dragged other members of the OUA hierarchy with him, the extreme being reached by Massachusetts Grand Sachem Alfred B. Ely, who propounded that even slaves were better suited (with appropriate education) to citizenship than those European immigrants "among us with habits of mind and body so formed and fixed under influences so totally different from . . . here."[19] This was hazardous language indeed for a movement that called itself "conservative."

Likewise, the OUA's faux-Indian lodge ritual and *The Republic's* regular articles on Indian antiquities and contemporary native American culture offered plenty of rhetorical opportunity to contrast the "native" feeling of the Indian with the "mercenary" adoption of citizenship by the naturalized immigrant. But led by Whitney, the OUA plunged onward. In early 1852, *The Republic* provided fanfare for OUA New York Chapter #41's induction of "a real North American," Indian activist and lecturer George Copway, ratifying a long-term relationship in which Copway played on nativism to enlist support for his proposed western Indian candidate state of the Union. The nativists used Copway to show how a combination of native birth, love of country, and Protestant education could produce an exemplary citizen. Consistent to the last, Whitney rose from the sickbed of terminal illness during his last Congressional session to denounce the depredations of white "savages" upon "civilized" Indians in Oregon and Washington and to bring into question the very premises of the emerging reservation policy.[20]

It would be historiographically convenient to write all of this off to a hyperbolic rhetoric that sought extremes of contrast to run down immigrants and Catholics. But it is not that simple. At the same time Whitney was defending the essential "Americanism" of native-born blacks, he was struggling mightily to persuade conservative northern Whigs and Southerners of all stripes that nativism was no cipher for abolition or free soilism. In championing Indian rights against the assaults of whites, the OUA was offending Westerners and Southerners simultaneous with renewed efforts to create chapters among them.

The same war between consistency and expediency was engendered by Whitney's treatment of religion and politics. While he adopted the standard nativist distinction between "religious" church and "political" church when referring to Roman Catholicism, he went one better, criticizing what he took to be political dabbling by any church, including the principal Protestant denominations. Theological and political thought, he insisted, were inherently at odds. Theology was "speculative" and unverifiable while republican politics was a "science." Churches—even Anglo-Saxon Protestant ones—should avoid taking public positions or pressuring parishioners on any subjects of political debate and clerics of all denominations should be barred from public office. Making good on its word, the OUA strongly objected to the new state constitutions of the 1850s that removed bars to clerical officeholding. Consistent this may have been, but it did not comport well with the popular enthusiasm in evangelical Protestant circles for concerted interdenominational political action that could counteract alleged Catholic influence upon government and the parties.[21]

Historians do not usually place the "rigid practice of economy in public expenditures" among the leading objects of antebellum nativism, but contemporaries listed it often enough and the OUA's Whitney tried hard to show that it was part and parcel of nativism's higher goals. One basis for it was the traditional republican fear of corruption: Give governors control over public wealth and they will abuse it in their own interest. But, perhaps more important, nativist parsimony was rooted in concern about the appropriate boundaries between local and national authority. Remember, one of their key positions was that only the nation should have anything to say about naturalization and enfranchisement, and they showed great sensitivity about local government overstepping its bounds.

But when Whitney tried to consistently apply this outlook, he stumbled into a quagmire. Sometimes, he merely found it necessary to oppose measures that everything else in nativist ideology indicated he should favor. Thus, as a Congressman, Whitney resisted funding a national school for consular officials which, as consistent critics of "political" consular appointments, nativists should have applauded.[22] And he got into trouble with nativist allies for taking a stand against prohibitionist Maine Laws in favor of moral suasion and individual conscience. His position was spelled out by C. D. Stuart, a regular contributor to *The Republic*, that reform "must be individual work, every man reforming himself." But these were relatively small prices to pay to preserve ideology.[23]

More dangerous was Whitney's position on the various homestead bills moving through Congress before and during his tenure in the House. He opposed them, calling each one "the land robbery bill." In Whitney's own New York constituency, this was not very popular and even less so in the states west of the Alleghenies where the OUA was intent on forming new chapters. The land was "national," Whitney insisted, and extreme care ought to be taken in giving it away. Of course, it did not help that the land would be given away, Whitney believed, to immigrants who would, accordingly, flood the West. Nor did it help that, in Whitney's eyes, the western states and territories were criminally liberal in extending to brand new residents—native or foreign-born—the right to vote. For this reason, in Congress, Whitney voted against both the admission of Oregon and the proposed constitution for the new state of Minnesota.[24]

Stuck with an unpopular position, Whitney sounded a populist note. Given away to homesteaders, the West would find its way by hook or by crook into the hands of "patricians." Divested of this valuable resource, government would look to higher taxes from everyone else. During the second session of the 34th Congress, Whitney took an especially strong position against distributing land in alternate sections to private railroad corporations unless it was for some obviously "national" object like tying east coast to west.[25]

The OUA's position—formulated by Whitney—on land, government, and the west was bound to bring trouble to the order, and it did. For if the nation controlled the public lands in the west, what authority did Congress have over the introduction of slavery into the territories? Could Congress act either to prohibit or to protect it? Did Congress only possess the right to do either until public land was organized by its inhabitants into a state? The inflexibility of the OUA's stance on the "national" character of the public lands did not leave much maneuvering room.[26]

Less troublesome, perhaps, but equally revelatory of Whitney's efforts to propagate a consistent nativist world view, was his championship of American "home" products, intellectual as well as material. Of course, it was nativist boilerplate to criticize the competition immigrants offered to American labor, but Whitney went a good deal further, arguing that it did no good to praise American workers and then buy fashionable foreign articles—among which, ever the engraver, he included art and literature. He repeatedly remarked the "anomaly presented between the political independence of this country, and her servile adherence to, and willing adoption of all literary opinion of a transatlantic character."[27] As good as his word, Whitney opened the pages of *The Republic* to young, unheralded American authors and poets and devoted regular attention to book and theater reviews. He was particularly proud of the effect it made when the famous American stage actor, Edwin Forrest, joined OUA Washington Chapter #2. Solicitous of struggling artists, Whitney created quite a stir in late 1851 when he criticized the financial management of the New York Art Union. Among his very last acts in Congress was to successfully remove a clause from the Coinage Bill which would have permitted the United States mint to compete with private engravers for a share of the business of manufacturing commemorative medallions.[28]

But these apparently innocent positions also had consequences—and dangerous ones. If native labor was to be defended, it had to be defended from an "aristocracy of wealth" as well as immigrant competitors. After all, Whitney reasoned, it was employers who took advantage of labor supply, not the supply itself, that drove down wages. At a time when bourgeois New Yorkers were celebrating A.T. Stewart's fabulous new department store, Whitney brought the attention of *The Republic's* readers to "the blood and flesh of . . . wives, widows, and children . . . coined into gold" in garret tailoring operations which kept Stewart's shelves full and called for a boycott. And, while Whitney had numerous friends on "change" (the stock and mercantile exchanges), he wondered about the efficacy of a proposed anti-gambling law that would stifle the recreation of the poor but leave "Wall-street, the private saloons of the money aristocracy" and their kind of gambling for "money or property" untouched.[29] Perhaps this explains why the OUA, usually identified with the conservative—and bourgeois—New York Silver Gray Whigs, displayed such hospitality to the more populist Order of United American Mechanics. In fact, for Whitney, the sticking point to united action between the nativist orders was much less the OUAM's labor activism than its retention of the twenty-one-year naturalization clause in its constitution. One wonders, though, how well union might have worked. Whitney's labor activism was of the nostalgic kind, a defense of the skilled "journeyman mechanic" who aspired to "dwell in his own cottage." This was more in keeping with the kinds of men who made up Whitney's original OUA Alpha Chapter, largely small retailers, craftsmen, and clerks mixed with neighborhood professionals. Consequently, while Whitney could wholeheartedly endorse a cooperative "Hat-Makers Union," he could not swallow the OUAM's call for a labor strike in Philadelphia.[30]

Thomas Whitney's efforts to assemble a coherent nativist ideology that was more than an unconnected series of expedient positions were not products of a self-destructive personality. Rather, Whitney pursued consistency because he saw it as the basis of political organization, as the basis of a party capable— because it had a world-view—of speaking on many issues. It has become historiographically fashionable to describe antebellum nativists as "anti-party," but the truth about many is that they were only "anti-parties." Like all would-be founders of new political movements, Whitney and most other nativist ideologists were resentful of the habitual loyalties of voters to the standing parties. The OUA itself emerged out of the disappointment of New York nativist politicos with the abandonment of the nativist ticket by former Whigs in 1844; Whitney would spend numberless editorials during the early 1850s bashing General Winfield Scott for being among those who used, then cast native Americanism aside.[31] But the OUA's chief complaint about the Whigs and Democrats as articulated by Whitney was that the parties had lost the ability to speak clearly on important public issues. It was alleged that the parties had become fragmented coalitions of diverse interests, that, accordingly, they adopted safe and fundamentally similar positions on key issues, and that (this, of course, a peculiarly nativist tenet) they had become willing to pay any price for a vote, allowing blocs of foreign-born voters to wield disproportionate influence. Whitney was particularly troubled by the imposition of national party labels and loyalties upon local issues; his participation in the New York City Reform League in 1852 was indicative of his frustration with municipal politics. *The Republic* treated it as evidence of the parties' bankruptcy that both the Whigs and Democrats turned to Presidential candidates with military credentials in 1852, pointing out that battlefield prowess was the lowest common denominator of political popularity.[32]

Whitney's response to the putative deficiencies of the old parties was to build a new one. Defending parties in the abstract as politically useful, Whitney employed the pages of *The Republic* to argue only that the contemporary parties' time was past.

Confronting a letter to the editor that asked whether the OUA was a "political institution," Whitney forthrightly answered that it was or aspired to be.[33] In fact, he viewed OUA chapters as local cells of a new "American" or "Union" party that would take its place alongside the existing party organizations. Given the irregularity of nominating procedures in antebellum America, one of Whitney's most appealing selling points was that nativist chapters would serve as neighborhood primary conventions. When Whitney was elected to the House as an American party member, he made sure that his first speech was a systematic exposition of the party platform. Party discipline was his special concern, and he bristled when legislators misrepresented what Whitney took to be American party orthodoxy.[34]

It was no accident that Whitney's chosen vehicle for propagating a nativist ideology and catalyzing the formation of a new political party was a fraternal benefit society. In fact, in light of the renewed attention historians have been giving to fraternal organizations in nineteenth century America, it is somewhat surprising that more has not been made of the role played by fraternalism in nativism's attractiveness to a mass following both in the antebellum period and later. In an age before social security or mutual life insurance, fraternal sickness, survivor, and funeral benefits had high value—especially for a peripatetic people who could no longer count on the support of an extended family and time-honored neighborliness. With credit reporting still in its infancy, there was no better business credential than fraternal membership or a transferrable lodge "withdrawal card" for a man on the move. "Brothers" provided customers, clients, and business contacts. If fraternity was useful, nativist fraternalism packed an especially strong ideological punch. For a movement concerned with unity and common culture, what made more sense than an order of "brothers"? If the problem with the political parties was that they were expedient coalitions called together to win elections, why not bind voters with similar outlooks to enduring organizations that had long-term acculturative and philanthropic objects?[35]

Whitney tried to fashion an Order of United Americans that modeled the sort of "nationality" he sought for the United

States itself. In place of the "hand of cold charity," the Order offered brotherly mutual obligation. In a mobile society where men were strangers, the "bond of the American brotherhood" created instant "friends." "It is national in its character, and almost holy in its origin: it springs from a love of country," Whitney enthused.[36] And, indeed, the OUA devoted substantial attention to the raising and distribution of fraternal benefits, to the dignified burial of the Order's dead, to the examination of new candidates for membership, and to commending mobile brothers to chapters afar. *The Republic* made the practical benefits of lodge membership plain, endorsing the hat emporium of "Brother Kellogg," the groceries of "Brother Haight," "Brother Souder's" ready-to-wear, and "Brothers Walnut and Radford's" oyster and dining saloon. The order's chapter rooms would be lyceums, providing continuing education on public issues and laboratories for personal leadership development. This, Whitney argued, was the appropriate function of "party."[37]

But like ideology itself, consistency in organizational matters had its costs. As the pages of *The Republic* clearly reveal, Whitney spent much of his time as an OUA trouble-shooter, responding to disputes over petty rules, adjudicating controversies over the distribution of fraternal benefits, and mediating intrachapter rifts. The opportunities that the OUA gave for political outsiders to become insiders were, in a sense, too effective. Ambitious men finding the way blocked to the chancellorship of old chapters repeatedly set off to create new cells they could call their own, fragmenting a few large and effective chapters into numerous small and weak ones. As in any organization, people grew restive with rules, were intolerant of personalities, and became jealous of rivals.[38] A tight organization was both the OUA's strength and its greatest weakness. In fact, once the native American movement had lost it bloom, the value of OUA lodge membership was so depreciated that it hemorrhaged brethren as much for the loss of practical fraternal value as for political impotency.

There is, of course, nothing inherently praiseworthy about ideological consistency or organizational sophistication. For all his sincerity, Thomas Richard Whitney espoused doctrines that we find quaint if not abhorrent. Whitney and his Order of United

Americans remind us, however, that mass movements like antebellum nativism have internal dynamics that we can ill afford to ignore. The Order of United Americans gained adherents not only because social and political developments on the outside directed men there but also because it had its own attractions, sometimes ideological and sometimes fraternal. Likewise, the fragmentation of nativism had internal as well as external causes. As Whitney, perhaps, discovered before his death, the constituency for a nativist mass movement was amoeba-like; when he prodded it into line on one side, it oozed out on another. It may be that the political discomfiture that Whitney experienced by painstakingly hewing to a nativist "logic" betrayed the bankruptcy of the ideology itself.

Notes

1. "Washington's Birthday," *The Republic* 3 (1852):156.

2. Gunnar Myrdal, *An American Dilemma: The Negro Problem and Modern American Democracy* (New York, 1944).

3. Albert C. Stevens, *The Cyclopedia of Fraternities,* rev. ed. (New York, 1907) pp. xviii, xvi.

4. Thomas R. Whitney, *The Union of States: An Oration Delivered before the Order of United Americans . . . on February 22, 1855* (New York, 1855), p. 17.

5. See Thomas R. Whitney to Millard Fillmore, July 25, 1856, Millard Fillmore Papers, State University of New York at Oswego, and Thomas R. Whitney, *A Defense of the American Policy as Opposed to the Encroachments of Foreign Influence* (New York, 1856), pp. 281–284 for discussions of the relationship between the OUA and Know-Nothingism; Whitney, *Defense of the American Policy,* p. 261.

6. "Growth of the Order," *The Republic* 1 (1851):284.

7. "Names and Addresses of the Delegates to Chancery, O.U.A., State of New York," *The Republic* 4 (1852):276–78.

8. To reconstruct the outlines of Whitney's early life see Stephen Whitney Phoenix, *The Whitney Family of Connecticut and Its Affiliates . . .*

From 1649 to 1878 (New York, 1878); Thomas R. Whitney, *The Young Draftsman's Companion* (New York, 1830); Thomas R. Whitney, *Evening Hours: A Collection of Poems* (New York, 1844).

9. OUA (November 18, 1848):4–5; John Hancock Lee, *The Origin and Progress of the American Party in Politics* (Philadelphia, 1855), 254; Frederic Hudson, *Journalism in the United States from 1690 to 1872* (New York, 1873), 283–87, 340; *The New York City Directory for 1848–49* (New York, 1849).

10. "The First Assembly District," *The Republic* 4 (1852):329; *The New York City Directory for 1854–55* (New York, 1855); "Death of the Hon. Thomas R. Whitney," *New York Daily Times* (April 13, 1858):4; U.S. Congress, House, *House Documents, Biographical Congressional Directory*, 57th Cong., 2nd sess., 1902–03, 920.

11. "A Weekly Organ," *The Republic* 4 (1852):53–4; "The Republic," *The Republic* 4 (1852):319; "Our Title Page," *The Republic* 1 (1851): 37.

12. "Magna Charta Chapter," *The Republic* 2 (1851):46; U.S. Congress, House, *Congressional Globe*, "State of the Political Parties," 34th Cong., 1st sess., 1856, Appendix: 352–53; U.S. Congress, House, *Congressional Globe*, "Votes for President and Vice President of the United States," 34th Cong., 3rd sess., 1857, 651.

13. "A Hint for Our Statesmen—Prospects of the American Republic," *The Republic* 3 (1852):255–257.

14. "Native Americanism," *The Republic* 3 (1852):308–309; Whitney, *Defense of the American Policy*, 135, 142.

15. "National Pride," *The Republic* 3 (1852):208–209; "Social Rights versus Political Rights," *The Republic* 4 (1852):157.

16. Whitney, *Defense of the American Policy*, pp. 126, 42, 33–5.

17. "Editorial: Reply," *The Republic* 3 (1852):262–263; Whitney, *Defense of the American Policy*, pp. 38–39, 19, 27–28.

18. "The Colored People," *The Republic* 3 (1852):40.

19. Alfred Brewster Ely, *American Liberty, Its Sources, Its Dangers, and the Means of Its Preservation—OUA Address, August 22, 1850* (New York, 1850):23.

20. "A Real North American," *The Republic* 3 (1852):105; U.S. Congress, House, *Congressional Globe*, 34th Cong., 3rd sess., 1857, 387, 916–19, 963; for a more thorough discussion of native Americans and "native Americans" see Dale T. Knobel, "Know-Nothings and Indians: Strange Bedfellows?," *The Western Historical Quarterly* 15 (1984):175–98.

21. U.S. Congress, House, *Congressional Globe*, 34th Cong., 1st sess., 1856, 152–53, 967–69; Whitney, *Defense of the American Policy*, 59–63;

"The Pulpit and Politics," *The Republic* 1 (1851):274; "Public Support of Private Institutions of Learning," *The Republic* 3 (1852):204–205; "Correspondence," *The Republic* 1 (1851):287.

22. U.S. Congress, House, "Consular and Diplomatic Bill," *Congressional Globe,* 34th Cong., 3rd sess., 1856, 214.

23. "Barnum's Museum," *The Republic* 3 (1852):101; C.D. Stuart, "Society Reforms," *The Republic* 2 (1852):194–95.

24. "The Land Robbery Bill," *The Republic* 4 (1852):216; "Where Shall We Land?," *The Republic* 1 (1851):178; U.S. Congress, House, "Admission of Oregon," *Congressional Globe,* 34th Cong., 2nd sess., 1856, 1455; U.S. Congress, House, "State Constitution for Minnesota," *Congressional Globe,* 34th Cong., 3rd sess., 1857, 519.

25. "Agrarian Laws," *The Republic* 3 (1852):186–87; "The Land Robbery Bill," The Republic 4 (1852):40–1; U.S. Congress, House, "Public Lands to Florida," *Congressional Globe,* 34th Cong., 2nd sess., 1856, 1221.

26. For an example of how Whitney tried to wiggle out of this dilemma see Whitney, *Defense of the American Policy,* pp, 201–03.

27. "The American Drama," *The Republic* 1 (1851):133.

28. "Amusements, Broadway Theater," *The Republic* 3 (1852):315; *New York Times* (January 9, 1852); U.S. Congress, House, "Cent Coinage Bill," *Congressional Globe,* 34th Cong., 3rd sess., 1857, 317, 342.

29. Whitney, *Defense of the American Policy,* p. 170; "The Way Men Build Marble Palaces," *The Republic* 4 (1852):103; "The Anti-Gambling Law," *The Republic* 2 (1851):81.

30. "New York Council, No. 10," *The Republic* 2 (1851):38; Whitney, *Defense of the American Policy,* p. 308; Directory, *Alpha Chapter #1 OUA* (New York, 1848); "A Valuable Invention," *The Republic* 2 (1851):276; "Strike," *The Republic* 3 (1852): 258.

31. "American Prejudice Against Americans," *The Republic* 2 (1851):269; "General Scott's Nativism," *The Republic* 4 (1852):46.

32. "The Next Presidency," *The Republic* 1 (1851):228; Whitney, *Defense of the American Policy,* pp. 217–20; "Foreign Demands for Public Office Intimidation of the Parties," *The Republic* 4 (1852):234; "The Municipal Party," *The Republic* 4 (1852):152–53; "General Scott in the Field," *The Republic* 2 (1851):82.

33. Whitney, *Defense of the American Policy,* p. 229; "Parties," *The Republic* 1 (1851):131; "Is It a Political Institution?," *The Republic* 3 (1852):214.

34. "A New Party," *The Republic* 4 (1852):328; "The Primary Elections," *The Republic* 3 (1852):309–310; U.S. Congress, House, "Organization of the House," *Congressional Globe*, 34th Cong., 1st sess., 1855, 52–53 and 1856, 172.

35. "The Future of Our Country," *The Republic* 3 (1852):207–08; "The Persecuting Order," *The Republic* 2 (1851):235.

36. "The Order: Its Fraternizing Influence," *The Republic* 1 (1851):284.

37. "Anniversary Celebration of Alpha Chapter," *The Republic* 2 (1851):282; "Duties of Chaplains of the Order," *The Republic* 3 (1852):321–22; "Ordinance No. 7 Relating to Candidates for Membership in the Order," *The Republic* 3 (1852):54; "Cards of Withdrawal," *The Republic* 3 (1852):269; "Business Notices," *The Republic* 2 (1852): 271–72; "Lectures," *The Republic* 1 (1851): 138.

38. See, for example, "Treason in the Camp," *The Republic* 1 (May 1851):238.

CHAPTER 2

Becoming American
Assimilation, Pluralism, and Ethnic Identity

David L. Salvaterra

Assimilation

"I was born, I have lived, and I have been made over."[1] With these words Mary Antin, an 1890s Russian Jewish immigrant, began her autobiography. Written in 1911 and published in 1912 at a time when Americans were very concerned about the impact immigration was having on their national character, Antin's account was surprisingly popular. Its popularity, according to Oscar Handlin, was due to the fact that it was both reassuring and representative.[2] It reassured Americans that the masses of recent immigrants could and would be remade, just as Antin claimed she had been remade, from immigrants into Americans. And, more importantly, her fellow Americans apparently accepted Antin's claim that her story was "illustrative of scores of unwritten lives."[3]

So thoroughly had she been remade by the experiences of immigration and assimilation that Antin regarded herself as having become a new person, totally different from the one she had been back in Polotzk, Russia. As she put it, in this process "*I* emerged, a new being, something that had not been before."[4] She felt so transformed that she regarded her earlier self as a "separate being"[5] and claimed "I can reveal everything; for she, and not I, is my real heroine. My life I have still to live; her life ended when mine began."[6]

Undoubtedly immigration and adjustment to a new culture and country were powerful experiences in the lives of those who underwent them. But what are we to make of Mary Antin's claim that a totally new person emerges from the process and that the "new" life is experienced as completely discontinuous with the "old"? Did all immigrants experience the same kind of decisive surrendering of old to new selves as one adjusts to a new land? Did they all experience these changes in more or less the same ways? Did they all make the adjustments in the ways Mary Antin did? In what sense was the older self "lost"? What was the "price" a person must pay in psychological and other terms while undergoing such a decisive loss and transformation? And finally, how were an immigrant's children, grandchildren and successive generations connected to the immigrant and his original culture?

The questions raised by Mary Antin's claims are at the heart of what is known today as "ethnic identity." Yet ethnic identity, as it is understood by scholars now, is a good deal more complex than Antin's account indicates. This essay will focus on the implications of Antin's claims and demonstrate that they are based on older understandings of what happens during the process of immigration and assimilation and to approach the subject by means of insights from both contemporary scholarship and other immigrant autobiographical sources.

Antin's views were powerful expressions of the traditional view of assimilation.[7] This view dominated discussions of the subject during the first seventy years of the twentieth century and was reinforced by popular understanding of the process of transformation. It might be summarized as follows: assimilation is equivalent to Americanization. But this proposition contained many assumptions that bear close examination. The individuals and groups involved were thought to bring a wholly different and homogeneous culture with them when they emigrated. When they arrived in the United States, a more or less automatic process of replacing that different cultural complex took place. The goal of this process was the complete replacement of the earlier culture by American culture. And this culture "swap" was both appropriate and good and constituted the total transformation of those involved from "immigrants" into "Americans."[8]

Symbolically the process was captured by the "melting pot" metaphor. Very different individuals and groups arrived here from many diverse areas and upon arrival their differences began "melting" away. Ultimately, of course, the "heat" in the "melting pot" blended and merged all into one homogeneous mass of undifferentiated American identity. This process was presumed to be unidirectional, inescapable, and salutary. It was the immigrant who was transformed; if the United States changed as the result of the process, the change was of secondary importance. The immigrant became American simply by coming to this country and being exposed to this culture.

The formation of a new being, as Antin called it, occurred whether or not the individual was involved consciously in the process. The outcome was progress, i.e. movement from a pre-industrial or pre-modern state to a modern one.[9] This was presumed to be beneficial on the two levels. It was good for the individual because he abandoned a temporary, undesirable and problematic status and achieved a permanent, desirable and un-problematic one. It also was good for the United States because a class of persons viewed chiefly as a serious social problem was transformed into citizens who conformed to American cultural and social values.

The term "melting pot" derives from the title of a play written by Israel Zangwill in 1908. No doubt the popularity of the play stemmed from the fact that it, like Antin's book, re-assured Americans about America's seemingly limitless capacity to melt all into one. Like her book, the play is also a celebration of Americanization and ever since it entered the popular im-agination the melting pot metaphor has been a staple of United States culture. In fact this is true to such an extent that it might be considered an important category of thought or cultural analysis.[10]

Scholarly interest in immigrants arose at virtually the same time as the publication of Zangwell's play and Antin's auto-biography. Record numbers of immigrants and concerns over their assimilation stimulated the first serious scholarly studies of ethnic phenomena at the University of Chicago in the first decades of the twentieth century. And the studies done by the sociologists at Chicago reinforced melting pot analyses in powerful and long-lasting ways.[11]

Albion Small, who founded the Chicago sociology department in the 1890s and chaired it from its beginnings through its formative stages, used Austro-German "conflict" sociological theories. Other early department members, especially William I. Thomas and Robert E. Park, applied "conflict school" thinking in their research and writings on immigrants. From the Europeans they derived the view that "traditional" or "peasant" culture and social organization differed greatly from "modern," "industrial" practices.

They saw the spread of industrialization as the explanation for migration in the first place and as the explanation for what happened to the migrants when they came into contact with the modern culture. Park refined these ideas into what has become known as the "ethnic cycle" or "interaction cycle."[12] According to Park, when individuals of more "backward" cultures encountered more "modern" ones, a cycle of initial contact, inevitable competition, accommodation and ultimately assimilation took place. That is, the modern would eventually "win" and be embraced by those who would inevitably surrender the premodern.

In the 1920s assimilationist sentiment was at its peak in this country. In fact, assimilationist assumptions were behind the restrictive federal government policies adopted during that decade. The Immigration Restriction Act of 1924 was the first such national policy ever adopted and drastically reduced the numbers of immigrants from the areas considered least desirable. Recent immigrants, particularly those from central and southern Europe, were the least "modern" and therefore hardest to "melt." Although the melting pot ideology had always been optimistic about America's melting capacity, some argued that excluding the least meltable ingredients from the pot would improve the "stew." By and large, however, the general scholarly and popular understanding of what took place would remain consistent for some time to come.[13]

In the 1960s sociologist Milton Gordon produced the fullest, most elaborate theoretical treatment of assimilation. He expanded Park's cycle and clarified the process through a seven stage model of the assimilation process. According to Gordon, there were seven possible levels of assimilation beginning with cultural or behavioral assimilation in which only acculturation occurs. The process then moved through structural assimilation, marital assimilation, identification assimilation, attitude reception assimilation, behavior reception assimilation, and finally civic assimilation.[14]

Movement through the successive stages involved progressive disappearance of differences. In cultural assimilation, or "acculturation," the newly arrived adopted only the culture of the new society. In the crucial second stage, structural assimilation, they were accepted into what social scientists call "primary group"[15] relationships. In the third stage, they intermarried or "amalgamated." In the fourth, they developed a shared sense of peoplehood with the culture's natives. In the fifth, prejudices against them disappeared and in the sixth, even discriminatory attitudes against them disappeared. Finally, they became so like the original population by the seventh stage that they had reached the point where their actions no longer provoked "value and power conflict."[16]

Gordon went beyond the melting pot analogy by demonstrating that there were lots of possibilities short of total assimilation and by specifying that any given group's assimilation might stop at any of the seven stages. He also maintained that a group's ability to assimilate might be inhibited by a number of factors, only some of which were under its own control. He shifted the focus away from the melting pot in that his model concerned mainly group changes rather than individual ones. Yet underlying his understanding were assumptions very compatible with a melting pot analogy.

He did this by means of a memorable hypothetical country he called "Sylvania." Sylvania "is made up of a population all members of which are of the same race, religion, and previous national extraction."[17] Then Sylvania experiences an influx of immigrants from "Mundovia." And Mundovians "differ in previous national background and in religion" from Sylvanians.

Eventually the group formerly constituting the Mundovians "has taken on completely the cultural patterns of the Sylvanians, has thrown off any sense of peoplehood based on Mundovian nationality, has changed its religion to that of the Sylvanians, has eschewed the formation of any communal organizations made up principally or exclusively of Mundovians, has entered into and been hospitably accepted into the social cliques, clubs, and institutions of the Sylvanians at various class levels, has intermarried freely and frequently with the Sylvanians, encounters no prejudice or discrimination (one reason being that they are no longer distinguishable culturally or structurally from the rest of the Sylvanian population), and raises no value conflict issues in Sylvanian public life."[18]

When they reached this point they achieved "the ultimate form of assimilation—complete assimilation to the culture and society of the host country."[19] And, although Gordon was careful to stipulate that this was an abstraction or "ideal type," it was clear from his discussion that this was what he felt could happen in the process of assimilation.

Quite apart from the difficulties of finding such countries as Sylvania and Mundovia, which are so culturally uniform and different from each other at the outset yet are so blendable in spite of initial differences, Gordon's ultimate or seventh stage was a melting pot: Mundovians "became" Sylvanians. Gordon did not really specify the complexities of moving from Mundovian to Sylvanian for the individuals involved; his focus was a higher societal or at least group one. Thus in his analysis, as in Chicago sociology and in melting pot ideology, the ones doing all the changing ("melting") are the immigrants. The changes were still unidirectional in that they brought about more and more thorough "Sylvanianization." And the ultimate outcome was still "good" in the sense that finally a common sense of peoplehood emerged due to the conversion of Mundovians into Sylvanians. This conversion allows serious value and power conflict to cease and presumably social harmony to prevail.

Pluralism

At roughly the same time as Gordon's book appeared, a significantly different perspective gained widespread popular support. Called "pluralism" or "cultural pluralism,"[20] it rejected the very bases of assimilationist or melting pot views.[21] Driven by the social upheavals of the 1960s and inspired by the various "liberation" movements of the time, pluralism celebrated and mandated diversity. Melting pot and assimilationist ideologies were depicted as coercive and destructive. Coercive because the immigrant was expected, in Geno Baroni's inelegant phrase, to "melt or get off the pot."[22] And destructive because it insisted upon eliminating valuable and legitimate human differences. When one people "melts" into another the outcome is no longer "good" but "bad," something irreplaceable is lost forever.

Additionally, assimilation ideology was now viewed negatively because it promoted homogenization. And homogenization resulted in vapid, characterless "mass" cultural blandness. This was underscored by fears about the impersonality and insipidity of mass culture and by individual alienation from it. People began to question: if I am just like everyone else, just who am I?[23] The focus shifted decisively from group to individual emphasis, from a need for social harmony to a need for personal meaning and fulfillment.

By the 1960s concerns about the ethnic element of America's national character had largely disappeared, mass immigration had long since ceased,[24] and the unique, the individual, the personal and subjective came to be valued and validated. Social harmony, moreover, was notably lacking in the decade and its lack came to be seen as more prevalent in our past than had been previously acknowledged. As the descendants of the new immigrants experienced significant social and economic mobility and left behind ethnic ghettoes to intermix with many combinations of other Americans, they expressed a renewed interest in their ethnic heritage and to value this heritage in ways their parents and grandparents never did.

This interest culminated in what was known as the "ethnic revival" or the "new ethnicity" of the 1960s and 1970s. Michael Novak declared some ethnics "unmeltable" and celebrated the

fact.[25] America, according to the supporters of the "new ethnicity," had always been able to thrive under conditions of far
greater diversity than we had imagined and undoubtedly would
continue to do so. Furthermore, ethnic diversity was now seen as
one of our country's great strengths. Ideologically, it seemed to
be closer to authentic Americanism to glory in diversity; it was
more "free" and "democratic."[26] Ethnic consciousness
flourished, ethnic studies programs and courses were
established at higher educational institutions, the study of
ancestral languages took on a greater importance to many
individuals, and ethnic cuisine, ethnic folk music and dress and
other manifestations of folk life became fashionable. White
ethnics became conscious of one another as they became
conscious of a shared historical experience and mobilized to
achieve political gains they felt were long overdue.

By the 1970s, pluralism had come to mean the opposite of
the melting pot.[27] Consider the following quote: "I'm a Jew
because I'm a Jew, and I would never have thought about
leaving Judaism, because what the hell for? . . . This is my
attitude: I was born a Jew and I'll die a Jew."[28] Similar dec-
larations of "unmeltability" were multiplied many times, re-
emphasizing the essential point that some, or all, portions of an
individual's sense of self must be preserved. Many Americans
sought a continuity between the past and the present and this
was both good and right.

And it was decidedly not true, at least in their minds, that
insistence on immunity from some or all assimilation made them
any less American. Quite the opposite. Michael Novak discovered and applauded what he termed the emergence of a new
and "unique psychological type: the pluralistic personality"[29] in
the United States. This individual was fully capable of loyalty to
ethnic heritage and to the public "superculture" of the United
States that merely "overlay[s]"[30] the particular ethnic cultures, all
of which retained their vitality and uniqueness.

Leonard Chrobot, a Polish-American priest, appended a
list of characteristics of what he called the "ideal" or "culturally
pluralistic Polish American" to his autobiographical reflections.[31]
He embraced at once both his past and his present, his "Pol-
ishness" and "Americanness." He was proud of both cultures,

did not feel any need for wholesale replacement of the one by the other. What he called for, instead, was valuation of both as equally valid, recognition that both contributed to who he was and would become in equally significant ways. And all of this made him very secure in his self-knowledge. "The ideal Polish American knows who he is."[32] "He knows the language, literature, and culture of at least two nations and is able to appreciate his own so much more."[33] "The mature Polish American must try to maintain the delicate balance between the old and the new ... [h]e must love and respect the land of his forefathers and his own land."[34]

Although pluralism has been used in a number of different ways in the past, it has recently come to displace assimilation as a form of "cultural coexistence."[35] It was important for the individual not to surrender all or most of his heritage. Part or parts must survive the Americanization process so that in the end the old culture in some form or another can coexist within the individual alongside the new culture. The old nativist fear that this would cause divided loyalty had been turned on its head. Cultural pluralists defined the phenomenon as a double rather than a divided loyalty and saw no conflict or contradiction between the past and the present. The parts are coequally shared and eminently combinable. In a new ethnic "mathematics"— cultural "addition" has taken place.

Scholars reinforced these popular perceptions with such works as Nathan Glazer and Daniel Moynihan's *Beyond the Melting Pot,* which declared that "the point about the melting pot is that it did not happen."[36] Andrew Greeley and others decried past efforts at forced Americanization.[37]

Ethnic Identity

Assimilation or pluralism? Cultural displacement or cultural addition? Were these the only alternatives? Are they necessarily antithetical? Are they universal? Do they exhaust the possibilities? Is there another, more satisfactory, way to look at the question? Recent scholarship has gone beyond assimilation and pluralism in a number of ways. The most important of these is that ethnicity and ethnic identity now dominate discussions.

"Ethnic" is a word that has had a long etymological evolution. It "derives via Latin from the Greek *ethnikos*"[38] and originally signified someone other than a Christian or Jew or, in other words, a pagan or heathen. Over many centuries it lost that meaning and acquired a generic one, coming to be applied in almost the opposite way to a group of people who shared some identity. Its current usage retains this sense of belonging, of membership in a certain group, rather than the outsider connotations of the original usage.[39]

"Identity," unlike "ethnic," is a term of surprisingly recent origin. It became a major conscious concern only in the 1950s due, in good measure, to the psychology of Erik Erikson.[40] It shared some of the same roots as the "new ethnicity" or cultural pluralist thought of the time in that its focus was the subjective individual's search for self. And the "new ethnicity" was itself an expression of many individuals' repossession of their ethnicity as a means of coming to terms with who they were, another way of asking and answering "Who am I?" But what exactly are ethnicity and ethnic identity?

"Who am I?" presupposes some perceived or felt difference to exist between two individuals and it presupposes a recognition of something identifiably unique in each individual that persists over time. Erikson felt it was "a process 'located' in the core of the individual and yet also in the core of his communal culture."[41] For Milton Gordon, surrounding an individual's "social-psychological core" were layers of identity attached in combination. Those layers closest to the core were the more fundamental to the individual's understanding of himself. Just beyond the core was national origin (what would today be called ethnicity), then just beyond that was religion, then race and finally nationality.[42] Other scholars understand the matter in different ways but there seem to be two basic views which differ over how the individual acquires the identity and maintains it but essentially concur that it is a complex and highly variable process.[43]

In 1973, at the height of the "new ethnicity," Nathan Glazer and Daniel P. Moynihan edited the first major treatment of ethnicity. In *Ethnicity: Theory and Experience*, they tried to account for the emergence of ethnicity and to specify how it operated in diverse specific cultural contexts. Many other theoretical and interpretive works followed *Ethnicity* and scholars have traced the meaning of ethnicity etymologically and historically.[44] And ever since these works ethnicity has been seen as a complicated and complex phenomenon. In a sense this involves attempts to elaborate upon things that both the assimilationist and pluralist models leave unspecified or unclarified. And when applied to understanding immigrant adjustment they shift the perspective and focus in significant ways.

Ethnicity is now understood to be a multifaceted, dynamic phenomenon. It emerges under certain circumstances and recedes or virtually disappears under others. Its content can be viewed as varying by individual and subject to change over time. It serves important purposes for individuals and is often utilized by them in functional and even in symbolic ways. Perhaps the most surprising recent findings have to do with how little relationship it can bear to ancestry. Finally, it is now understood to be surprisingly persistent, having survived in European-descended people to the fourth and fifth generations and beyond, albeit in greatly altered form.[45]

For most of the current century one of the givens of immigrant studies was summed up in Horace Kallen's observation that no one can change his or her grandfather.[46] That is, each person is a product of an unalterable ethnic makeup which is partly determined before and permanently transferred to an individual at birth. Ethnic heritage, therefore, is physical because it is genetic. It is also genealogical in that it is determined by gene concentrations unique to them and their individual families.

Cultural factors, of course, also play a similarly important part in this evolutionary process. One's "birth culture" is an assemblage of values, attitudes and behaviors, or "traits." One inherits cultural traits along with phenotypic traits and they are just as immutable and inescapable a legacy as that of one's ancestors. The cultural traits shared by one's ancestors were seen to be virtually identical to the gene pools they shared. Thus genealogy and culture interacted, overlapped and reinforced one

another and produced individuals who were indelibly stamped
with distinctive language, dress, diet, religion and other
distinguishing characteristics. Ethnicity, to put it in today's
terms, was seen as "primordial," "fixed," a matter of genes and
genealogy at birth and later on a matter of internalizing the
cultural traits of the homeland as a youth.[47]

If such a possessor of fixed traits remained within his or
her original culture no significant changes would occur. But emigration placed that person in contact with a new and discretely
different cultural "package." His genetic and genealogical
makeup persisted but his internalized original culture found
itself in competition for his allegiance with an alternative culture,
that of his new land. Mere exposure to this other culture dictated
that his initial culture would be supplanted at a pace that varied
from one individual to another.

What affected the pace of the change from the birth culture
to the "adopted" culture was the decision of the immigrant to
settle in an ethnic enclave in the culture of adoption. Within the
enclave the native tongue stood a better chance of survival
because it could be freely used. Ancestral religion could continue
because fellow communicants outnumbered worshippers of
other faiths or they may be effectively excluded altogether.
Within the enclave, also, a network of institutions, organizations
and individuals existed to keep the original culture as intact as
possible. Immigrant voluntary societies, fraternal organizations,
social, religious, and benevolent associations formed a cohesive
network which kept the original as alive as possible. So also did
the economic and cultural arrangements and institutions operated by fellow ethnics. It was here that one could most comfortably
dress, talk, eat, do business with and live one's original way of
life among primary group members who essentially shared it.
Here one's birth culture was replicated to the fullest extent
possible by others who valued it.[48]

Life in such an enclave was viewed by Milton Gordon and
others as constituting a "subculture."[49] As the immigrants
moved away from the enclave or subculture with its ethnic
support systems they exposed themselves more directly to the
model culture. Beyond the enclave or subculture there were no
buffers to help maintain traits and the immigrants invariably

adopted the dominant alternative. Intermarriage, spatial and socioeconomic mobility could carry one beyond the familiar confines of the enclave "community" fastest and most decisively. The essentially "defenseless" individual, immersed in the dominant culture, adapted, acculturated, and assimilated. The only role assigned to the adapting individual was that his or her absorption in the new culture was conditioned by the amount and type of "human capital" he/she brings to the process. Individual differences in intelligence, economic, social and psychological skills helped determine the speed and completeness with which his absorption took place.[50]

Undoubtedly there is much truth to the subculture v. dominant culture understanding. It surely must be easier to eat kosher food in an area where kosher butchers, groceries and restaurants are readily available. One is also a good deal more likely to speak Yiddish, maintain traditional Sabbath and holiday observances, and wear a yarmulke. It is a neighborhood where synagogues and rabbis are available, where few gentiles live and where many other individuals value those same things.

Social scientists and historians generally accepted this account of matters until fairly recently. Even proponents of the "new ethnicity" felt it was, in the main, an accurate representation of what happened. Then troubling questions began to surface that called this conventional wisdom into question. How can a resurgence of ethnicity be possible at the very time when those most involved in it and committed to it should have been expected to have become the most thoroughly assimilated? They had indeed moved away from the ethnic ghetto and out into the suburbs, had intermarried and had experienced significant socioeconomic mobility. Despite all of that change over time, they were more, not less, ethnically conscious and committed just at the time when assimilationists would have predicted complete absorption. How could it be that just the opposite was happening? Perhaps the nature of ethnicity needed closer examination. If pluralists were correct in assuming that ethnicity persists, were they also correct in explaining how and why? Many of their explanations hinged on some version of "Hansen's Law,"[51] that the "grandson remembers what the son forgets."

What they felt was at work was a generational dynamic which involved a "third generation return."[52] The original immigrant was ethnic by default, so to speak, having been given physical and cultural traits in his donor culture. By removing to the new host culture, he always remained culturally marginal both because of his permanent legacies from the homeland and because he had no opportunity or incentive to melt due to the buffers of his enclave community. Further, many immigrants positively resisted melting, reckoning it an abandonment of the "old country." His children, on the other hand, the "second generation," often grew up within the enclave but rejected its values because they were natives of the host culture, were educated in its schools, were more at home using its language, dress, values and traits. These would be the classic "hyphenate" Americans who often led "double lives" and had classically dual identities. They were in an intermediate stage between immigrants and Americans, they were "ethnics."[53]

Their children, the "third generation," were so far removed from the immigration experience and the ancestral culture physically and psychologically that they should have been thoroughly assimilated. Surely they had both physically and psychologically moved beyond the subculture to the larger culture. This expectation was reinforced by the alacrity with which their second-generation parents abandoned the cultural legacy of the immigrant ancestors. But were not the "third" and "fourth" generations the very mainstays of the "new ethnicity"? By embracing ties to the world of their grandparents were they merely obeying the operations of "Hansen's Law"?[54]

Their primordial heritage, psychically submerged by their parents' generation, resurfaced. The third generation was more comfortably American, no longer felt the sting of prejudice or ridicule experienced by their parents or the "guilt" the second generation felt for being "different." Different was "good" because it was nonthreatening to American culture and nationality so the third and later generations are much more free to embrace differences.[55]

Aside from surprise at the persistence of ethnicity, new questions arose from several other quarters. A broad anthropological conception of culture was adopted by social scientists and historians, and this made it possible to view questions about cultural transmission in a new light, one which allowed for far greater participation of the individual in the process.[56] It was also possible to understand that what were formerly viewed as "pre-modern" and "modern" were simplistic judgments, themselves cultural constructs or at least culturally conditioned.[57] They obscured the fact that donor cultures were anything but unitary and also the fact that a good deal of immigrant adjustment is now regarded as having taken place prior to migration.[58] And concern with ethnic identity itself raised some fundamental questions.

What if ethnicity is not primordial? What if it is culturally constructed, even a social "invention"?[59] Several scholarly advances made it possible to view it in this way. If it were strictly a primordial matter, how could it possibly be transmitted across generations? Specifying the precise contents of the genetic-cultural endowment of any given individual proved to be far more problematic than imagined. How much more difficult it was, then, to specify the precise endowment of an entire ethnic group.[60]

If ethnicity is primordial, membership is unproblematic, it simply belongs to those who share the physical-cultural legacy, the genes, the genealogy and the cultural package. Social scientists expended a great deal of energy attempting to specify such things, just what makes one "Polish" or "Italian," for instance.[61] But just what distinguishes one ethnic group from another is often more complicated than it might at first seem because intragroup differences are often just as great or greater than differences between members of the supposedly same ethnic group.[62] Also the realization that there never has been a single, monolithic "Polish" or "Italian" culture complicated the picture.[63]

Then social scientists suggested that a more fruitful way of looking at this issue might be to shift the focus. Frederick Barth, an anthropologist, suggested that emphasis should be given to "the ethnic *boundary* that defines the group, not the cultural stuff that it encloses."[64] Barth and his followers also insisted that we recognize that these boundaries are "social boundaries," that is, they are socially constructed and socially maintained and do not necessarily connect back to any discretely identifiable primordial characteristics.[65] In other words, membership is not automatic, based on an unalterable inheritance of genes and genealogy, but artificial in a sense, based as it is on on-going perceptual judgments. It is expressive of our urge to differentiate among the great masses of other humans, to select some as "like" us and some as "others," not "like us." Foregoing membership, therefore, must be a far different matter than merely a culture swap.

Taking this approach yet another step away from a primordialist understanding of ethnicity, Herbert Gans and other sociologists identified what they referred to as "symbolic ethnicity" or "situational ethnicity."[66] They were attempting to account for ethnicity's persistence beyond the point of assimilation. How did a sense of "differentness" survive beyond the third generation, the initial generation whose connection to the ancestor's culture is wholly historical, that is, based on absolutely no direct contact. The ancestry connection was so tenuous for such individuals, and the ethnic group to which the ancestors belonged had so long ago disappeared, that for these persons ethnicity, while undeniably real, must also be indisputably nonprimordial. On what could it be based, then, and what could it mean to such individuals?

In contemporary America ethnicity is, according to sociologist Mary Waters, "a dynamic and complex social phenomenon."[67] It is still based on information people have about their ancestry but their information is often incomplete, subjective, selective and even erroneous and this is essentially the one and only connection to the primordial. Nor is their construction of ethnic identity consistent throughout their lives. Indeed, Waters suggests that there is something like a life-cycle of changing ethnic identification for individuals and she further suggests that individuals choose identities from among various possibilities or they can even voluntarily choose to eschew an ethnic identity altogether.[68]

Sociologist Richard Alba suggests that there is currently a new ethnic group in the process of formation in the United States, the "European-American."[69] This new identity is based generically on descent from any European country and the specific country of origin makes no real difference. If Alba is correct this is a most striking and surprising example of what is known as "ethnogenesis," the process by which an ethnic group comes into being. Further, it is, according to Alba, not ancestry-based but based instead on ethnic identity. That is, it is not based on "descent" (primordialist) but on "consent," an individual's self-understanding.[70] If an ethnic group can come into being now, in the late post-European immigration phase of American history, how much more complex have the processes been in the past?

Many scholars have offered their own ideas on this complex issue. April Schulz suggests that assimilation be seen as a complex bargaining process in which those involved play a more direct role than has ever been acknowledged and that adjustment be seen as a mutual process whereby the immigrant adjusts to America and America adjusts to the immigrant.[71] Kathleen Conzen and others have demonstrated that ethnic festivals contained complex meanings among which were ones that enabled immigrants to appropriate Americanization on the group's own terms.[72] Kerby Miller suggested that ethnic identity for Irish Americans had a conscious ideological component. Werner Sollors has talked about "cultural mergers and secessions"[73] which allows us to view cultural contact and transmission as a process in which the former "victims" can be assigned a great deal more volition, choice and control than formerly believed.

We now realize that much more than human capital and settlement in an ethnic enclave are involved in the assimilation process. Significant institutional and attitudinal structural constraints limited immigrant life-chances.[74] Comparative and even cross-cultural studies have documented that members of the same immigrant group have had significantly different experiences of adjustment depending on the areas in which they settled.[75]

Historians of immigration have both broadened and deepened our understanding of all processes involved by extending discussions back to the donor countries and by identifying several of the major patterns discernible in migration. They have shown how selective it has been in terms of who migrates, from what parts of what specific countries and how specific it has been in terms of immigrant destinations and concentrations in certain jobs or trades in their new countries. In addition, these scholars have taught us to redefine just who was an "immigrant," to be dissatisfied with the classic new versus old immigrant dichotomy, and to replace it with a perspective that is globally and historically inclusive. And finally, they have established the "network" contexts of migration, destination and adjustment.[76]

What affect will all of this have on interpreting the processes of adjustment? It might be best now to view assimilation and pluralism as having been related dialectically in terms of historical usage rather than dichotomously.[77] And recent scholarship suggests they may well have been related dialectically in terms of historical experience as well. Neither assimilation nor pluralism alone explains why one individual enthusiastically embraces a new culture and abandons an ancestral one.[78]

Nor do they explain why another individual from the same original culture resists adjusting in all ways possible.[79] Nor do they suggest the entire range of individual responses that surely lie in-between. Nor do they, finally, offer any real clues as to the appearance or disappearance of ethnic groups over time.[80]

The experience of Mary Antin offers some concluding observations. Antin was enthusiastic about assimilation and reported a total transformation of self. But one must realize that embracing America was made all the easier for her because she rejected both her mother country and her ancestral religion. In her memoirs her pre-migration experiences were interpreted in a uniformly negative way, associated as they were in her mind with the persecution and oppression she felt. And her conception of America, by striking contrast, was uniformly and naively positive. Becoming American for her meant education and opportunity, a chance to leave behind a past experienced as constricting and limiting.

For every Mary Antin there were countless others who experienced adjustment in other and often fundamentally divergent ways. While she remembered her homeland with shame and embarrassment many others, especially of the original immigrant generation, found that their adopted land failed to measure up either to their expectations or to what they remembered of home. And while Antin eagerly and indiscriminately embraced all aspects of Americanization, many others resisted, bargained, conceded, cajoled and balanced components of a more complicated multiple-element identity. And it surely does justice to their historical experiences to recognize their daily adjustments as well as to recognize the ways in which they changed America in the process of becoming transformed from immigrant into hyphenate American into ethnic and finally just American.

NOTES

1. Mary Antin, *The Promised Land* [1912] (Princeton, 1969), p. ixx.

2. Handlin's foreword to the most recent edition of Antin's book was written in 1969, see Ibid., pp. v–xv.

3. Antin, *Promised Land*, p. xxi.

4. Ibid., p. xx.

5. Ibid.

6. Ibid., p. xix.

7. Social scientists refer to this as the "straight-line" view of assimilation. Ewa Morawska, "The Sociology and Historiography of Immigration," in Virginia Yans-McLaughlin, ed., *Immigration Reconsidered: History, Sociology, and Politics* (New York, 1990), pp. 187–238; See also Olivier Zunz, "American History and the Changing Meaning of Assimilation," *Journal of American Ethnic History* 4 (1985):53–72.

8. Stow Persons, *Ethnic Studies at Chicago, 1905–1945* (Urbana, 1987); Persons calls this the "Anglo-American burden," see chapter 1. Oscar Handlin's works are characteristic of this approach. See Handlin, *Boston's Immigrants: A Study in Acculturation*, rev. ed. (New York, 1972), and Handlin, *The Uprooted* (New York, 1951).

9. Philip Gleason, *Speaking of Diversity: Language and Ethnicity in Twentieth-Century America* (Baltimore, 1992). Especially relevant are chapters 1–3.

10. Werner Sollors, *Beyond Ethnicity: Consent and Descent in American Culture* (New York, 1986), chapter 3.

11. Robert E.L. Faris, *Chicago Sociology, 1920–1932,* rev. ed. (Chicago, 1970). This contains brief biographical sketches of the early members of the department at Chicago along with titles of doctoral and master's dissertations done by their students at Chicago up to 1935 in appendixes. See also Persons, *Ethnic Studies at Chicago,* and Fred Matthews, *Quest for an American Sociology: Robert E. Park and the Chicago School* (Montreal, 1977).

12. Persons, *Ethnic Studies at Chicago,* see especially chapter 4.

13. Gleason, *Speaking of Diversity,* see especially chapter 2.

14. Milton Gordon, *Assimilation in American Life: The Role of Race, Religion, and National Origin* (New York, 1964), see chapter 3, table 5, "The Assimilation Variable," p. 71 for a summary of the stages.

15. "Primary group" relations are those that take place on a "face-to-face" basis among people who are related in some way. They can either be actual relatives or merely fellow countrymen but in either case they live in close proximity and share many characteristics in common and the relationships would normally be marked by easy familiarity.

16. Gordon, *Assimilation in American Life,* chapter 3.

17. Ibid., pp. 68–70.

18. Ibid., p. 69, emphasis added.

19. Ibid., p. 69.

20. Horace Kallen coined the term "cultural pluralism," see Kallen, *Culture and Democracy in the United States* (New York, 1924), pp. 67–125, and outlined what he called a "democracy of nationalities," p. 116. Kallen also called cultural pluralism "dissimilation," see Persons, *Ethnic Studies at Chicago,* p. 20; see also Gordon, *Assimilation in American Life,* chapter 6, and John Higham, *Send These to Me: Jews and Other Immigrants in Urban America,* [1975] (Baltimore, 1984), pp. 198–232; see also Milton Gordon, "Models of Pluralism: The New American Dilemma," *Annals of the American Academy of Political and Social Science* 454 (1981):178–188.

21. Or, at least, it appeared to reject the bases of assimilationist thinking. Gleason in *Speaking of Diversity* notes that "pluralism" has undergone a significant shift in meaning since Kallen coined the term in 1924 and also that as Kallen and others came to use it later it actually shared some features with assimilationist thinking. As they have actually been used historically in this country the usages "overlap and relate to each other in a dialectical manner." See chapters 3 and 6–8; the quote is from page 49.

22. Geno Baroni, *National Catholic Reporter* (May 6, 1977), quoted in Gleason, *Speaking of Diversity*, p. 36.

23. Gleason, *Speaking of Diversity*, especially chapter 5.

24. Large-scale immigration from Europe, at least, has virtually ceased while immigration from Asia and Latin America has become much more important. Roger Daniels, *Coming to America: A History of Immigration and Ethnicity in American Life* (New York, 1990); Al Santoli, *New Americans: An Oral History of Immigrants and Refugees in the United States Today* (New York, 1988); Thomas Sowell, *Ethnic America: A History* (New York, 1981); Thomas J. Archdeacon, *Becoming American: An Ethnic History* (New York, 1983).

25. Michael Novak, *The Rise of the Unmeltable Ethnics: Politics and Culture in the Seventies* (New York, 1971); see also Joseph A. Ryan, ed., *White Ethnics Life in Working Class America* (Englewood Cliffs, NJ, 1973); Andrew Greeley, *Why Can't They Be More Like Us? America's White Ethnic Groups* (New York, 1971), and Nathan Glazer and Daniel Moynihan, *Beyond the Melting Pot*, 2nd ed. (Cambridge, MA, 1970).

26. Gleason, *Speaking of Diversity*, see especially chapters 6–8.

27. See ibid. and note 25 above.

28. Howard Simons, *Jewish Times: Voices of the American Jewish Experience* (New York, 1988), p. 199.

29. Michael Novak, "Pluralism in Humanistic Perspective," in William Peterson, Michael Novak, and Philip Gleason, *Concepts of Ethnicity* (Cambridge, 1980), pp. 39–46.

30. Ibid., pp. 44–45.

31. Leonard F. Chrobot, *Who Am I? Reflections of a Young Polish American on the Search for Identity*, Monograph No. 4 (Orchard Lake, MI, 1971); for Polish-Americans in general, see John J. Bukowczyk, *And My Children Did Not Know Me: A History of the Polish-Americans* (Bloomington, 1987). Bukowczyk discusses Polish-American identity throughout but see especially chapters 4–6 and epilogue.

32. See Chrobot, *Who Am I?*, pp. 17–18; the quote is from p. 17.

33. Ibid., p. 18.

34. Ibid., p. 13. It may be worth pointing out that Chrobot does not use a hyphen between Polish and American, suggesting, perhaps, a rejection of "hyphenate consciousness."

35. Gleason, *Speaking of Diversity*, chapter 3.

36. Glazer and Moynihan, *Beyond the Melting Pot*, p. 290.

37. See note 25 above for some of the best-known examples.

38. William Peterson, "Concepts of Ethnicity," pp. 1–26 in Peterson, Novak, and Gleason, *Concepts of Ethnicity*, p. 1.

39. Sollors, *Beyond Ethnicity*, pp. 21–26; Nathan Glazer and Daniel Patrick Moynihan, eds., *Ethnicity: Theory and Experience* (Cambridge, MA, 1973), pp. 2–26.

40. Gleason, *Speaking of Diversity*, chapter 5.

41. Ibid., p. 127.

42. Gordon, *Assimilation in American Life*, Chapter 2 and figure 1, p. 27.

43. Richard D. Alba, *Ethnic Identity: The Transformation of White America* (New Haven, 1990), pp. 21–30, who adds to Erikson's views of the matter the perspective supplied by contemporary social psychology's self-concept.

44. Glazer and Moynihan, *Ethnicity: Theory and Experience*. They were struck by both the relative newness of the concept and its persistence among later-generation European Americans.

45. Peterson, "Concepts of Ethnicity" and Harold R. Isaac, "Basic Group Identity: The Idols of the Tribe," in Glazer and Moynihan, *Ethnicity: Theory and Experience*, pp. 29–83; Donald L. Horowitz, "Ethnic Identity" in Ibid., pp. 111–140. Peterson's essay originally appeared in Stephan Thernstrom, Ann Orlov and Oscar Handlin, eds., *Harvard Encyclopedia of American Ethnic Groups* (Cambridge, 1980), pp. 234–242. Other relevant essays from that source are Harold J. Abramson, "Assimilation and Pluralism," pp. 150–160; Philip Gleason "American Identity and Americanization," pp. 31–58; Michael Novak, "Pluralism: A Humanistic Perspective," pp. 772–781 (both of which are reprinted along with Peterson's essay) in Peterson, Novak, and Gleason, *Concepts of Ethnicity*, and Michael Walzer, "Pluralism: A Political Perspective," pp. 781–787.

46. Persons, *Ethnic Studies at Chicago*, p. 20. As Persons puts it: "One might change one's clothes or one's spouse, but not one's grandfather."

47. Today known as "primordialism," the concept was first introduced by Edward Shils, "Primordial, Personal, Sacred and Civil Ties," *British Journal of Sociology* 8 (1957), pp. 130–45, and reinforced by Clifford Geertz and others. See James McKay, "An Exploratory Synthesis of Primordial and Mobilizationist Approaches to Ethnic Phenomena," *Ethnic and Racial Studies* 5 (1982):395–420.

48. Morawska, "The Sociology and Historiography of Immigration," Yans-McLaughlin, ed., *Immigration Reconsidered*; see also John Higham, "From Process to Structure: Formulations of American

Immigration History," pp. 11–41, and Fred Matthews, "Paradigm Changes in Interpretations of Ethnicity, 1930–1980: From Process to Structure," pp. 167–188, both in Peter Kivisto and Dag Blanck, eds., *American Immigrants and Their Generations: Studies and Commentaries on the Hansen Thesis after Fifty Years* (Urbana, 1990).

49. Gordon, *Assimilation in American Life*, chapter 2, especially pp. 34–59. Peterson suggests the concept "subnation" be substituted. See Peterson et al., *Concepts of Ethnicity*, p. 3.

50. See note 48 above.

51. "Hansen's Law" was articulated by Marcus Lee Hansen in an address to the Augustana Historical Society of Rock Island, Illinois in May, 1937. The text of the address is included in Kivisto and Blanck, *American Immigrants and Their Generations*, pp. 191–203. In his address, entitled "The Problem of the Third Generation Immigrant," Hansen maintained that the problem of the first generation, the immigrant, is solved by Americanization. The problem of the second generation, the children of the immigrants, is "[h]ow to inhabit two worlds at the same time" (p. 193). They solve the problem by "escape" (p. 193), by rejecting their parents' world. Eventually their children, the "third generation," will obey "the almost universal phenomenon that what the son wishes to forget the grandson wishes to remember" (p. 195). Will Herberg first called this "Hansen's Law" in *Protestant-Catholic-Jew: An Essay in American Religious Sociology* (New York, 1955), in which he used the concept to explain how America had become a religious "triple melting pot," pp. 30–31.

52. Philip Gleason, "Hansen, Herberg, and American Religion" in Gleason, *Speaking of Diversity*, pp. 231–249, points out that its current usage is far different from that which Hansen originally intended.

53. Joseph Swastek, "What is a Polish American?" *Polish American Studies* 1 (1944), pp. 34–44.

54. Leonard Covello is a good example of someone who was trying hard to live in two worlds. At home he had to respect the values of his father yet at school he was becoming Americanized. His teacher had dropped the letter "i" from his last name (originally Coviello) and Leonard thought nothing of it. His father, however, did not want to sign his report card, saying "From Leonardo to Leonard I can follow, a perfectly natural process. In America anything can happen and does happen. But you don't change a family name. A name is a name. What happened to the i?" The confrontation is described in Covello's memoir: Leonard Covello with Guido D'Agostino, *The Heart Is the Teacher* (New York, 1958), pp. 29–31, and the quote is from pp. 30–31. For information

on the ethnic ghetto that Covello called home, see Robert A. Orsi, *The Madonna of 115th: Street Faith and Community in Italian Harlem, 1880–1950* (New Haven, 1985), especially chapters 2 and 4.

55. Ryan, *White Ethnics*, contains a good selection of such sentiments. As Leonard Covello put it: "Throughout my whole elementary school career, I do not recall one mention of Italy or the Italian language or what famous Italians had done in the world, with the possible exception of Columbus, who was pretty popular in America. We soon got the idea that "Italian" meant something inferior, and a barrier was erected between children of Italian origin and their parents. This was the accepted process of Americanization. We were becoming Americans by learning how to be ashamed of our parents" (pp. 43–44).

56. Alice Kessler-Harris, "Social History," in Eric Foner, ed., *The New American History* (Philadelphia, 1990), pp. 163–184. In the same volume relevant material is also included in Leon Fink, "American Labor History," pp. 233–250, and James P. Shenton, "Ethnicity and Immigration," pp. 251–270.

57. As Werner Sollors puts it, we have come to recognize "the general cultural constructedness of the modern world. What were the givens in intellectual pursuits until very recently have now become the problematic issues." Werner Sollors, ed., *The Invention of Ethnicity* (New York, 1989), p. x.

58. John Bodnar, *The Transplanted: A History of Immigrants in Urban America* (Bloomington, 1985); Yans-McLaughlin, *Immigration Reconsidered*.

59. Sollors, *Invention of Ethnicity*. This collection of essays emphasizes "the importance of language in the social construction of reality," p. x.

60. Alba, *Ethnic Identity*, chapters 2 and 3.

61. Martin N. Marger, *Race and Ethnic Relations: American and Global Perspectives*, 2nd ed. (Hayward, CA, 1991), pp. 12–26.

62. Ibid.

63. Daniels, *Coming to America*; Bodnar, *The Transplanted*; and Yans-McLaughlin, *Immigration Reconsidered*.

64. Fredrik Barth, ed., *Ethnic Groups and Boundaries: The Social Organization of Culture Differences* (Boston, MA, 1969), "Introduction," pp. 9–38; the quote is from p. 15.

65. Ibid.

66. Herbert Gans, "Symbolic Ethnicity: The Future of Ethnic Groups and Cultures in America," *Ethnic and Racial Studies* 2 (1979):1–20;

Jonathan Okamura, "Situational Ethnicity," *Ethnic and Racial Studies* 4 (1981):452–465; McKay, "Primordial and Mobilizationist Approaches," pp. 399–401; Mary C. Waters, *Ethnic Options: Choosing Identities in America* (Berkeley, CA, 1990), pp. 1–8; William L. Yancey, Eugene P. Ericksen, and Richard N. Juliani, "Emergent Ethnicity: A Review and Reformulation," *American Sociological Review* 41 (1976):391–403; George Devereux and Edwin M. Loeb, "Antagonistic Acculturation," *American Sociological Review* 7 (1943):133–147, and George Devereux, "Ethnic Identity: Its Logical Foundations and its Dysfunctions," in George de Vos and Lola Romanucci-Ross, eds., *Ethnic Identity: Cultural Continuities and Change* (Palo Alto, CA, 1975), pp. 42–70.

67. Waters, *Ethnic Options,* chapter 2; the quote is from p. 16.

68. For the life-cycle concept, see Ibid., pp. 36–46.

69. Alba, *Ethnic Identity.*

70. The "consent" and "descent" concepts are from Sollors, *Beyond Ethnicity,* which "takes the conflict between contractual and hereditary, self-made and ancestral definitions of American identity—between consent and descent—as the central drama in American culture," pp. 5–6. In our terms descent relations would be primordial and consent ones would be voluntary.

71. April Schultz, "'The Pride of the Race Has Been Touched': The 1925 Norse-American Immigration Centennial and Ethnic Identity," *Journal of American History* 77 (1991), pp. 1265–1295; see also Victor Greene, "Old-Time Folk Dancing and Music Among the Second Generation, 1920–1950," in Kivisto and Blanck, *American Immigrants and Their Generations,* pp. 142–163.

72. Kathleen Neils Conzen, "Ethnicity as Festive Culture: Nineteenth-Century German America on Parade," in Sollors, *The Invention of Ethnicity,* pp. 44–76; Orsi, *The Madonna of 115th Street,* especially chapters 2, 7–8.

73. Kerby A. Miller, "Class, Culture and Immigrant Group Identity in the United States: The Case of Irish-American Ethnicity," in Yans-McLaughlin, *Immigration Reconsidered,* pp. 96–129; Miller, *Emigrants and Exiles: Ireland and the Irish Exodus to North America* (New York, 1985).

74. Sollors, *Beyond Ethnicity,* p. 14.

75. Samuel L. Baily, "Cross-Cultural Comparisons and the Writing of Migration History: Some Thoughts on How to Study Italians in the New World," in Yans-McLaughlin, *Immigration Reconsidered,* pp. 241–253; Baily, "The Adjustment of Italian Immigrants in Buenos Aires and New York, 1870–1914," *American Historical Review* 88 (1983): 281–305; see also Dino Cinel, *From Italy to San Francisco: The Immigrant Experience*

(Stanford, CA, 1982). Japanese Americans who settled in Hawaii had significantly different experiences than those who settled on the west coast of the mainland. See David L. O'Brien and Stephen S. Fugita, *The Japanese American Experience* (Bloomington, 1991).

76. Charles Tilly, "Transplanted Networks," in Yans-McLaughlin, *Immigration Reconsidered,* pp. 79–95.

77. Gleason, *Speaking of Diversity,* p. 49.

78. Mary Antin would be a classic example. For another, see Richard Rodriguez, *Hunger of Memory: The Education of Richard Rodriguez* (Boston, MA, 1982).

79. Gay Talese, *Honor Thy Father* (New York, 1992), reports that his own father "always encouraged me to take pride in my ethnic heritage, a heritage he identified with such names as Michelangelo and Dante, Medici and Galileo, Verdi and Caruso" (p. xv); Talese, however, felt "an alien, an outsider . . . different . . . in almost every way, different in the cut of my clothes, the food in my lunch box, the music I heard at home on the record player, the ideas and inner thoughts I revealed on those rare occasions when I was open and honest. I was olive-skinned in a freckle-faced town, and I felt unrelated even to my parents, especially my father, who was indeed a foreigner—an unusual man in dress and manner, to whom I bore no physical resemblance and with whom I could never identify." Talese, *Unto the Sons* (New York, 1992), p. 4. He preferred baseball and American popular culture to his father's tastes. Talese also describes a neighborhood in Brooklyn: "Except for the absence of a mountain, it could have passed for a Sicilian village. The dialect and manner of the people were the same, the cooking was the same, the interior of the homes seemed the same." *Honor Thy Father,* p. 52. One of the residents of that neighborhood "neither spoke nor wrote English despite living in America for thirty-two years." Ibid. Jerre Mangione in *Mount Allegro: A Memoir of Italian American Life* [1941] (New York, 1989), describes relatives who were similarly reluctant to assimilate, see chapter 7. And Richard Rodriguez relates the same situation for his father; Rodriguez, *Hunger of Memory.*

80. Will the experiences of the most recent groups be the same as the experiences of those who came earlier? See Paul James Rutledge, *The Vietnamese Experience in America* (Bloomington, IN, 1992). See also note 24 above.

CHAPTER 3

Us and Them
Personal Reflections on Ethnic Literature

Betty Ann Burch

A book discussion group made up of people from business, the clergy, and academe came face to face recently with the frequent conflict between ethnicity and education. A seminary professor was concerned that one of her students—a Native American woman—was having difficulty bridging the gap between what she was learning and doing at school and her home and tribal life. Another member of the group added that his African American students were having similar difficulties reconciling the culture of a large university with life in their neighborhoods. These are cultural conflicts without obvious solutions.

Such student anxieties underscore the marginality of minorities in contemporary American society. Just as poignant and pervasive but often forgotten today is the alienation experienced by immigrants who came to this nation in the decades from 1880 to 1920. Eastern and southern Europeans—Jews, Poles, Italians, Croatians, Greeks—lived through a sense of marginality similar to that faced by today's minorities. We are fortunate that the children of these immigrants captured their parents' experiences in novels and short stories during the 1930s and 1940s.

These ethnic authors wrote movingly of their own experiences as cultural interpreters for their parents and about their parallel search for their own identity as individuals caught between two cultures. These authors—James T. Farrell, Henry Roth, Jerre Mangione, and Thomas Bell are but four examples—

movingly traced the search for an American identity among European immigrants and their children in the twentieth century.

Preoccupation with identity is self-evident in the large number of ethnic novels that focus on adolescent development. The children of immigrants who turned to fiction used this genre to detail the marginality of an ethnic childhood caught between two cultures. In this effort, these ethnic writers clarified the dilemma of the marginal person, so their work is of practical value to other minority students in pondering the roots of their anxieties in contemporary society.

The value of ethnic fiction, therefore, especially in an historical or sociological context, is without question. The skill of the ethnic novelist—the passion, the pathos, the authenticity— breathes life into otherwise dull historical facts and sociological statistics. Historians of ethnicity analyze past events; sociologists evaluate the behavior and culture of ethnic groups. It is the ethnic novelist, however, who can most effectively involve today's students in the daily life of immigrants and help these students to better understand a distant time and a clash of cultures.

In providing this unique perspective on immigrant life, ethnic writers steered a course independent from the mainstream of American literature. In fact, even a cursory reading of the ethnic novels of the 1930s and 1940s underscores the uniqueness of this literary genre.

Unlike mainstream American literature, ethnic fiction of the 1930s and 1940s rarely focused on a lone hero—the confident sheriff, for example—who faces evil in the middle of the street and proves his manhood in a dramatic life-and-death struggle. On the contrary, the ethnic hero is a marginal man, full of self-doubt, the son of an immigrant family struggling in a new country. Moreover, he carries the burden of identity: What does it mean to be an American? Am I an American? Where do I fit in American society?

For the most part, ethnic novelists tell the stories of men and boys who are never alone. Even after they leave their parents' home, they are not on their own. In fact, the protagonists in most ethnic novels quickly join extended families of friends or fellow countrymen. They room with like-minded people, live in their own ethnic neighborhoods, and work with their own kind. The ethnic hero is a man in a crowd.

But ethnic authors also tell stories within stories. Their novels were more than simple tales of immigrants and their children as they faced the travails of acculturation and assimilation. Some novelists focused on the nuances of how their own people perceived and reacted to American society. Others wrote of the warmth and love of their extended immigrant families, showing how their fellow countrymen established foundations and fortifications for survival in America. Still others concentrated on the conflict between American ideals and parental aspirations. Finally, there were some ethnic novelists who wrote of the limitations of ethnic culture versus the freedom of American society.

Whatever the sub-theme, ethnic novelists portrayed heroes who had the full range of life experiences from success to failure. Some heroes became disillusioned or disgusted with American society. Others were left in limbo—confused and unhappy because they were not accepted as Americans but not able to return to the families and the culture of their youth. Still other heroes rose above harsh circumstances to make it in America. Yet it is not too much to say that there is a pervasive sadness in much of the ethnic fiction of the 1930s and 1940s.

These authors wrote of American cities, farms, factories, and families from a working-class point of view. They were the sons and daughters of working-class men and women, and they wrote of the sweatshop, the street, the saloon, and the tenement. In fact, many of these novelists began their working lives alongside their fathers in the factory and the union hall. They wrote of what they knew: hardship, violence, alcoholism, early death, and the struggle for a better life.

To be sure, economic security was a pervasive theme in most ethnic novels. The deep-to-the-bone weariness of farm and factory work, the tragic deaths of principal wage earners, the broken health and poverty of older workers, the insensitivity and violence of factory managers: these are but some of the sobering facets of the immigrants' almost constant concern about economic security.

Another important element in many if not most ethnic novels is the presence of strong female characters. Ethnic novels of the 1930s and 1940s show women working both inside and outside the home. These characters are factory workers, farm hands, and domestics (most often called "hired girls"). Even female characters bound to the home by young children are portrayed as taking in wash or renting rooms to boarders. The point was clear: everyone in the immigrant community worked to support their families.

These female characters also displayed wisdom and courage. They gave advice and counsel and often served as the conscience of their husbands and boyfriends. These women were not compliant; they argued their beliefs, they goaded, they scolded. They even withheld their affection until their men changed their behavior.

Ethnic novelists, perhaps even more than other writers, saw their world through the prism of personal experience. Thomas Bell, who Anglicized his name from Belejcak, for example, never ceased to look at the world through the lens of his immigrant childhood experiences of degradation and exploitation. More important, in novels such as *Out of This Furnace* (1941), he never stopped asking why Anglo-Saxon America did not live the ideals professed in the Declaration of Independence, the Constitution, and the other revered documents of the past.

Even in his final autobiographical work, *In the Midst of Life* (1961), Bell continued to speculate about the quality of life that could be lived in America if its affluence and ideals were blended into a democratic culture. He believed that there had to be a sufficient level of material comfort for every American to have the dignity that is his or her birthright.

Yet Bell saw material success as a means, not an end. Living at the survival level, he believed, did not allow people the time or energy to observe, to learn, to ponder, and ultimately to become whole human beings who could then help their fellow citizens to achieve affluence.

Bell also wrote about the tragedy of American assimilation that was forced upon Eastern European children in this country. One of his characters, for example, says that America had taken away the lullabies of his people, their customs and values, and had substituted super-patriotic but hypocritical platitudes.

In *Out of This Furnace,* one character bemoans how Slovak and other Eastern European children have to learn American songs in school. "If we were to sing some of our songs and explain what we were about," adds the character, "would it surprise them [the factory owners and the school board] to learn we sang about such things and had such feelings? If we told them how we lived in the old country, how we worked the land, the crops we grew, the little money we saw from one year's end to another, our holidays and festivals—would they realize that even though we spoke different languages we were still men like themselves, with the same troubles and the same hopes and dreams? I hoped we might learn to respect one another, that we might even become friends" [p. 196]. Bell believed that he and his people were forced to learn American ways too quickly and that America was less of a nation for not embracing more of the ethnic culture of its newest residents.

Bell and other ethnic writers argued that immigrants could move from their native cultures into the American mainstream without abandoning their roots. Indeed, their fashion, cuisine, language, literature, and music would add an unprecedented texture to the nation.

The work of Bell and other ethnic writers of the 1930s and 1940s helped to expand the definition of American literature. By 1980, "American literature" had come to be accepted as literary work by citizens and residents from all classes, races, and regions of the country. More important, this expanded definition accepted the concept of marginality as a fundamental American experience. "Where do I fit in to American society?" was a question asked by characters—Anglo as well as ethnic—in thousands of short stories and novels over the past five decades.

Feelings of marginality—especially among the immigrants—intensified in the public school. This is not surprising given that one of the often-stated principles of our educational system is to mold the coming generation into American citizens. One by-product of inflicting this process on the children of immigrants was to strip these young people of their ethnic heritage.

Many ethnic writers of the 1930s and 1940s wrote of this experience, but none more movingly than Thomas Bell. He wrote critically of the holiday celebrations in public schools among other aspects of this experience. Bell wrote repeatedly that the schooling received by immigrant children was unrelated to their lives at home and on the streets. School learning was one thing; street learning was another.

Thirty years after Bell's complaint, another writer touched the same nerve. In his widely discussed book, *The Rise of the Unmeltable Ethnics* (1971), Michael Novak wrote of this same sense of displacement still to be found in the public schools. "If you are a descendent of southern and eastern Europeans every-one else *has* defined your existence," noted Novak. "A pattern of 'Americanization' is laid out. You are catechized, cajoled, and condescended to by guardians of good Anglo-Protestant atti-tudes. . . . The entire experience of becoming American is sum-marized in the experience of being made to feel guilty" [p. 62].

The immediate impact of ethnic fiction was as marginal as the writers themselves. Even though their work was reviewed in the magazines and newspapers of the day, reviewers often missed the major theme of this work—the search for personal identity and the burden of being marginal in American society. It was long after publication that the reading public as well as literary critics discovered the primary message of ethnic fiction.

Bell's *Out of This Furnace,* for example, is considered a minor classic and remains in print today precisely because it is a beautiful saga of three generations of Slovak men and women living on the margins of American society. Nearly as important, it demonstrates to new generations of readers the struggle for dignity in the world of work. It needs no apology to be included in the canon of American literature.

Perhaps what makes Bell's work so valuable is that he is able to write so authentically from the immigrant's perspective. Henry Roth's *Call It Sleep* is another successful book of this gen-re. Not to be overlooked, of course, are works such as Willa Ca-ther's *My Antonia* that portrays the vitality of Antonia through the eyes of Jim, a boy of colonial Virginian ancestry.

Yet the price of acceptance for ethnic Americans and their literature has been high. There has long been an undercurrent of

hostility to ethnic culture. In fact, there are far too many incidents of ethnic violence. "Why can't they be like us?" has been a
question asked by native-born Americans since the middle years
of the nineteenth century. Even Americans whose families were
but one or two generations removed from Ellis Island have
asked that question of more recent arrivals. The price paid by
immigrants and their children is low self-esteem or possibly a
sense of victimization. The price paid by American society is a
loss of vitality, creativity, and talent from those outside the mainstream.

Ethnic literature is something of a tonic in remedying this
unfortunate situation. It is often through books that the host
society can learn of the worth of its newest arrivals. How little
we know of the Haitian boat people, and how much we need to
learn before Americans will accept these unfortunate souls.
Through literature, immigrants can begin to define their place in
American society.

Will we ever eliminate marginality in American society? It
is an impossible question to answer. To be sure, we have symbols such as Israel Zangwell's "melting pot" and the Statue of
Liberty that lull us into a false sense of security that all immigrants will eventually be assimilated into American society.

But the melting pot is a poor symbol for what happens
between immigrants and American society. The notion that
many different cultures would be combined in a common pot
called America and that after sufficient "stirring and cooking"
would emerge a common culture is an amusing folktale, but it is
too simple to be accurate. This is not to say, however, that the
melting pot is completely invalid. Certainly, the children and
grandchildren of American immigrants quickly come to realize
how different they are from Europeans of the same ethnic ancestry.

The problem of the melting pot extends, in part, from
academic theory. Social scientists at the turn of the century
theorized that ethnic groups would gradually abandon their native customs and values and embrace their American counterparts. But this seemingly harmless process ran roughshod over
individual identities, and contemporary social theorists have

abandoned the melting pot as an analogy for becoming American.

Today there is a progression of theories about immigrant assimilation—from acculturation to cultural pluralism to structural pluralism. The most recent construct is "autonomous" pluralism, which posits that each immigrant group has its own culture, heritage, set of values, and a unique presence, all of which are worthy of preservation within American society.

Yet assimilation theories are the tools of social scientists. For most Americans, ethnic pluralism is explained through American literature in one form or another. In fact, it is the stories written by the people who have lived the immigration experience and endured marginality and the pressure to assimilate that offer the most vivid testimony. In focusing on their stories, historians and other academics do this nation a great service by consciously incorporating in its history the culture, talents, and energy of all the people who make up this great land.

Alice Walker succinctly captured the essential value of ethnic literature in an essay published in 1984. "I believe that the truth about any subject only comes when all sides of the story are put together and all their different meanings make a new one," she wrote in *In Search of Our Mothers' Gardens*. "Each writer writes the missing parts to the other writer's story." It is for this reason that we are so much in debt to the ethnic novelists of the 1930s and 1940s. It is for this reason that their work should and will endure.

PART II

Haven in a Strange New Land

Introduction

There is nothing quite so private and personal as a home and family. Indeed, "family has always been regarded as sacred," notes Tamara Harevan and John Modell in an essay in the *Harvard Encyclopedia of American Ethnic Groups.* "Its significance as a private retreat from the outside world, the guardian of tradition and barometer of social change has been elevated to mythic proportions in American culture." Without question, therefore, any study of the impact of European immigration must also tell the story of immigrant families.

Perhaps the most interesting facet of European immigrant family life was that the typical household had so many members at so many different stages of evolution from ethnic to American. To be sure, the immigrant family was essentially nuclear, but because of economics, a great many immigrant families included grandparents, cousins, and even boarders in transitional stages between leaving Europe and establishing roots in America. Each immigrant household, therefore, was a collection of individuals of several generations and family relationships with different concepts and appreciations of American culture.

The glue that kept these households together was as much economic as it was familial. Few immigrant heads of household arrived in this country with the skills needed to support their families by themselves. As Mary Elizabeth Brown notes in the essay that follows, most male heads of

households earned little more than half of the money
needed to support themselves and their wives and
children in the United States. The basic need for food and
shelter, therefore, kept these immigrant families working
in common cause.

Economics also determined the responsibilities of
each family member. Fathers worked full-time, of course.
Mothers generally stayed at house raising the children and
caring for elderly family members and the house, but they
also supplemented family income by taking in wash and
renting spare rooms to boarders. The oldest children went
to work usually by the age of twelve, in some families as
young as ten. Only the youngest children—those born in
America—were allowed the luxury of an education that
was more than basic literacy in English.

Economic survival meant more to these immigrant
families than just food and shelter, however; it also meant
owning property. Purchasing their own home was almost
a universal desire among European immigrants. Most
immigrants had been landless peasants in Europe. To own
property in America was both a symbol and a measure of
success—something to boast about in letters back to the
old country. In their essay below, Gordon and Carolyn T.
Kirk explain the nature of home ownership among
immigrant families.

Even though some immigrants objected to
compulsory education for their children, many immigrant
families embraced schooling and other social services.
Those services that strengthened the family unit—health
care, job services, and home economics for example—were
accepted with gratitude. "Despite the challenge these
agencies posed to cherished tradition," note Harevan and
Modell, "immigrant parents generally cooperated with
them, both because of the assistance they offered and because of the advantages their teaching and assistance
promised for their children. Yet whenever possible,
immigrant families continued to exercise their own choices
in response to the cultural premises." Mary Elizabeth
Brown underscores this point in the essay that follows.

The adaptation of immigrant families to American culture was, therefore, a mix of resistance and acquiescence. The process required negotiation between millions of immigrant families and the society at their doorsteps. Just as important, it required negotiation within the family between parents and their children. The process was as dynamic as it was drawn out.

The process of adaptation was hard, especially for parents. In Europe, the father had been head of the household and his commands were obeyed; but in America, everything was turned upside down. "Often it was necessary for the fathers to turn for enlightenment to their sons," wrote Oscar Handlin. "Accepting that role, the immigrants nevertheless resented it. It reversed the proper order of things. They could remember how they themselves had feared and respected the father and they were embittered by their own failure to evoke the same fear and respect from their children." It was a pessimistic point of view of immigrant family life to say the least.

In recent years, however, a new generation of scholars has accentuated the positive aspects of immigrant family life in the United States. The books by John Bodnar, James Bensen, Thomas Kessner, and Josef Barton, among others cited in the bibliography, provide details. More to the point, Gordon and Carolyn T. Kirk provide additional evidence on the varying commitment to home ownership among different ethnic groups.

Among the more recent European immigrants, the family has remained an extraordinary and vital force. The essay by Mary Jane Capozzoli Ingui in this section shows how the almost symbiotic relationship between Italian American mothers and their daughters has prospered, at least in New York. The work of Virginia Yans McLaughlin provides additional evidence of these close Italian ties. Other scholars—Gary Kunkelman and Edward Zivich to cite only two—suggest that close family ties are a common aspect of European immigrant family life in the twentieth century.

The European immigrant family is, therefore, something of a paradox. Did the process of immigration destroy the ethnic family unit, or did it forge a bond of unity between family members that was passed on from generation to generation? The slim body of literature on the subject only suggests some answers. Far more research needs to be done on this topic before we can detail the nature of this haven in a strange new land.

CHAPTER 4

Home Is Where the Heart Is
Immigrant Mobility and Home Ownership

Gordon W. Kirk, Jr.
Carolyn Tyirin Kirk

In the late nineteenth and early twentieth centuries, immigrant mobility and property accumulation, particularly home owner-ship, were assumed to be closely intertwined. Both historians and contemporary students of the urban immigrant experience concur that the vast majority of immigrants strongly desired to become home owners and that the ownership of a home was both the most common form of property acquisition and surpris-ingly widespread among working-class immigrants; rates of immigrant home ownership did, however, vary both by cities and stages in the family life-cycle.[1] Furthermore, as we shall see, scholars do not agree either on the meaning of home ownership or its impact on immigrant mobility and their standard of living.

The purpose of this essay is three-fold. First, we will out-line the main issues surrounding the meaning of home owner-ship and its relation to the mobility of immigrants and their children.[2] Next we will examine issues surrounding the nature of the sacrifices that have been attributed to immigrants in their quest for ownership and the purported impact of those sacrifices on their standard of living. Last, we will examine several hypo-theses regarding the relationship between immigrant home own-ership and both the sacrifices and standard of living which bear directly on the relationship between home ownership and mobility.

I

Sociological theorists have traditionally viewed property
ownership as a major component of the concept of class. Following Max Weber, "'property' and 'lack of property' are considered
the basic categories of all class situations," although economic
class situations are further differentiated by the kind of property
owned. In the American context, however, sociologists from
Lloyd Warner to Herbert Gans argue that owning a house also is
a symbol that the family has "arrived" in terms of social status.
In other words, home ownership suggests a higher social class in
both economic and social status terms than does renting.[3]

Both old world traditions and the values of American society have also emphasized the importance of property ownership. Numerous studies clearly demonstrate that part of the
culture of late nineteenth and early twentieth-century immigrants included the old world emphasis on property ownership
as a measure of social class. The social worker Edith Abbott
found that immigrants in Chicago believed in "the superior social status of the man of property." Similarly, among the foreign
stock in the Back of the Yards area of Chicago, the old world
desire for property "translated into ownership of one's home."
William Thomas and Florian Znaniecki also argued that possession of property provided "the main condition of social standing
of the family" for the Poles in both Europe and America. For
Italians in Buffalo, according to Virginia Yans-McLaughlin, emigration provided "a way to avoid loss of status and to fulfill their
desire to own property." As these observations and those of others indicate, many immigrants viewed home ownership as closely tied to status, economic attainment and social position in
American society.[4]

The dominant values of American society did not conflict
with these immigrant aspirations and, if anything, may have reinforced immigrant attitudes toward the importance of home
ownership. Middle-class reformers and Americanizers both encouraged home ownership and equated it with social advancement. Regarding immigrants in Boston's Zone of Emergence,
Robert Woods noted that the "ownership of property is one of
the surest indications that emergence is emergence indeed."

Similarly, Herbert Hoover remarked to the Conference on Home Building and Home Ownership in 1931 that the "renter has never been accorded the full status of the owner."[5]

Furthermore, reformers and Americanizers saw ownership promoting citizenship and social order. Abbott viewed ownership as an indication of both good citizenship and part of becoming American and Woods felt ownership spurred an interest in "government, neighborhood, and the general community." Many testifying before the Industrial Commission of 1901, industrial leaders such as Henry Ford and the Detroit Americanization Committee, and advocates of savings and loans, also emphasized the conservative effects of home ownership, such as a reduction in labor violence and unrest among the working class.[6]

Beginning with John Bodnar's important essay in 1976, historians have offered a more complex and enriched interpretation of the meaning of immigrant working-class home ownership. While not totally dismissing its relevance to enhanced status or upward mobility in either old or new world terms, he and others have suggested it also served as a "surrogate for limited occupational mobility" and offered a "means of solidifying their precarious economic status." The nineteenth-century capitalist transformation—by increasing the likelihood of irregular employment, industrial accidents and other dangers inherent in industrial society—heightened immigrant and working class family insecurity. This changing set of circumstances prompted them and their children to adopt a defensive strategy, particularly by the end of the nineteenth century, in which home ownership became an integral part. Indeed, Olivier Zunz has extended the argument to suggest that "ownership was more an emblem of immigrant working-class culture than of the established middle-class native white American culture."[7]

In short, by owning their own homes, immigrants gained some marginal control over their social and economic environment. Ownership provided independence from the dictates of landlords regarding the number of people in the household. Possession of one's home further offered some security and stability by providing a hedge against rising rents, a means of forced savings and increased equity, supplemental income, and security in retirement. Rear houses or additions to existing structures could also be used to help newly married children. The security provided by a home, however, had limitations. For example, with the advent of the Great Depression, as Lizabeth Cohen has noted, "owning a home did not offer the kind of security . . . that it had in the 1920s."[8]

In addition to questioning the meaning of immigrant home ownership, historians have advanced two sets of arguments suggesting that home ownership may have impeded the mobility of immigrants and their children. One version advocated by Matthew Edel, Elliot Sclar, and Daniel Luria maintains that home ownership constituted an unwise investment which impeded the intergenerational occupational mobility of both the native- and foreign-born working class. Since ownership tied up the meager capital of the working class which limited future investment and is not generally as profitable as most alternatives, Edel et al. maintain that "home ownership did not impart any advantage to working families over renters." Ownership also placed them "at the mercy of a competitive housing market which they in no way controlled." Thus, the onset of an economic depression forced workers either "to sell their homes in order to survive unemployment, or move to another locality in search of a job." The empirical support for this argument rests upon a reexamination of a subsample of Stephan Thernstrom's data for 1880 from his study of occupational mobility in Boston that they argue demonstrates that father's home ownership adversely affected the upward occupational mobility of their sons. However, Eric Monkkonnen's reexamination of their statistical analysis indicates, if anything, a positive relationship between home ownership and sons' upward mobility.[9]

A second variation of the argument that home ownership impeded occupational mobility rests on the view that immigrants sacrificed their children's education by relying on the income of their children in order to become home owners. That is, they had their children leave school at an early age to work so that the family could purchase a home. The end result of this strategy was that the chances for improved occupational status of the children suffered. This argument, first advanced by Thernstrom to explain the lower intergenerational mobility rates of unskilled Irish in Newburyport, has been applied to other immigrant groups in the late-nineteenth and early twentieth centuries.[10]

These conclusions tend to rely on aggregate- rather than individual-level data which frequently show high levels of immigrant ownership and low levels of schooling and occupational attainment by immigrant children. Employing individual-level data, Joel Perlman has found a positive relationship between parental home ownership and school attendance among immigrant children in Providence. He cautions, however, that correlations of this nature are dealing with families who already are rather than being in the process of becoming home owners. Such families, having already purchased their homes, may no longer have to rely on the labor of their children. All of this serves to underscore Bodnar's observation regarding the difficulty of verifying any conclusion regarding home ownership of immigrants and the school attendance of their children.[11]

The above studies have enriched our understanding of the meaning of immigrant home ownership and have clearly indicated that it was not simply the fulfillment of a middle-class ideal. This, however, has led to a tendency to excessively downplay the importance of home ownership for immigrant mobility. That the motivation for home ownership also included a quest for security in an uncertain social and economic environment and/or served as an alternative to limited occupational mobility does not mean that ownership was irrelevant to improved social position. That immigrants and their children placed heavy emphasis on home ownership and that their ownership rates frequently surpassed those of the native stock population indicates both a congruence between immigrant aspirations and achievements and that ownership clearly represented a mark of success for immigrants. That it also provided them with greater security against the vagaries of capitalism is consistent with Weber's formulation of class where ownership means improved life chances.[12]

II

While agreeing on the immigrants' desire for a home and disagreeing about the meaning of home ownership for mobility, historians and contemporary observers have generally concurred that immigrant home ownership in the late-nineteenth and the early decades of the twentieth century resulted in large part from substantial sacrifice of their standard of living. The extent, degree, and variety of these sacrifices, moreover, were great. Robert Slayton has contended among the foreign-stock population in the "Back of the Yards" area in Chicago "No sacrifice was too great . . . even if they have to starve their families to get the money."[13]

More specifically, the types of sacrifices attributed to immigrant homeowners fall into three general categories. First, both Roger Simon and Olivier Zunz have argued strongly that immigrants sacrificed quality to reduce the costs of home ownership. Both have demonstrated that the infrastructure of homes owned by immigrant populations in Milwaukee and Detroit fell below the quality of housing owned by the native-stock population. In Milwaukee this stemmed from the strategy of delaying the installation of vital city services in order to forestall tax assessments that would increase the cost of ownership. In addition, Zunz has suggested that in Detroit a dual housing market existed which enhanced the possibility of home ownership for unskilled immigrants. While the formal market served the native-stock middle class, an informal housing market based on owner-built housing with local help on unimproved land and inferior city services existed for German and Polish Americans. From these studies, one would expect the physical quality of foreign-stock owned homes to fall below that of the native-stock population. The delaying of vital city services and the concept of the dual-housing market, for example, both suggest that immigrant-owned homes would be less likely to have indoor plumbing, hot water and bathroom facilities than those of the native-stock population. Such amenities, Richard Lieberman has suggested, offer additional indicators of social position.[14]

Owning a home, others have argued, often meant sacrificing some of the other amenities associated with home ownership. The most frequently cited amenity was privacy. Both contemporary observers and historians have suggested that immigrants took in boarders or rented out parts of their homes to help retire mortgages. Edith Abbott's study of Chicago tenements reports that immigrant home owners would frequently "live in the dark and sometimes damp basement flats or other undesirable rooms which they cannot rent." On the other hand, that freedom from landlords' restrictions on the size of households is cited as one of the advantages of immigrant home ownership also suggests greater crowding.[15] Given these observations, one would also expect foreign-stock-owned housing to be more crowded than native-owned housing.

In addition to living in more crowded dwellings, contemporary observers and historians have implied that immigrants scrimped on their expenditures and sacrificed their standard of living in order to become homeowners and pay off mortgages. Margaret Byington wrote of the "heroic efforts to buy the house" and the "great thrift exercised" by the foreign born of Homestead, and Edith Abbott reported that children in the home-buying family are "too frequently underfed" and "too poorly dressed." With the exception of some of the household budget data for Homestead, little is known about the specific impact of home ownership on the family expenditures of immigrants. The presumption is that these families spent less on necessities such as food and clothing than their native-stock counterparts.[16]

Although generalizations abound, little effort has been made to examine systematically the above propositions regarding the sacrifices made by immigrants and their children to become home owners. Moreover, many studies have looked at poor and working-class immigrants and implicitly compared them to middle-class and upper-middle-class native stock. Such implicit comparisons would lead to incorrectly attributing sacrifices to ethnicity rather than class.

III

Employing data collected by the U.S. Bureau of Labor Statistics (BLS) 1917–19 Cost of Living Study used to calculate the original weights for the cost of living index, we will now focus on some of the issues regarding home ownership and sacrifice. In order to more fully understand the degree to which immigrants and their children either sacrificed and/or benefitted from owning rather than renting their homes, two types of comparisons will be made. First, we will compare foreign-stock home owners and renters to each other with respect to the types of sacrifices associated with the dream of home ownership. Then, foreign-stock home owners and renters will be compared to "American" home owners and renters in order to determine if foreign- and native-stock Americans from the same broad socioeconomic stratum differ from each other.

These data, which include 12,817 families of wage earners and salaried workers in 99 cities from a number of northeastern, midwestern and southern states, provide extensive information pertaining to the income, expenses—including owner and rental expenditures—and demographic characteristics of the households surveyed. Although not a statistical sample in the modern sense, the BLS took great effort to insure its representativeness and instructed interviewers to select families that "represent proportionally the wage earners and the low and medium salaried families of the locality." Other instructions included limiting the sample to families with two parents and at least one child, with three or fewer lodgers, and without boarders except for friends or relatives temporarily boarding. The households were to be an "economic family" including friends and those outside of the nuclear family who were "supported from a common family fund." The BLS also limited the sample to those families in which the husband was either a salaried worker earning less than $2,000 annually or a wage earner. Charity or slum families were excluded as were non-English-speaking families who had resided in the United States for less than five years, assuring that those in the sample had a minimal level of acculturation. More importantly, the selection criteria means that the sample is representative of a broad spectrum of urban working- and middle-class families.[17]

The BLS did not specifically ask for the national identity of those households participating in the study. Fortunately, 1,972 families, 15.4 percent of the households, reported a national identity (including "American") that was recorded in response to the question on race in the interview schedule. The precise meaning of national identity, however, is not entirely clear. We cannot be certain whether the foreign nationality given meant the respondents were born in that country or merely described themselves as being of foreign descent even though born in the United States. Thus our measure of foreign stock includes not only foreign born but also those who identified with a particular ethnic group. Those reporting an ethnic identity, including American, resided in only 22 of the 99 cities included in the sample with as few as one each from Chippewa Falls, Wisconsin and Dover, New Jersey and as many as 247 from Detroit.[18] This suggests that some interviewers exceeded their instructions and asked respondents their nationality. That those reporting a nationality are concentrated in a smaller number of cities strengthens the comparative results that follow because we are comparing households from the same areas which helps to control for the structural impact of cities on home ownership rates.

To eliminate ambiguity, we have also excluded 42 families from the subsample who reported both rental and home ownership expenses as well as 129 families who reported income from boarders and lodgers. Their inclusion would not only skew measures of food expenditures and crowding but also, given instructions to canvassers, would not accurately represent the larger population with boarders and lodgers.

Other than the narrower range of cities represented, this subsample of families differs only slightly demographically and economically from the remaining 10,845 families who did not specify a national identity. Husbands and wives in our subsample are on average one year younger, and total family income averages $45 less per year or 97 percent of the income of the larger group (p <0.001). On the other hand, the average household size (4.6) for both subsamples is identical, and husband's mean income as well as percent of family earnings spent on food and net income saved for the year do not differ significantly (p >0.10). In other words, to the extent that the larger sample represents a fair cross section of two-parent working- and middle-class families, our subsample of those reporting a nationality is representative of that broad socioeconomic stratum.

A broad overview of selected characteristics of foreign and native-stock home owners generally indicates greater differences between home owners and renters in both groups than differences between the two ethnic groups. Overall, home owners were older, lived in larger households, and had larger household incomes than renters both among immigrants and "Americans" with the income differential greater among the native group (see Table 1). Renters in both groups had virtually identical profiles. By contrast, foreign-stock home owners had slightly smaller family incomes and larger households than native stock owners. That over 90 percent of the family income came from husband's earnings in all four groups is due partially to the exclusion of households with boarders and lodgers (a major source of wife's economic contribution within the home).

Table 1. Selected Characteristics
of Owners and Renters by Ethnicity*

| | Foreign-Stock | | Native-Stock | |
	Owners	*Renters*	*Owners*	*Renters*
Husband's age	39.0	34.9	39.2	35.3
Wife's age	35.3	31.0	34.9	31.7
Household size	5.1	4.6	4.6	4.5
Mean annual income	$1,514	$1,409	$1,553	$1,405
Percent annual income from husband's earnings	91.8%	93.9%	91.6%	92.3%
Number of cases	177	416	288	920

Source: See notes at end of chapter.

Consistent with those who argue that home ownership was of greater importance to immigrants and their children than to native-stock Americans, a higher percentage of ethnic Americans (29.8 percent) owned homes than did native Americans (23.8 percent) overall in our sample (see Table 2). Dividing both groups into income and age quartiles demonstrates that this difference persisted, controlling for both family income and husband's age with the exception of both the highest income quartile and the youngest age quartile where ownership rates are virtually the same. Finally, with the exception of the foreign stock's highest income quartile, both groups are similar in that ownership rates increased with age and income.

Table 2. Percentage Owning Homes by Family Income Quartiles, Husband's Age Quartiles and Ethnicity*

	Income				
	Lowest Quartile ($446– 1,196)	*Second Quartile* ($1,197– 1,420)	*Third Quartile* ($1,421– 1,722)	*Highest Quartile* ($1,723– 4,760)	*Overall*
Foreign-Stock	18.1	28.9	38.8	33.9	29.8
Native-Stock	12.9	21.4	31.1	32.7	23.8
	Husband's Age				
	Lowest Quartile (20–30)	*Second Quartile* (31–35)	*Third Quartile* (36–41)	*Highest Quartile* (42–74)	*Overall*
Foreign-Stock	12.5	27.9	37.6	43.1	29.8
Native-Stock	13.0	21.9	26.7	35.1	23.8

Source: See notes at end of chapter.

Addressing the issue of sacrifice directly by examining several indicators of the quality of homes indicates that buying a home actually bought a higher standard of living according to American middle-class standards not only for the native stock but also, and more significantly, for the foreign stock (see Table 3). Specifically, ownership for both groups meant a free-standing house, more space and less crowding. Of all the variables examined in this study, the clearest difference between renters and home owners is shown by the proportion who lived in detached single-family dwellings—those houses most frequently depicted as middle-class.[19] Over 85 percent of owners in both categories lived in such middle-class housing while fewer than 50 percent of renters did. Furthermore, owned dwellings for both groups averaged over one room larger than rented housing. Even taking into consideration the larger households of owners, home ownership, as indicated by the data on persons per room, provided improved living standards and increased privacy over renting. Although foreign-stock home owners were slightly less likely to live in a free-standing house and were slightly more crowded than native-stock owners, these data indicate a major improvement, rather than sacrifice, in the standard of living of immigrant owners over renters.

Table 3. Housing Characteristics of Owned and
Rented Homes by Ethnicity*

	Foreign-Stock		Native-Stock	
	Owned	*Rented*	*Owned*	*Rented*
Structure				
Percent detached				
single-family	86.4	34.5	91.3	49.9
No. of rooms	5.2	4.1	5.3	4.2
Persons/Rm.	.98	1.12	.87	1.07
Quality				
Percent hot running				
water inside	31.6	18.5	43.4	26.1
Percent bathroom				
inside	55.9	40.1	66.0	58.3
Percent water closet				
inside	67.8	67.5	73.6	67.0
Percent sole use of				
WC/privy	93.2	84.9	96.5	87.3
City Services				
Percent running water				
inside	93.2	97.1	88.5	90.2
Percent sewer				
connection	85.3	88.5	81.9	85.2

*Source: See notes at end of chapter.

Moreover, for each of six specific ethnic groups—German, Irish, Italian, Polish, Scandinavian, and Slavic (excluding Polish) —that had at least ten home owners and renters each, this pattern of improved quality of housing with ownership persisted for each of the above indicators. Similarly, each group of foreign-stock owners was more likely to live in larger and free-standing homes than native-stock renters. Although Italians (1.24), Slavs (1.22), Poles (1.24) and Germans (1.09) had slightly larger numbers of persons per room than native-stock renters (1.07), all owner groups had fewer persons per room than their ethnic cohort who rented. These results indicate an improved standard of living for foreign-stock home owners over all renters and suggest that our image of immigrants may be skewed by a traditional overemphasis on the unskilled and the Progressive Era investigations of slum areas.[20]

Ownership also brought other amenities associated with middle-class housing. For both nationality groups, owned dwellings were more likely to be equipped with hot running water and an inside bathroom, although over two-thirds of all households had indoor water closets. Home ownership also meant greater privacy, as indicated by the percentage with sole use of a water closet or privy although, again, the vast majority of both renters and owners had such private facilities. These differences between owners and renters also held for all specific ethnic groups except for the Poles, where 73 percent of Polish home owners had sole use of a privy or water closet compared to 77 percent of renters.

The data, though, do suggest that significant differences did exist among ethnic groups. Consistent with the dual-housing market thesis, both foreign owners and renters, particularly the Italians, Slavs, and Poles, were far less likely to have hot running water and an inside bathroom than either their home-owning or renting counterparts among the native-stock population.[21] Yet, since foreign-stock home owners were more likely than foreign-stock renters to have such amenities, these findings do not indicate that ownership represented sacrifice and a lower standard of living but rather suggest that as either renters or owners they faced some discrimination in the housing market.

Finally, our results show little support for the practice of delaying the installation of city services as part of the price for becoming a home owner that Simon found among the Poles of Milwaukee. Although the homes of renters were slightly more likely to be hooked up to water mains and sewage lines, over four-fifths of both owners and renters, native and foreign-stock, had such city services, a finding clearly at variance with images of great sacrifice by delaying city services. In short, these slight percentage differences do not suggest that the practice of delaying the installation of city services was widespread among those in our sample.[22]

Although the quality of owned homes exceeded that of rented dwellings, ownership status and perhaps its concomitant improvement in quality may have been achieved by scrimping elsewhere in the family budget. Those making this argument most commonly cite food and clothing as areas of substantial sacrifice. Our data indicate that among working- and middle-class households, foreign- or native-stock, such sacrifices were simply not made. In absolute dollars owners and renters spent about the same amount per capita per year in food controlling for age and gender of households (see Table 4). Similarly, owners and renters spent about the same percentage of household income on food and clothing.[23] The slightly higher percentages spent by the two renter groups can perhaps be best explained by

Table 4. Budget Characteristics of Owned and
Rented Homes by Ethnicity*

	Foreign-Stock		Native-Stock	
	Owned	*Rented*	*Owned*	*Rented*
Annual Expenditures				
Food/cap.[a]	$78	$80	$83	$81
Percent of Income Spent On:				
Housing[b]	24.9	22.5	25.4	23.1
Food	36.7	37.7	35.5	38.1
Clothing	15.7	16.3	14.3	14.9
Other	18.3	17.9	20.7	19.9
Surplus	4.4	5.6	4.1	4.0

a. Household size is weighted as follows by gender and age based on relative average weights at that time: males over 14=1, women over 14=0.9, children 11–14=0.9, children 7–10=0.75, children 4–6=0.4 and children 0–3=0.15. See Royal Meeker, "What is the American Standard of Living?," *Monthly Labor Review* 9 (1919), 3–5.

b. Includes mortgage or rent, water and property taxes, fuel and light, and furniture.

Source: See notes at end of chapter.

their lower incomes; that is, families with smaller incomes will spend a higher proportion on food.

Owners did spend slightly higher percentages of their income on housing and on such "discretionary" items as school supplies, lodge dues, insurance, health care, entertainment, etc. Higher discretionary expenditures, if anything, indicate that owners enjoyed a higher standard of living. That both owner groups and native renters saved 4 percent while foreign-stock renters saved 5.6 percent of their income may have been the result of ethnic renters building greater savings towards the goal of buying a home. Nevertheless, these minor variations in the budgetary expenditures of foreign- and native-stock owners and renters do not support the contention that the foreign stock sacrificed more than others to become home owners.

Finally, although precluding a definitive exploration of the relationship between buying a home and intergenerational mobility, the data do not indicate that immigrants removed their children from school and sent them to work at an early age in order to purchase a home. Among households owning their homes, only 19 and 16 percent of the foreign- and native-stock respectively received any income from their children. Furthermore, those figures drop to 11 and 10 percent when including only children 14 and under. Similarly, only 14 percent of the households of either renter group reported earnings from children with those figures falling to 8 and 6 percent for children under fourteen among foreign- and native-stock respectively. That the overwhelming majority of all groups in our study did not rely on children's income, and particularly the earnings of young children, gives virtually no support to the contention that immigrants and their children differed substantially from native-stock Americans or that they achieved ownership through sacrificing children's futures either by the children of renters working to help save for a house or by the children of owners working to help maintain a home.

IV

Recent explorations of home ownership have produced a consensus that ownership among immigrants and their children was both strongly desired and surprisingly widespread. Debate,

however, persists regarding its meaning for their social advancement and standard of living. Without providing compelling
evidence, some maintain that ownership retarded mobility either
because it was an unwise economic investment or required
children to sacrifice their chances for upward mobility by entering the labor force at an early age. Others deemphasize or challenge the importance of ownership as an indicator of advancement and maintain that it was part of a working-class defensive
strategy against the uncertainties of industrial capitalism and
may have served as a surrogate for occupational mobility. Although enriching our understanding of the meaning of ownership, this view has inordinately downplayed the meaning of
ownership for advancement. This is particularly true given the
congruence between the aspirations of the foreign stock and
their achievements and that ownership marked an improvement
in their life chances consistent with Weber's formulation.

Closely related to this issue is the contention that ownership required immigrants to make tremendous sacrifices in their
standard of living. If true, this suggests that ownership did not
represent upward mobility for the foreign stock. Little effort,
however, has been made to test systematically those propositions
regarding sacrifice and a reduced standard of living by comparing comparable groups of native and foreign stock. In order to
examine these issues more fully, we used the BLS 1917–19 Cost
of Living Study that included a broad spectrum of working- and
middle-class native- and foreign-stock Americans. This enabled
us to compare both native and foreign renters and owners to
determine more precisely the degree to which foreign-stock
home owners sacrificed their standard of living. Since the BLS
study excludes families with paying boarders, however, issues
revolving around the use of income from boarders could not be
pursued.

Our examination clearly suggests that home ownership
resulted in both an improved standard of living and no sacrifices
over renting. Although to a slightly lesser degree than native
owners, immigrant owners, by being more likely to live in free
standing houses and larger and less crowded dwellings than
foreign-stock renters, began to approach a middle-class life style.

Similarly their dwellings were more likely than foreign-stock renters to possess amenities such as a private privy or water closet, an inside bathroom, and hot running water. Such patterns, with one exception, also existed for the six specific ethnic groups we examined. Similarly, foreign-stock owners in our sample did not delay the installation of city services such as water and sewage connections. For the foreign stock, then, ownership represented an improvement in the quality of their housing and by inference their standard of living.

Similarly, ownership for the foreign stock in our sample did not, as some have suggested, result in budgetary sacrifices. The budgets of both owners and renters provide no evidence that owners sacrificed on the necessities of food, clothing, and shelter to finance the purchase or maintenance of a house. Likewise, our data provide no evidence that the households from this broad socioeconomic stratum relied on the income of their children either to save for the purchase of a house or to maintain a home.

In sum, whatever sacrifices foreign-stockowners made did not distinguish them from either native owners or immigrant renters. This does not suggest that their lives were easy or that sacrifices were not made, but rather they were not unique to those in the broad socioeconomic strata included in our sample. This further suggests that those who have argued for disproportionate sacrifices may have implicitly and mistakenly compared poor and working-class immigrants and their children to middle and upper-middle-class native-stock Americans. In so doing, they have underestimated the importance of home ownership as a mechanism for achieving both an improved standard of living and social advancement for a broad spectrum of ethnic Americans.

NOTES

* The data and tabulations utilized in this study were made available by the Inter-university Consortium for Political and Social Research. The

data for Cost of Living in the United States, 1917–1919, were originally collected by the Bureau of Labor Statistics. Neither the collector of the original data nor the Consortium bear any responsibility for the analyses or interpretations presented here.

1. John Bodnar, *The Transplanted: A History of Immigrants in Urban America* (Bloomington, 1985), p. 180; John Bodnar, Roger Simon, and Michael Weber, *Lives of Their Own: Blacks, Italians and Poles in Pittsburgh, 1900–1960* (Urbana, 1982), pp. 153–54; Robert Barrows, "Beyond the Tenement: Patterns of American Housing, 1870–1930," *Journal of Urban History* 9 (1983):402–418; Michael B. Katz, Michael J. Doucet, and Mark J. Stern, *The Social Organization of Early Industrial Capitalism* (Cambridge, 1982), p. 141; Carolyn Tyirin Kirk and Gordon W. Kirk, Jr., "The Impact of the City on Home Ownership: A Comparison of Immigrants and Native Whites at the Turn of the Century," *Journal of Urban History* 7 (1981):471–498.

2. Since much of the literature on home ownership often refers to the immigrant community which includes both immigrants and their children, we will use immigrant to refer to both the first and second generation in both our discussion of the literature and our data analysis.

3. Max Weber, "Class, Status, Party," in H.H. Gerth and C. Wright Mills, eds., *From Max Weber: Essays in Sociology* (New York, 1946), p. 182; W. Lloyd Warner and Leo Srole, *The Social Systems of American Ethnic Groups* (New Haven, 1945), pp. 79–81; Herbert J. Gans, *The Levittowners: Ways of Life and Politics in a New Suburban Community* (New York, 1967), pp. 286–287.

4. Edith Abbott, *The Tenements of Chicago, 1908–1935* (Chicago, 1936), pp. 379–82; William Thomas and Florian Znaniecki, *The Polish Peasant in Europe and America* (New York, 1958), p. 162; Bodnar, et al., *Lives of Their Own*, pp. 153–154; Bodnar, *The Transplanted*, p. 181; Kirk and Kirk, "The Impact of the City on Home Ownership," Virginia Yans-McLaughlin, *Family and Community: Italian Immigrants in Buffalo, 1880–1930* (Ithaca, 1977), pp. 35–36; Eric Monkkonen, *America Becomes Urban: The Development of U.S. Cities & Towns, 1780–1980* (Berkeley, 1988), pp. 182–183; Robert A. Slayton, *Back of the Yards: The Making of A Social Democracy* (Chicago, 1986), p. 37.

5. Bodnar, et al., *Lives of Their Own*, p. 153; Robert A. Woods and Albert Kennedy, *The Zone of Emergence: Observations of the Lower Middle and Upper Working Class Communities of Boston, 1905–1914*, ed. by Sam Bass Warner, Jr. (Cambridge, MA, 1969), pp. 39, 132; Jan Cohn, *The Palace or the Poorhouse: The American House as a Cultural Symbol* (East Lansing, 1979), pp. 237–38.

6. Abbott, *The Tenements of Chicago*, p. 381; Cohn, *The Palace or the Poorhouse*, pp. 237–238; Woods and Kennedy, *The Zone of Emergence*, p. 39; Jules Tygiel, "Housing in Late Nineteenth-Century American Cities: Suggestions for Research," *Historical Methods* 12 (1979):84–97; Olivier Zunz, *The Changing Face of Inequality: Urbanization, Industrial Development, and Immigrants in Detroit, 1880–1920* (Chicago, 1982), pp. 311–318.

7. John Bodnar, "Immigration and Modernization: The Case of Slavic Peasants in Industrial America," *Journal of Social History* 10 (1976):49–50; James R. Barrett, *Work and Community in the Jungle: Chicago's Packing House Workers, 1894–1922* (Urbana, 1987), p. 271; Bodnar, et al., *Lives of Their Own*, pp. 153–180; Helena Flam, "Democracy in Debt: Credit and Politics in Paterson, N.J.," *Journal of Social History* 18 (1985):441; Caroline Golab, *Immigrant Destinations* (Philadelphia, 1977), p. 148; Tamara K. Hareven, *Family Time and Industrial Time: The Relationship Between the Family and Work in a New England Industrial Community* (Cambridge, 1982), p. 360; Richard Harris, "Working Class Homeownership in the American Metropolis," *Journal of Urban History* 17 (1990), p. 46; John Modell, "Changing Risks, Changing Adaptations: American Families in the Nineteenth and Twentieth Centuries," in *Kin and Communities: Families in America*, ed. by Allen J. Lichtman and Jean R. Challinor (Washington, D.C., 1979), pp. 128–129; Slayton, *Back of the Yards*, p. 131; Zunz, *The Changing Face of Inequality*, p. 161.

8. Kirk and Kirk, "The Impact of the City," pp. 473–474; Bodnar, et al., *Lives of Their Own*, p. 154; Abbott, *The Tenements of Chicago*, pp. 379–382; Lizabeth Cohen, *Making a New Deal: Industrial Workers in Chicago, 1919–1939* (Cambridge, 1990), p. 233.

9. Daniel D. Luria, "Wealth, Capital, and Power: The Social Meaning of Home Ownership," *Journal of Interdisciplinary History* 7 (1976), pp. 267–269; Matthew Edel, Elliot D. Sclar, and Daniel Luria, *Shaky Palaces: Homeownership and Social Mobility in Boston's Suburbanization* (New York, 1984), pp. 134–149; Monkkonen, *America Becomes Urban*, pp. 296–298; Stephan Thernstrom, *The Other Bostonians: Poverty and Progress in the American Metropolis, 1880–1979* (Cambridge, MA, 1973).

10. Stephan Thernstrom, *Poverty and Progress: Social Mobility in a Nineteenth Century City* (Cambridge, MA, 1964), p. 186; Yans-McLaughlin, *Family and Community*, pp. 47–48; Hareven, *Family Time and Industrial Time*, pp. 360–361; David Hogan, "Education and the Making of the Chicago Working Class, 1880–1930," *History of Education Quarterly* 18 (1978), pp. 244–245; Gary Ross Mormino, *Immigrants on the Hill: Italian-Americans in St. Louis, 1882–1982* (Urbana, 1986), p. 117.

11. Bodnar, *The Transplanted*, p. 182; Joel Perlman, "Working Class Homeownership and Children's Schooling in Providence, Rhode Island, 1880–1925," *History of Education Quarterly*, 23 (1983):176–186.

12. Bodnar, et al., *Lives of Their Own*, p. 154; Weber, *Class, Status, Party*, p. 181.

13. Slayton, *Back of the Yards*, p. 31.

14. Roger Simon, "The City-Building Process: Housing and Services in New Milwaukee Neighborhoods, 1880–1910," *Transactions of the American Philosophical Society* 68 (1978):446–448; Zunz, *The Changing Face of Inequality*, p. 161, 170–176; Olivier Zunz, "Neighborhoods, Homes and the Dual Housing Market," *Michigan History* (1982):40; Richard K. Lieberman, "A Measure of the Quality of Life: Housing," *Historical Methods* 11 (1978):129–134.

15. Margaret Byington, *Homestead: The Households of a Mill Town*, with an introduction by Samuel P. Hays (Pittsburgh, 1974), pp. 155–157; Abbott, *The Tenements of Chicago*, pp. 179–182, 385; Woods and Kennedy, *The Zone of Emergence*, pp. 39, 132; Simon, "The City-Building Process," pp. 448; Yans-McLaughlin, *Family and Community*, pp. 175–176; Zunz, *The Changing Face of Inequality*, pp. 170–176; Bodnar, et al., *Lives of Their Own*, p. 154.

16. Abbott, *The Tenements of Chicago*, p. 385; Byington, *Homestead*, pp. 56, 155; Slayton, *Back of the Yards*, p. 31; Bodnar, "Immigration and Modernization," pp. 49–50; Bodnar, et al., *Lives of Their Own*, p. 153; Bodnar, *The Transplanted*, pp. 181–182; Yans-McLaughlin, *Family and Community*, p. 176.

17. For a complete description of the data set including the original question see Inter-University Consortium for Political and Social Research, *Cost of Living in the United States, 1917–19*, principal investigator, Bureau of Labor Statistics (Ann Arbor, 1986). See also Royal Meeker, "What Is the American Standard of Living?," *Monthly Labor Review* 9 (1919):1–13, for a fuller discussion of the original study.

18. The number of households and the cities represented in the sample are as follows: Calumet, Michigan, 21; Chicago, Illinois, 12; Chippewa Falls, Wisconsin, 1; Cincinnati, Ohio, 235; Corsicana, Texas, 69; Dallas, Texas, 72; Detroit, Michigan, 247; Dover, New Jersey, 1; Duluth, Minnesota, 87; Grand Rapids, Michigan, 74; Houston, Texas, 92; Lawrence, Massachusetts, 7; Little Rock, Arkansas, 58; Minneapolis, Minnesota, 80; New Orleans, Louisiana, 125; New York, New York, 4; Oklahoma City, Oklahoma, 83; Pittsburgh, Pennsylvania, 115; St. Louis, Missouri, 204; St. Paul, Minnesota, 91; Virginia, Minnesota, 60; Wichita, Kansas, 63.

19. Sam Bass Warner, Jr., *Streetcar Suburbs: The Process of Growth in Boston, 1870–1900* (Cambridge, MA, 1960), p. 8.

20. See also Barrows, "Beyond the Tenement."

21. Specifically, the proportion of owners and renters respectively having hot running water were Italians, 15 and 14 percent; Slavs, 9 and 0 percent; and Poles, 13 and 4 percent. The proportion of owners and renters respectively having an inside bathroom were Italians, 23 and 26 percent; Slavs, 46 and 20 percent; and Poles, 40 and 15 percent.

22. With the exception of Irish home owners with 71 percent of houses hooked up, no other group of owners had fewer than 80 percent with sewer hookups, and all of the Polish home owners had sewer connections. Scandinavian owners had the lowest proportion (89 percent) of hookups to water mains of any owner or renter group.

23. None of the six ethnic groups varied by more than three percent in any category of expenditures from the overall pattern of expenditures.

CHAPTER 5

Parents and Children
Fundamental Questions about Immigrant Family Life

Mary Elizabeth Brown

This essay addresses three questions about the immigrant family as a focal point for historical research. First, what are the components of the typical immigrant family? Second, how does the immigrant family relate to both public and private social institutions? Third, how do individuals fare in the immigrant family setting? Even though most of the examples used in this essay concern Italians in New York City in the late nineteenth century, these three questions can be used in any context to study any group of immigrants to this country.

Defining the Immigrant Family

Defining the "immigrant family" is a significant problem because historians do not use a single definition of the term. Many of the first scholars in Italian-American studies, for example, used a definition found in Edward C. Banfield's *The Moral Basis of a Backward Society* (1958). Banfield examined conditions in one town in post World War II southern Italy, and defined families as nuclear units. He explained family relationships to society as "amoral familism," in which each unit tried to "maximize the material, short run advantage of the nuclear family [and] assume that all others will do likewise."[1]

At the opposite extreme from Banfield's suspicious and miserly family unit is the Italian immigrant family of popular culture and immigrant memoirs—the extended, multi-generational family that is bound together by ties of blood, marriage and affection.

Most historians accept this second definition of immigrant family, but add that economics must be included among the ties that bind family members together as a unit. Adding economics allows the definition of family to expand to include even boarders and lodgers as well as blood relations.

Defining the immigrant family, therefore, may be a moot point. Implicit in recent historical scholarship is the supposition that nineteenth-century immigrant families were too flexible and open-ended to be captured in a single definition. The concept of the immigrant family unit is stretched to suit the specific conditions and hardships facing various immigrant groups.

Italians, for example, did not migrate as family units. Between 1880 and 1910, over three-fourths of the Italians arriving in the United States were males travelling alone.[2] These "birds of passages," as they were called, sought long-term temporary jobs in the United States to earn money to support their families in Italy. Many of these immigrants chose to leave the United States after a few years. It is estimated that over 1.5 million of these men returned to Italy permanently.

Three events in the first quarter of the twentieth century transformed most Italian sojourners into permanent residents in this country. First, the outbreak of war in 1914 made crossing the Atlantic difficult. Second, immigration restrictions in 1924 reduced annual Italian migration to the United States from over 100,000 individuals to under 5,000. Third, after 1922 the Italian government restricted the migration of males who were eligible for Italian military service. Virtually all Italian migrants to the United States between 1914 and 1924 faced the consequences of these three different restrictions.

Most important, these restrictions forced Italian men to choose between Italy and the United States. And of those who chose America, a substantial number settled in New York City.

By 1930, over 14 percent of the population of New York was either Italian-born or had two Italian-born parents.[3] Wives and mothers took responsibility for bringing the children to America to join their husbands and fathers.[4] Thus reunited, the Italian immigrant family established a home and augmented its income by boarding and lodging compatriots and relatives.

Newly reassembled on the western side of the Atlantic, the Italian immigrant family differed significantly from its American counterpart. To be sure, Italian immigrant families were most often headed by the father. Even though the father was the man of the house, he was rarely the sole support of his family. Before World War I an average New York City family needed $876 per year, but according to economist Robert Foerster, a typical Italian laborer averaged only $390 per year.[5] To close the income and expenditure gap, most Italian families put other family members to work. Louise C. Odencrantz's 1919 study of Greenwich Village Italians found that these immigrant families averaged 6.8 members and 4.8 workers per household.[6]

Family members did not go out to work at random, however. When the father's earnings did not cover expenses, other family members were asked to join the work force in a predetermined order. First, the oldest children went to work. Odencrantz's study found that 94 percent of the sons and 95 percent of the daughters over the age of 14 contributed to their families' income. Second, mothers went to work; in Odencrantz's study, 76 percent of these mothers contributed to family income through wages earned outside the home. (This figure omitted the unpaid labor that women performed in the home, such as tending to boarders and lodgers.)[7] Some families were even more desperate. Fully 28 percent of Odenkrantz's Italian American families included children under the age of 14 who worked for wages.[8]

Louise Boland More's 1907 study of 15 Greenwich Village Italian families reinforces this point about the fragile nature of immigrant family economics.[9] More's families had an average annual income of $846.80, but the husband's portion was only $487, about 58 percent of the total. Children, wives, and boarders contributed the balance. Yet even though the husband's income fell far short of what was needed, it was still the foundation of family survival. Fatherless immigrant families suffered an even lower standard of living.

This is not to say that the typical two-parent immigrant family had a stable income base. Sometimes husbands or wives died or deserted the family before the children were fully grown, and as the children matured they contributed variable amounts of income to the support of the family. Male children traditionally kept a portion of their earnings for their personal use and females joined a new family unit upon marriage.[10] All of these factors precipitated shifts in immigrant family income from year to year.

A final change in family structure and income came about when parents became too old to work and depended on their children for support. According to Colleen Johnson, who interviewed multi-generational families in central New Jersey, many immigrant families adapted to this change by assigning the responsibility for parental care to adult daughters.[11]

Johnson's research indicated that the most important factor inhibiting family accommodation of the elderly was a coincidental economic situation—the so called "baby boom" that followed World War II. Large numbers of young children in the household made it difficult for Italian-American daughters also to care for their parents. Other problems with this relationship stemmed from the difficulty of parents accepting their diminished role in the family unit.[12]

The mutability of Italian families in Greenwich Village was a characteristic shared with immigrants in other cities. Virginia Yans-McLaughlin, for example, showed how Italian immigrants in Buffalo, New York, brought "a flexible tradition" to this country, enabling them to support themselves in a city whose climate and economy were very different from southern Italy.[13] Hasia Diner and Janet Nolen described Irish women going forth alone to find work to support themselves and sometimes families as well.[14] The immigrant family's flexibility suggests possibilities for further research on other stages of the migration and assimilation process, especially on how a family adapts as its pioneer generation ages.

The Immigrant Family and Social Institutions

Immigrant families, especially those living in cities and those near the poverty level, came into frequent contact with social settlements, hospitals, asylums, schools, and other social institutions. Rather than relying exclusively on their own resources, immigrant families used both public and private social institutions to achieve some of their goals.

One of the most important social supports for the Italian immigrant family was the Catholic Church. Yet the popularity of the Italian Catholic parish is somewhat ironic. In the late nineteenth century, when Italian migration consisted primarily of transient male workers, the American Catholic hierarchy had concluded that the Italian immigrants were an irreligious people. However, families settled down to raise children, Greenwich Village's Italian community supported two national parishes and augmented the membership of several territorial parishes.

The purpose of these national parishes was to ease the transition from being an *Italian* Catholic to being an *Italian-American* Catholic. The sermons during Mass and other religious services were delivered in the Italian language, and parish workers supported the new families with a web of social services, including what are now called day care centers.

Although most Italians did not support Catholic education, some Italian parents actually preferred the parochial school because the public school made their children "less respectful and obedient and more independent."[15] In addition to school, Italian-American children were kept busy with various parish activities, including acolytes, choirs, drama groups, team sports, and summer camps. All of these efforts were to keep the children under both parental and Church control.[16]

The American Catholic clergy supported these parish programs because they were effective alternatives to similar programs offered by local Protestant churches and civic philanthropies. Parish leaders feared that immigrants would be lured away from the Church by these non-Catholic activities.[17]

These fears were not warranted, however. Many immigrant families accepted Protestant social services without leaving the Church. Despite the hierarchy's emphasis on parochial schools, most Italians sent their children to public schools. They also accepted the help of private non-Catholic philanthropies. The Children's Aid Society, Greenwich House, and The Charity Organization Society were three such enterprises in the Italian neighborhoods of Greenwich Village.[18] In short, immigrants took help where they found it.

Political organizations also functioned as surrogate social institutions. Public officials needed votes to stay in office and they earned those votes by performing services for their constituents. The alderman might extricate a wayward son or daughter from the court system, gain the release of a loved one confined to a state hospital, or find work for the unemployed. Most important, support was provided to impoverished families in the form of money, food, recreation, education, and even funeral services if needed. In short, political organizations filled in for the lack of a responsive public social service system.

The experience of Italians in Greenwich Village was not unique. Linda Gordon has shown how Boston's social services agencies assisted immigrant women during moments of crisis. Diane C. Vecchio's study of Italian women working for the Endicott-Johnson Shoe Company in upstate New York indicates that one appeal of working for this particular company was that management encouraged the labor force to think of itself as a big family and also to think of what employment at Endicott-Johnson could do to provide income and benefits to support a family.[19] Much of the recent historical research underscores not only the resourcefulness but also the vulnerability of immigrant families.

Members of the Family

In his classic volume *The Uprooted*, Oscar Handlin describes an immigrant family on their way to church. "Papa, Mama and the boys and girls covering the paved walk in a pair of uneven rows," Handlin wrote. "They no longer cohered as a family and, as individuals, could scarcely say how they stood to one another."[20] Their life experiences, their longings, even their dreams differed so greatly, depending as they did on their age at emigration. The family was not an irreducible unit, but composed of individuals. One cannot study the effects of immigration without examining how it divided immigrant parents from their children.

Children generally were the first family members to attract public attention. Were the children at school? Were they old enough to be at work? Were they sick or malnourished? Progressive reformers at the turn of the century wanted to know.

Certainly no reformer more than Jacob Riis was sensitive to the needs of immigrant children.[21] After observing the growth and development of his own children, Riis began looking in the mouths of children in the sweatshops. Many parents put their children to work as soon as possible and lied about their ages. But the mouth told the story; a lack of rear molars, which come in at age 12 or 13, showed who was below the legal working age.

Riis was shocked at the number of underage workers in the sweatshops, but the immigrants had another perspective. In Italy, education was secondary to economic security. Indeed, Italian families measured their success in America in terms of wages and property. It would take another generation before education became a paramount concern of Italian American families.

This lack of interest in education concerned social reformers at the turn of the century. They feared that Italian and Italian-American adolescents had a predilection for criminal activity.[22] Most Italian-American youth were suspected of criminal behavior, a prejudice that lasted well into the 1950s. In the 1920s, for example, young Italian boys were presumed to be delinquents while their older brothers were thought to be bootleggers. Italian ancestry seemed to be proof enough.

Not everyone gave in to this form of prejudice, of course. But even those social reformers who rejected such generalizations looked for reasons why Italian boys seemed so rebellious. After spending most of his adult life as a teacher and principal in New York's Italian neighborhoods, Leonard Covello concluded that the friction between Italian family characteristics and the expectations of the educational establishment made it difficult for Italian-American boys to succeed in school.[23]

Irwin L. Child focused on the larger society and pictured the second generation as being adrift between two shores. These young men did not fully accept their Italian heritage because they wanted to be Americans, but old-fashioned American prejudice prevented their acceptance as anything but Italians.[24]

Even Italian-American parents accepted, however reluctantly, the notion that their boys were in trouble. Both Greenwich Village parishes, for example, sponsored teen programs during the 1950s because parents perceived their neighborhood as full of criminal temptation and their sons as particularly vulnerable to such temptation.

Parents and reformers were less concerned about the girls. Young Italian-American girls generally were confined to a world made up of equal parts home, school, work, market, and church. They were hemmed in with rules reinforced by corporal punishment, psychological coercion, and social ostracism. For the most part, the small contribution of girls to the delinquency problem was confined to unsupervised dating.[25]

Italian immigrant memoirs and feminist historians have raised the question of whether or not immigration was a wise choice for adult women. For example, Edward Corsi's mother brought him and his siblings to New York to join their stepfather. The youngsters acclimated well to American life and the stepfather toiled dutifully in a local piano factory to support his family. But Corsi's mother could not adjust to her new home; she returned to Italy lonely and heartbroken and died within a year.[26] In a similar vein, a recent study by Robert Orsi indicated how Italian immigrant communities honored Italian mothers for maintaining family life but also blamed them for the social deterioration of the family unit caused by migration.[27]

Obstetrics exemplifies the impact of immigration on the lives of Italian women. Women in Italy and America had distinctly different birthing experiences. In Italy, midwives provided primary neonatal care and the vast majority of births in Italy took place in private homes. In the United States, however, Italian immigration coincided with what has been called "the medicalization of childbirth."[28] Physicians predominated and their care extended from the diagnosis of pregnancy until after delivery; most births took place at a hospital. Immigrant women came to the United States with a preference for midwives, but accepted the American method without much resistance. Was the loss of female community worth the increased comfort? Immigrant women have left little testimony on this most intimate of family activities.

Living standards were another source of ambiguity and differing perspectives. Progressive reformers like Jacob Riis often depicted Italian families as living in dire poverty, but the Italians themselves had a very different perspective. Italian families rarely had the luxury of eating meat in Italy, but meat became a staple part of their daily diet in America.[29] Perhaps even more revealing, Italian women did not feel deprived in sharing a single cold water faucet among all their neighbors on one floor of a tenement because that was an improvement over laborious trips to haul water from a village well in their native Italy.[30]

Immigration had a similar impact on the individuals in other immigrant families. One New York City police report that accused Jewish boys of "hooliganism" (a word redolent of attitudes toward Irish boys) led to a brief revival of the European kehillah.[31] Migration gave Jewish women educational opportunities that their culture had previously reserved for men only.[32] Ongoing concern with juvenile delinquency and recent feminist scholarship have made valuable contributions to the study of children and women. The next challenge may be to study immigrant men, and to analyze changes in their roles as husbands and fathers.

Understanding Family Issues: Mobility as an Example

Immigrant social mobility may be defined broadly as a movement from ethnic culture to American culture. This process is sometimes called assimilation, but as Milton Gordon explains, assimilation is more complex than a single definition can imply. Social mobility also may be defined as an improvement in economic status. Whatever the definition, social mobility is affected by the three themes discussed above.

Oscar Handlin's *The Uprooted* gave historians their first picture of social mobility, and it was a dismal scene. Migration traumatized the first generation and the second generation was suspended between two cultures. It was not until the third generation that the immigrant family felt at home in America. In 1964 Rudolph Vecoli used new evidence to test Handlin's thesis and found it wanting.[33] By 1985, Handlin's theories had been so thoroughly disputed that John Bodnar titled his survey of urban immigration *The Transplanted*.[34] Uprooted or transplanted, a dominant element in immigrant assimilation was a change in family life.

If the family was indeed transplanted rather than uprooted, it was because of its flexibility. As early as 1943, Paul J. Campisi charted the shift in family priorities.[35] The first generation of immigrants was "adult-oriented," but assimilated families made decisions to benefit the youngest generation instead of the eldest.[36] Rather than removing their children from school and thereby sacrificing their future for the sake of short-term income, newly assimilated Italian Americans continued their children's education. This major shift in attitude represented the change from Italian to American in family orientation.

In addition to altering its priorities to suit the situation, the immigrant family took advantage of both public and private social institutions to achieve economic security. Two books on comparative immigrant socioeconomic mobility underscore the importance of education to the future prosperity of immigrant families.

Cleveland's Italians, for example, concentrated their efforts on achieving status and wealth through the accumulation of property and the acquisition of local businesses. In this environment children were sent to work rather than to school. Even though the father might move from laborer to shopkeeper, he found it difficult to pass on his hard-earned upward mobility to the next generation.[37]

New York Italians followed a different path, however, one that increasingly emphasized education. Even though New York Italians did not acquire wealth and property as quickly as their countrymen in Cleveland, the children of these New Yorkers were more likely to reach the next rung of the socioeconomic ladder than their second-generation cousins in Cleveland.[38]

Climbing the economic ladder affected different family members in different ways. Italians did not treat their children equally, especially when it came to education. The boys were sent to college to prepare them for a useful trade or career. Girls, however, were rarely allowed to go beyond high school. Most Italian-American parents believed that their daughters would achieve their economic status through marriage, not through a career. It was only the most liberal parent or the most persistent daughter who went to college in the decades prior to World War II.[39]

Like everything else in immigration studies, measuring assimilation leads the researcher back to the question of standards. Should assimilation be measured by contemporary standards or those of the immigrants themselves? A personal experience may be useful here. The Greenwich Village Italians I interviewed always elaborated on their decision to remain in the city rather than move to the suburbs. It was not that they couldn't afford to move, they noted; of course they could. No, they wanted to stay in the city and they wanted me to know that they had good reasons for doing so. It was clear that they were sensitive about this decision to stay and believed that they were being judged harshly for not having joined the trek to suburbia.

My interviews with Greenwich Village Italians underscores this essay's central point. When studying immigrant families, it is important to allow variations in the concept and definition of family. It is also important that by concentrating on immigrant family life that one not lose sight of the other social institutions of immigration and assimilation. Finally, any study of the family should remember to balance concern for the group with proper respect for the individual.

NOTES

1. Edward C. Banfield, *The Moral Basis of a Backward Society* (New York, 1958), p. 58.

2. Silvano M. Tomasi, *Piety and Power: The Role of Italian Parishes in the New York Metropolitan Area, 1880–1930* (New York, 1975), p. 22.

3. Ira Rosenwaike, *Population History of New York City* (Syracuse, 1972), p. 204.

4. Edward Corsi, *In the Shadow of Liberty: The Chronicle of Ellis Island* (New York, 1937).

5. Robert F. Foerster, *The Italian Emigration of Our Times* (Cambridge, 1924), p. 379.

6. Louise C. Odenkrantz, *Italian Women in Industry* (New York, 1919), p. 192.

7. By contrast with European immigrants, African-American mothers went to work before any of their children went to work. See Elizabeth H. Pleck, "A Mother's Wage: Income Earning among Married Italian and Black Women, 1896–1911," in Michael Gordon, ed. *The American Family in Social-Historical Perspective,* 2nd ed. (New York, 1978), pp. 490–510.

8. Odenkrantz, *Italian Women,* p. 169. For more on child labor, see John Zuccni, *Little Slaves of the Harp: Italian Child Street Musicians in Nineteenth-Century Paris, London and New York* (Montreal, 1992), and David Nasau, *Children of the City at Work and at Play* (New York, 1985).

9. Louise Boland More, *Wage Earners' Budgets: A Study of Standard and Cost of Living in New York City* (New York, 1907), p. 85.

10. Kathy Peiss, *Cheap Amusements: Working Women and Leisure in Turn-of-the-Century New York* (Philadelphia, 1986).

11. Colleen Leahy Johnson, *Growing Up and Growing Old in Italian-American Families* (New Brunswick, NJ, 1985).

12. Eugene J. Cacciola, M.D., "Ethnic and Cultural Variations in the Care of the Aged: Some Aspects of Working with the Italian Elderly," *Journal of Geriatric Psychiatry* 15 (1982):197–208.

13. Virginia Yans-McLaughlin, *Family and Community: Italian Immigrants in Buffalo, 1880–1930* (Ithaca, NY, 1982).

14. Hasia R. Diner, *Erin's Daughters in America: Irish Immigrant Women in the Nineteenth Century* (Baltimore, 1983); Janet Nolan, *Ourselves Alone: Women's Immigration From Ireland, 1850–1920* (Lexington, 1989).

15. Nicholas J. Russo, "The Origin and Progress of Our Italian Mission Work in New York," *Woodstock Letters* 25 (1896):141.

16. "A Short History of Our Lady of Loretto, New York," *Woodstock Letters* 46 (1917):181.

17. Judith N. DeSena, "The Participation of Italian American Women in Community Organizations," in Dominic Candeloro, et al., eds., *Italian Ethnics: Their Language, Literature, and Lives* (New York, 1990), pp. 185–189.

18. Mary Elizabeth Brown, "Italian Immigrant Catholic Clergy and an Exception to the Rule: The Reverend Antonio Demo, Our Lady of Pompei; Greenwich Village, 1899–1933." *Church History* 62 (1993):41–59.

19. Diane C. Vecchio, "Italian Women in Industry: The Shoeworkers of Endicott, New York, 1914–1935," *Journal of American Ethnic History* 8 (1989): 60–86.

20. Oscar Handlin, *The Uprooted*, 2nd ed. (Boston, 1973), pp. 216–217.

21. Jacob Riis, *How the Other Half Lives: Studies Among the Tenements of New York* (New York, 1971), p. 123

22. Federal Writer's Project, *The Italians of New York* (St. Clair Shores, MI, 1976), pp. 50–80.

23. Leonard Covello, *The Social Background of the Italo-American School Child: A Study of Southern Italian Family Mores and their Effect on the School Situation in Italy and America* (Leiden, Netherlands, 1967).

24. Irwin L. Child, *Italian or American? The Second Generation in Conflict* (New Haven, 1943). Sociologist Alejander Portes has taken up the subject of post-1965 second generation Americans.

25. Dorothy Reed, *Leisure Time of Girls in a "Little Italy"* (Portland, OR, 1932).

26. Corsi, *In the Shadow of Liberty*, p. 23.

27. Robert Anthony Orsi, *The Madonna of 115th Street: Faith and Community in Italian Harlem, 1880–1950* (New Haven, 1985), pp. 107-149.

28. Angela D. Danzi, "Old World Traits Obliterated: Immigrant Midwives and the Medicalization of Childbirth," in Candelero, et al., eds., *Italian Ethnics*, pp. 215–230.

29. John F. Mariani, "Everybody Likes Italian Food," *American Heritage* 40 (1989):123–131.

30. Donna R. Gabaccia, *From Sicily to Elizabeth Street: Housing and Social Change among Italian Immigrants, 1880–1930* (Albany, 1984), p. 93.

31. Arthur Goren, *New York Jews and the Quest for Community* (New York, 1970).

32. Sydney Stahl Weinberg, "Longing to Learn: The Education of Jewish Immigrant Women in New York City, 1900–1934," *Journal of American Ethnic History* 8 (1989):108–126.

33. Rudolph J. Vecoli, "*Contadini* in Chicago; A Critique of *The Uprooted,*" *Journal of American History* 51 (1964):404–417.

34. John Bodnar, *The Transplanted: A History of Immigrants in Urban America* (Bloomington, IN, 1985), Chapter 2.

35. Paul J. Campisi, "Ethnic Family Patterns: The Italian Family in the United States," *American Journal of Sociology* 53 (1947–48):443–449.

36. Herbert Gans, *The Urban Villagers: Group and Class in the Life of Italian Americans* (New York, 1962).

37. Josef J. Barton, *Peasants and Strangers: Italians, Romanians, and Slovaks in an American Society, 1890–1950* (Cambridge, 1975).

38. Thomas Kessner, *The Golden Door: Italian and Jewish Mobility in New York City, 1880–1915* (New York, 1977).

39. Leslie Woodcock Tentler, *Wage Earning Women: Industrial Work and Family Life in the United States, 1900–1930* (New York, 1979); and Miriam Cohen, *Workshop to Office: Two Generations of Italian Women in New York City, 1900–1950* (Ithaca, NY, 1993).

CHAPTER 6

Mothers and Daughters
Nassau County Italian American Women

Mary Jane Capozzoli Ingui

Scholarly research concerning the persistence of ethnicity has neglected the so-called "third generation," the grandchildren of immigrants. This neglect is due, in part, to the difficulty of targeting this group using conventional sources such as the census.[1] Yet assimilationists and pluralists agree that ethnicity in some form—even if it is only as "symbolic identification," as Herbert Gans has suggested—persists in suburban areas among middle-class, third-generation white ethnics.[2]

The following essay on the life and work of third-generation Italian American women in Nassau County, New York, results from interviews and questionnaires from seventy-seven women who were of Italian heritage on both the mothers' and fathers' sides. It derives from a larger study of three generations of Nassau Italian American women published in 1990.[3]

The following portrait of the third generation departs from what Virginia Yans-McLaughlin terms the traditions of male superiority and familism in shaping immigrant women's lives.[4] Like their mothers before them, the daughters of second-generation families were subject to close supervision in their social relationships, especially with men. Yet, in contrast to the second generation in this study, the third generation faced less stringent family controls. Self-assertion and initiative emerged as guiding forces in the lives of the grandchildren; ultimately, most found support in family.

Although they were not chaperoned on dates, these young women were subject to other types of control. For example, 85 percent reported that they had a curfew, usually midnight. As Ann Marie remarked, "There were always some limitations up until the day I married and left home." In another case, Rayna recalled that her mother believed that her reputation had been ruined because she had been at a picnic in Suffolk County with a young man from 7 A.M. to 8 P.M. "You don't even do that when you're engaged," her mother told her. On the second date, he wanted to go to Bear Mountain and "that was the end of Larry [because] there was no way I would be able to go. . . . She was really old-fashioned in that respect," Rayna recalled. Like the second generation, one-third of these interviewees reported that their parents had to meet the young men they dated.[5]

Supervising and guiding these women through their young adult years before marriage also involved providing information about sex. Compared to their mothers, a larger proportion of these third generation women said they had learned about sexual intercourse before marriage. These third-generation mothers also were more likely to have informed their daughters about menstruation than previous generations.[6] Likewise, discussions concerning birth control, divorce and abortion were more common than in previous generations.

Dating for the third generation usually began at age 17, although it varied from 15 to 19—not much of a difference from the second generation. While over half of the third generation (58 percent) indicated that they could date anyone, results from questionnaires as well as interviews indicated that these women usually dated Catholics but not necessarily Italians. Half reported that the majority of their dates were with Catholic men. Over one-third (37 percent) reported dating men of Italian descent or those who were mostly Italian-American.[7]

Almost without exception, the third generation decided when and whom to marry without parental interference. Love was a more important reason for marrying than was the case for their parents. Both generations met their future spouses in similar ways, however: through family, friends, and work. At their marriages, the third generation tended to be a bit younger (average age 23, for husbands 25 years old) than their mothers had been at marriage, but like them, they nearly all chose to be married in the Catholic church.[8]

Third-generation women were less likely to marry Italian-American men than were the first and second generations. About 60 percent married men of Italian descent, usually those who were also third generation and another 6 percent chose men who were part-Italian.[9] By comparison, 80 percent of first-generation and 67 percent of second-generation women married Italian men.

Despite the high rate of endogamy, the third generation, like their mothers, rated religion more important than ethnicity. Of the 95 percent who were Catholic, 85 percent married Catholics. And two-fifths of these women reported that marrying a Catholic was more important to their parents than "marrying Italian." Of those women who did not marry Italian, most chose German or Irish mates, which is a pattern consistent with the literature on Italian Americans as well as with my findings on first- and second-generation Nassau women.[10]

After their marriages, third-generation women and their husbands usually rented apartments in Brooklyn, Queens, or Nassau. Only about a fourth, fewer than the second generation, reported living with parents or in-laws. After accumulating some money over several years, the third generation purchased homes in Nassau County not far from parents or other relatives, most of whom also lived in Nassau County or in New York State.[11]

The third generation continued a trend begun by their mothers of settling in ethnically diverse neighborhoods. Despite the increasing numbers of Italians in Nassau since World War II, only 15 percent of interviewees characterized their neighborhoods as "Italian." Three-fourths of interviewees said their neighborhood was "mixed."[12]

Other differences in degree are evident in the education and employment histories of these women. Like their mothers before them, third-generation women worked before marriage and there were few of the inhibitions concerning women working that existed among the first generation. The second generation had moved into clerical positions and their daughters continued to enter that field as opportunities became available. The third generation also was more likely than their mothers to hold high white-collar positions. Mirroring Richard Gambino's findings regarding Italian women's employment, these trends also reflect the general post-World War II tendency of American women to enter clerical, service and professional positions.[13]

Examination of the jobs held by these third-generation women before marriage indicates that 50 percent of them worked in clerical positions, 25 percent in traditional female professions (teaching, nursing, librarianship, chemistry), and 13 percent in service occupations. The remainder worked in the graphic arts, textile design, and clothing design.

Third-generation women explained that it was not as important for them to contribute to the family income as it had been for the first and second generations. Instead of turning over their paychecks to their parents when single, 80 percent paid room and board. There was a shift toward laboring for their own needs and independence, rather than for the family. In fact, 25 percent of these women said their mothers saved their board for them until they married.[14]

A majority of these women lived at home until marriage, keeping most of the money they earned. The exceptions were five of the thirty-three interviewed who had lived away from home while attending school. Only a fourth of those who provided information said they had considered moving out and living on their own. The rest of these women either had never thought of moving out or said that such an idea was unacceptable.

Besides living at home, daughters were tied to their families in other, more subtle ways. For instance, requiring daughters to find work close to home through family or neighborhood networks was another means of restricting their independence. Less than one-fifth indicated that they had received any counselling from their parents regarding career choices, yet when advice was given, it usually concerned which jobs to avoid.[15]

These neighborhood and family ties, which constituted important means of social control, were maintained among 33 percent of the third generation who worked for or with relatives or friends at some time in their lives. Twenty-five percent explained they had obtained jobs through relatives or friends.

Finally, 33 percent held at least one job which was close to their home when they were single. These figures are actually lower than the findings for the second generation, indicating a tendency away from such practices.

When they were involved in the roles of wife or mother, third-generation women were just as likely to be employed outside the home as the second generation. While difficult to track and measure, since women often move in and out of the work force throughout their lives, the work patterns of the third-generation women suggested that more of them worked and had longer working lives than their mothers. Like other American women, these Italian-American daughters have been entering the work force in increasing numbers and are more apt to continue working after taking time out for child-rearing.

Like their mothers, most of the third generation worked for financial reasons. A second income helped pay for their children's schooling and to buy items for their homes, finance vacations, or purchase luxuries. The others (20 percent), similar to the second generation, gave noneconomic reasons for working: "I really wanted to do something for myself," said a 34-year-old woman, "to find out about me and what I could do."[16]

Although it is difficult to gauge whether these women were more successful than their mothers in attaining social mobility, because women move in and out of the work force and usually work in segregated positions, a crude estimate was worked out by using a woman's first and last full-time job. Three-fourths of the respondents remained in the same work throughout their working lives. This figure is not significantly different from the proportion of the second generation who were also fixed in their clerical or teaching positions.

About one-fourth of these women did attain a measure of social mobility, however. Half of this subgroup did so through a promotion. Gloria, for example, began her working life as a file clerk and later became an executive secretary. The other half of the subgroup, a larger proportion than those of the second generation, improved its job status through education. While Debbie worked as a secretary after high school, she later attended college and graduate school and became a reference librarian. This case exemplifies a recent American trend (beginning in the

1960s) of more middle-class women moving from clerical into professional positions.[17]

Like the second generation, almost all (92 percent) third-generation women were white-collar workers and held the same types of jobs as their mothers. This trend continued with their daughters, the fourth generation, with research suggesting that 95 percent had white-collar jobs, usually clerical. While most of the second-generation women were clustered in low-level white-collar positions, particularly clerical, almost equal numbers of third-generation women (45–47 percent) held high- and low-level white-collar jobs. That more third-generation women could be found in the high white-collar category may indicate a trend toward women having careers with long-range plans of improvement and not simply jobs to earn money for the family or themselves.

Within the high white-collar category, teachers (20 percent), educational administrators (8 percent), nurses (6 percent), and store and sales managers (6 percent) accounted for the largest number of third-generation women. This pattern continued for their fourth-generation daughters, where three-fifths of them held low-level white-collar positions. Of the 35 percent in professional/managerial positions, most had jobs similar to their mothers: teacher, nurse, librarian.

The largest number of third-generation low-level white-collar workers were salespersons (10 percent) and secretaries (10 percent). When the latter was combined with clerical occupations (clerk, bookkeeper, administrative assistant), they represented almost one-third of the lower white-collar workers. These proportions were lower than among the second generation, where 45 percent were clerical workers. Focusing on the figure for salespersons alone, it can be observed that the percentage of salespersons in the third generation (10 percent) was substantially higher than the second (3 percent), probably reflecting the growth of the service sector of the economy since World War II.

Although the economy generated more service occupations over the last thirty years, and more opportunities for women have been opened in the professions dominated by men, the movement of Italian-American women can largely be attributed to their educational achievement. The table below shows that the third generation was somewhat more educated than the second. These third-generation women were more likely to have attended college and/or received a degree than their mothers; a graduate degree was also more common for the third generation. Rayna, for example, said she was the first woman in her extended family to attend college, one of a number of interviewees who emphasized the importance of obtaining a college education. In 1963 Jo became the only female college graduate on both her mother's and her father's side of the family.[18]

This trend toward education beyond high school continued with the fourth generation. They entered the work force with as much education as and often more education than their mothers. More of the fourth generation had college degrees and had done graduate work than their mothers. Fewer were merely high school graduates, although fewer had advanced degrees. Since one third of these young women were still in school when they were interviewed, this figure is probably lower than one would expect in comparison to older third-generation women.

Table 1. Women's Highest Level of Education
(In Percentages)

	Generation		
Level	*Second*	*Third*	*Fourth*
Grammar school	5	3	0
High school: some	7	1	
graduate	38	34	23
Business/trade school	17	10	13
College: some	12	18	19
graduate	11	14	29
Graduate school: some	2	3	13
degree	8	17	3

Source: Interviews and questionnaires from 181 second- and 77 third-generation women.

In addition to their own educational background and the importance placed on a college degree, the parents of third-generation women were more inclined to recognize the importance of higher education. Only 7 percent of the second generation stated that their parents had encouraged them to go to college, while 29 percent of the third generation mentioned that their parents had encouraged them to attend. Of those second-generation women who expressed a favorable attitude toward education for their daughters, 42 percent stressed the importance of college.

Of those third-generation women who attended college for a year or more, 30 percent went away from home. Of the 70 percent who went to college locally, several said that they could have gone to an out-of-town college but instead chose to stay at home. Such a proportion is in marked contrast to the 5 percent of second-generation women who actually attended colleges away from home. In choosing to go away, these women were asserting their independence. As JoAnn stated: "I wanted the freedom to decide when to come in and the opportunity to make my own mistakes."[19]

Despite this trend of allowing daughters to go away, interviews indicated that Italian mores were still operative since the majority of these third-generation women, like the second generation, commuted to colleges in the New York metropolitan area. For instance, Debbie's parents believed that "an 18-year-old girl should not go away from home." Rayna's father said "something terrible would happen" to her if she went away.[20]

Finally, in their personal narratives, these third-generation women also discussed Italian traditions. While hard evidence was limited, interviews suggested a greater departure for the children of the third generation. Such a change seems to be a result of the attitude of third-generation women themselves. Several third-generation women said that Italian traditions were not being passed down and a few women felt that they were unimportant anyway.[21]

Few third-generation women mentioned the traditional child rearing values of respect, obedience and the family's importance—themes echoed by the first and second generations. The only statement concerning the supervision and protection of daughters came from Catherine in discussing the possibility of sending her daughters away to college. Only about one fifth reported that they had tried to instill in their children the idea of the closeness of the family, particularly with reference to holiday gatherings.[22] Most of these third-generation women could not specify anything Italian that they wanted to pass on or had passed on to their children other than recipes. More typical was Lucille's sense of regret that her two children were losing their ethnic identification: "The last Italian is my grandfather and I'm sure they'll remember him because they're old enough to remember him, but they won't really have the stories or the closeness, and their children's children are going to have nothing as far as Italian goes except an Italian name."[23]

Other developments which indicate a decreased emphasis on ethnicity were also evident. Like their mothers, most daughters of third-generation women dated men whose ethnic backgrounds were diverse. However, when compared to the third generation (38 percent), they were more likely to date men of various faiths (55 percent). Despite this departure, most (73 percent) finally married Catholic men, although less frequently than the third generation (85 percent). Being Italian also proved to be less important, since only half of them (47 percent) married a man who was Italian or part-Italian, whereas 65 percent of the third generation did so. Religion and ethnicity were thus becoming less important criteria in mate selection for the fourth generation.

In many ways, the lives of third-generation Italian American women in Nassau county were not vastly different from their second-generation counterparts. Third-generation daughters worked when single as did their mothers. They were a bit more likely to hold white-collar positions than their mothers. Their financial contributions to their families were not as crucial as they had been for their mothers, and more of these women kept more of the money they earned than did the second generation. Like their mothers, most lived at home until marriage and did not receive constructive advice concerning their working futures. These women made less use of kin or friendship networks when looking for work and were less apt to have a job close to home.

On the whole, third-generation women attained higher levels of education than their mothers and parental support for education was higher than that exhibited by the Italian born. More of these women went away to college than their mothers, but like the latter, the majority enrolled in institutions close to home.

Although less severe than among the first and second generations, social restrictions for third-generation women were still evident. Even though most began dating at about the same age as their mothers and most had to observe curfews like the second generation, they were less likely to date Italian men than was the previous generation.

More third-generation women than second received information about sex before marriage. There was also more open discussion between mothers and daughters, not only about sex, but about birth control, divorce, and abortion.

As married adults, most settled not too far from their relatives, a pattern also found among second-generation women. Marrying an Italian Catholic or a non-Italian Catholic was less important to them. They were more likely to work and to stay in the labor force after they had children. They were also more apt to hold professional white-collar jobs than their mothers.

In raising the fourth generation, limited evidence suggests the continuation of a few of the trends exhibited by the third generation. More young fourth-generation women are or will be receiving higher education; more are working and white-collar jobs continue to be prevalent. Religion and ethnicity tend to be less important in choosing spouses than it was for their mothers. Most mothers did not mention respect, obedience, the importance of the family, or even the supervision of their daughters as part of their upbringing. Except for the food, and possibly the religious symbols, Italian customs do not hold the importance they did for earlier generations.

Fourth-generation daughters will thus move away from their Italian heritage. It is the women of this generation who will chart their own course in life without feeling that they are betraying their Italian heritage.

NOTES

1. However, some speculative information regarding the third generation is provided in: Richard Gambino, *Blood of My Blood* (Garden City, NY, 1974), pp. 241–242, 159, 270, 273. One recent attempt to shed some light on the third generation is: Carmella Sansone-Pacelli, "Ethnic Identification in Third-generation Italian-Americans," in Francis X. Feminella, ed., *The Italians and Irish in America* (Staten Island, NY, 1985), pp. 141–149.

2. Mary C. Waters, *Ethnic Options* (Berkeley, 1990), pp. 6–7.

3. Mary Jane Capozzoli, *Three Generations of Italian American Women in Nassau County, New York, 1925–1981* (New York, 1990).

4. Virginia Yans-McLaughlin, *Family and Community: Italian Immigrants in Buffalo, 1880–1930* (Ithaca, NY, 1977), pp. 260–265. See Virginia Yans-McLaughlin, "Metaphors of Self in History: Subjectivity, Oral Narrative, and Immigration Studies," in Yans-McLaughlin, ed., *Immigration Reconsidered* (New York, 1990), pp. 254–290, for an analysis of the outlook of Italian women interviewees who were New York City garment workers.

5. Interviews with: A.Z., Valley Stream, 9/16/81; R.P., Garden City, NY, 8/4/81.

6. Interviews with: J.P., Merrick, 5/4/81; J.B., Westbury, 9/24/81; A.Z., Valley Stream, 9/15/81.

7. Almost one-fourth dated men who were of various religious persuasions; 56 percent indicated that the men they dated came from various ethnic backgrounds. Second-generation women reported the following figures regarding their daughters' dating: 45 percent all or mostly Catholic; 33 percent from all religions; 10 percent Italian or mostly Italian; and 46 percent from all ethnic backgrounds.

8. Interviews with: C.M., Glen Head, 1/20/82; R.P., Garden City, 8/4/81; J.P., Merrick, 5/4/81; J.B., Westbury, 9/24/81; L.P., Merrick, 1/5/81; N.I., Elmont, 7/6/81.

9. An intermarriage rate of 50 percent was reported for Italians nationwide in the late 1970s. See James S. Olson, *The Ethnic Dimension in American History* (New York, 1979), p. 435.

10. One in ten married men who had two ethnic backgrounds.

11. Twenty-eight percent lived in Nassau, 51 percent elsewhere in the State, mainly in the metropolitan area.

12. Interviews with: P.G., Glen Cove, 8/11/81; I.S., Plainview, 6/25/81; J.G., Merrick, 8/4/81; A.G., Merrick, 4/5/81.

13. Gambino, *Blood of My Blood*, p. 90. Top categories of women's jobs were clerical, food service, teaching, sales, typist, bookkeeper, hair dresser, servant, nurse, dietitian, therapist. Alice Kessler-Harris, *Women Have Always Worked* (Old Westbury, NY, 1981), p. 146.

14. Interviews with: N.I., Elmont, 7/6/81; G.S., Bellmore, 6/4/81; C.M., Glen Head, 1/20/82; J.P., Merrick, 5/4/81; Cf. Richard Gambino, "La Famiglia," in J. Ryan, ed., *White Ethnics* (Englewood Cliffs, NJ, 1973), p. 51.

15. Interview with J.P., Merrick, 5/4/81; Gambino, *Blood of My Blood*, pp. 40, 364.

16. Interview with J.P., Merrick, 5/4/81.

17. Interviews with: G.B., Garden City, 9/16/81; D.A., Westbury, 7/9/81; L.Z., Plainview, 7/9/81.

18. Interviews with: R.P., Garden City, 8/4/81; J.B., Westbury, 9/24/81. Second-generation women reported that 32 percent of their children were college graduates, 18 percent with graduate degrees.

19. Interviews with: C.M., Glen Head, 1/20/82; J.B., Westbury, 9/4/81; L.W., Merrick, 5/6/81; J.P., Merrick, 5/4/81.

20. Interviews with: G.M., Uniondale, 9/2/81; N.I., Elmont, 7/6/81; D.A., Westbury, 7/9/81; R.P., Garden City, 8/4/81.

21. E.g., interview with C.M., Glen Head, 1/20/82.

22. Interviews with: L.P., Merrick, 1/5/81; J.P., Merrick, 5/4/81; C.S., Garden City, 2/27/82.

23. Interview with L.P., Merrick, 1/5/81. When asked if she cooks Italian, "I make a good roast beef, that's about all," said Camille (interview with C.M., Glen Head, 1/20/82).

PART III

Agents of Acculturation

Introduction

The long process of becoming an American was facilitated by many agents in American society, including religion, education, and employment. Religion was a spiritual and psychological bridge between the old world and the new. If an immigrant was no longer a European and not yet an American, he was always and forever a Jew, or a Catholic, or a Lutheran. Education was largely an American institution that focused on the youngest members of the immigrant family. If the school was something of a threat to the old ways, it also was the path to the new. Immigrant children learned to live in both worlds. Employment was both necessary and fearful as an agent of acculturation. To survive, to sustain one's family, an immigrant worker had to adapt to American ways. A failure to learn English or pay attention to the American boss could lead to dismissal, injury, or even death. Church, school, and factory were vital forums in the Americanization process.

The central role of religion in the acculturation process has not yet been fully explored by scholars. In his landmark essay, "Religion and Ethnicity in America," Timothy L. Smith articulated the interdependence of ethnicity and religion. Religion was vital to the mental health of a people who had uprooted themselves, migrated, and resettled in a new land. Familiar religious symbols and ceremonies were anchors of continuity in otherwise tumultuous lives. "Migration was often a theologizing experience," concluded Smith, "just as it has been when Abraham left the land of his fathers, when the people of Exodus followed Moses into the wilderness, and when Jeremiah urged the exiles to make the God of their past the hope of their future." Indeed, for millions of immigrants, religion was the bridge between a European past and an American future.

If religion was the most important agent of acculturation it also was the most diffuse. Immigrants were left to use their faith in their own way, but education was another matter. Schools—both public and parochial— were established with a common purpose: to shape the hearts and minds of the young, to form them into good Americans or Catholics or both. Indeed, it can be said that education was the most intensive and focused agent of acculturation.

This is not surprising in that the education of children was an extension of family life. In Europe, most formal education was done in the home, but migration to America changed all that. American law required immigrants to send their children to school, an institution apart from the family. The culture, language, and religion of the old country had no place in school and this worried immigrant parents.

The response of immigrants to public schooling was mixed. The majority accepted these institutions with little complaint. Some groups successfully lobbied for inclusion of foreign language instruction in the curriculum and others, most particularly Jews, established supplementary education programs to teach culture and religion.

The most visible and vocal resistance to public schooling came from immigrant Catholics. The school was seen by many immigrants—particularly the Irish, Germans and Poles—as a means of preserving both faith and culture, an extension of both religion and family. Yet the parochial school was essentially an American institution and except for religion and language instruction, the curriculum mirrored the content of the public schools. In a sense the parochial school was a half-way house, easing the transition of some immigrant children from the old world to the new. The pace of Americanization in these private schools was not as vigorous as that in the public school, but the direction was the same.

A third and often brutal agent of Americanization was employment. Arriving in this country with little more than the clothes on their backs and trunks full of memories, these immigrants needed jobs to support their families. The work they found was unskilled and arduous. By 1910, the foreign-born and their children made up the vast majority of workers in mining, manufacturing, most of the unskilled professions. The sheer number of so many foreign-born workers speaking so many different languages presented a challenge to every factory and mine manager. Some chose to group immigrant workers by national origin with a fellow countryman as foreman. Work orders were given in Polish or Italian or Croatian, depending on the work gang.

But such gangs were only a short-term solution. Factory managers needed a flexible workforce made up of individuals who could communicate with one another regardless of ethnicity. The challenge of the factory floor was to teach these different workers a common language, to follow directions, and to work as a team. "The workplace was by its nature an authoritarian environment," notes James Barrett, "and foremen and other supervisors were always 'teaching' immigrants—to do what they were told, to act promptly, to keep working." These foremen used a mixture of English and foreign languages to get their message across.

If foremen were the harshest of teachers, they were not the only teachers in the workplace. "There were other teachers," adds Barrett, "—older, more experienced, sometimes politicized workers, who conveyed different notions of what was right and what was wrong in the workshop and in the United States as a society." The oppressive nature of Americanization in the workplace led to worker solidarity and assimilation.

Religion, education, and employment all served as agents of acculturation. The three essays that follow underscore this point. Pastors spoke to the heart, teachers to the mind, and foremen to the hands. Together they reinforced the message that the United States was one nation of many peoples and cultures that lived and worked together in harmony. It was a message that most immigrants accepted without question. Indeed, most embraced the message with enthusiasm.

CHAPTER 7

The Religious Factor in Immigration
*The Dutch Experience**

Robert P. Swierenga

Economics explains the "why" of immigration but religion largely determines the "how" of immigration and its effects. Although most immigrants left their homelands in the hope of economic betterment, religious institutions facilitated the move,
guided the newcomers to specific destinations, and shaped their
adjustment in the new land. Religion was the very "bone and
sinew" of immigrant group consciousness and the "focal point"
of their life.[1] One of the first scholars to recognize this was Oscar
Handlin, who wrote in *The Uprooted* (1951) that "the very process
of adjusting immigrant ideas to the conditions of the United
States made religion paramount as a way of life."[2] A few years
later, Henry S. Lucas, in a masterful study of Dutch immigration,
observed that "for years religion determined the pattern of
Dutch settlement in America."[3]

    The church community was a "shelter in the time of
storm," a provider of benevolent and charitable services, an employment agency, and the center of social and cultural life. The
newcomers embraced it with a fervor unknown even in the Old
Country. Nativist attacks forced ethno-religious groups to close
ranks, and even internal conflicts between Americanizers and
anti-Americanizers served to define the boundaries of the community.[4] In turn, the communities were shaped by the interaction of successive waves of immigrant groups, each with its
unique religious heritage.

Whatever forces instigated the migration to North America, religious communities and their leaders played crucial roles in the move itself and in determining the ultimate destinations. The churches as institutions created immigration organizations, clerical and lay leaders personally promoted and participated in it, and the church communities created a supportive emotional and psychological environment in the sending and receiving areas. Immigrants faced a personal crisis due to a sense of loss, rootlessness, and social degradation; but religious faith offered stability and helped resolve tensions.

Religiously based immigrant aid societies commonly helped members to emigrate. In the 1840s, for example, Dutch Reformed clerics and lay patrons formed organizations such as the Utrecht-based Christian Association for Emigration to North America. At least a dozen clerics themselves emigrated with some or all of their congregations.[5] Dutch Catholics were somewhat less organized and the church hierarchy opposed overseas emigration, but several mission-minded priests founded emigration societies such as the Nederlandsche Catholijke Kolonies and the U.S.-based Catholic Colonization Society. American priests organized the latter in 1911 to prevent the dispersion of coreligionists by planting colonies.[6]

American churchmen with ethnic roots also assisted immigrants. At the outset of the Dutch Calvinist migration in the mid-1840s, the Reverend Isaac N. Wyckoff of the (Old) Dutch Reformed Church of Albany, New York, formed the Protestant Evangelical Holland Emigration Society, which became the model for a similar New York City organization.[7] Subsequently, Reformed immigrant congregations in the Midwest established common revolving loan funds, derived from annual levies on the entire membership, to provide passage money for eligible relatives who were chosen by lot. The sponsored family pledged to settle in one of the participating church colonies and to repay the loan with a small interest charge as soon as possible. Dutch churches and synagogues also established benevolent and burial societies, health and accident funds, and insurance cooperatives, all mandated by the law of charity.

Not only did churches directly promote and fund immigration, but they created ethnic colonies where religion gave "form and substance" to community life. Religious solidarity provided an even stronger bond than ethnic identity alone, and ensured the long-term success of nearly all church-centered colonies. Dutch Calvinists especially, it was said, "stick together not primarily on the bases of ethnicity or nationalism but on the basis of their religion."[8] Consequently, the Dutch Reformed were indifferent to their Catholic, Jewish, or secularist countrymen even when they lived in close proximity in the cities.[9]

While immigrant religion ensured cultural maintenance, it also led to conflict both within and without. Churches with hierarchical ecclesiastical structures such as the Roman Catholic Church had to deal with lay challenges to clerical authority.[10] Every immigrant settlement also faced new conflicts stemming from the internal pressures of Americanization and external intergroup rivalries and conflicts with the dominant Anglo-Protestant host society.[11]

Some ethno-religious communities were racked with theological controversies carried from the Old Country as part of their cultural baggage. Recent studies of Dutch Reformed and Norwegian Lutheran schisms illustrate the divisive nature of such an inheritance. But internecine theological disputes were also a form of "ritual conflict," incomprehensible to outsiders, that helped maintain cultural walls against the wider American community. Commenting on one such Dutch colony in Amsterdam, Montana, Rob Kroes remarked: "In their attempts at reaffirming the boundary in strict and unambiguous terms, they did not shrink from cutting into their own flesh." "Honest wars" of religion thus worked both ways, creating factions within the camp based on common bounds of discourse that simultaneously walled them off from the society.[12]

Religion thus provided continuity for the immigrants by bridging the Old and New Worlds, which made gradual adjustment to American culture possible and even bearable. At the same time, every group had battles between conservative "slow Americanizers" and liberal "fast Americanizers." Indeed, much of the theological conflict was a reflection of this process of assimilation. The traditional forces believed that "language saves faith" and "in isolation is our strength." Liberals advocated rapid language changeover and the desirability of becoming "good Americans," in every respect.[13]

Multi-ethnic religious groups struggled with endemic nationality conflicts, as for example, the Sephardic versus Ashkenazic Jews in the early nineteenth century and the German versus East European Jews later in the century. Other classic battles were the Irish and German struggles in American Catholicism and later the East and South European challenge to the more assimilated northern European Catholics.[14]

While a few immigrants were secularists, for the vast majority religion and ethnicity were so closely intertwined as to be indistinguishable.[15] As Jay Dolan noted in his book, *The Immigrant Church:* "In New York Irish and German parishes were located within walking distance of one another, but they were as distinctive as German beer and Irish whiskey. They reinforced the ethnic differences of the people and enabled neighbors to build cultural barriers among themselves. As the center of their religious life the neighborhood parish exhibited the piety of the people, and the differences in piety proved to be more striking than the similarities of the urban environment."[16]

If religion strongly influenced the process of immigration and subsequent adjustment to American life, it is necessary to differentiate the effects of religion per se from the equally powerful forces of national identity. For immigrants from countries dominated by one religion, such as Irish, Italian, French, or Czech Catholics, nationality and religion were interwoven. Which beliefs and practices arose from religious identity and which from national identity? Was the puritanical streak among Irish Catholics in America a product of traditional Irish rural life, or religious defense against American Protestantism, or both? Did Dutch Calvinists in America seemingly revel in theological disputes and schisms because they were Dutch or because they were Calvinists?

One possible method to employ to address this differentiation problem is to study immigrants from countries such as the Netherlands and Germany where religions were regionally segmented, and to compare to immigrant behavior of the different religious subgroups. Dutch emigration in the nineteenth century affords such an example. Reformed and Roman Catholic emigrants have been identified and traced from their communities of origin to their communities of destination in the United States. Nearly 62,000 Hollanders emigrated in the years 1835 to 1880, with more than 90 percent going to the United States. For each family or single person, the official records compiled by Dutch government officials specify name, age, religion or denominational affiliation, occupation, social class, presumed reason for emigrating, intended destination, place of last residence, and year of departure. These Dutch emigration records have been merged with U.S. population census records of Dutch-born nationals in 1850, 1860, and 1870.[17] The linked file permits comparisons between Catholics and Protestants within the same nationality group, which reveal the role of religion, as distinct from nationality (or ethnicity), in shaping the total immigration experience.

The emigration began in the mid-1840s in conjunction with a widespread agricultural crisis caused primarily by the failure of the potato crop. The food problem followed a decade of religious dissension within the privileged Hervormde (Reformed) church headed by the monarchy, which had been accompanied by police suppression of dissenters and Seceders. The religious persecution strengthened the emigration mentality already strong among rural peasants who had long suffered from poverty, land hunger, and a pinched future.[18] Cheap lands in America and improved means of ocean transportation provided an irresistible lure. Some 20,000 persons emigrated in the decade 1846–1856, more than one-fourth being Seceders. Among both Calvinists and Catholics, families and church groups emigrated in large numbers led by their preachers and priests.

The religious factors in Dutch emigration are evident both in the Old Country and in the New. At home, Catholics were more reluctant than Protestants to emigrate and fewer did so. In America, Catholics settled in cities mainly and assimilated more rapidly than Protestants. Catholics were less prone to emigrate overseas because of cultural and clerical pressures against it, as well as regional differences.[19] One of the earliest brochures that warned against emigrating came from the pen of a "Catholic citizen" and was published in 1846 in the Catholic center of 's Hertogenbosch. The pamphlet's inflammatory title, "Think Before you Start! A cordial word to my Countrymen concerning the illness in our Fatherland called 'Emigration'," is sufficient to indicate the strident nature of the text. The desire to emigrate, said the writer, is a "strange disease" that afflicts "a blind crowd," who in the mistaken hope of getting away from "cares and troubles" will instead find a hard, lonely, and despised life in the United States.[20]

Catholics comprised 38 percent of the Dutch population in 1849 but made up only 17 percent of the total emigrants in the years through 1880. Hence, to match their share of the population, more than twice as many Catholics should have emigrated. Seceders, on the other hand, were heavily overrepresented, particularly in the first wave that followed the bitter government repression of the 1830s. Seceders comprised 49 percent of all Dutch emigrants in the years 1845 to 1849, yet they formed only 1.3 percent of the total population in 1849. The new liberal constitution of 1848, which granted complete religious freedom, sharply reduced the Seceder propensity to emigrate. Nevertheless, Seceders numbered 18 percent of the emigrants, but they claimed only 3 percent of the Dutch populace in 1869. Thus six times as many Seceders departed the fatherland as their share of the total population. Hervormde church members were also overrepresented but by only 7 points. They numbered 55 percent of the population in 1849 but comprised 62 percent of all emigrants.

Calvinists overshot and Catholics undershot their proportion of the population in every province except the very minor province of Drenthe. Notably, Catholic emigrants were heavily underrepresented in the three urban provinces (Noord Holland, Zuid Holland, and Utrecht), which indicates that urban Catholics were less likely to emigrate than rural. In the traditional Catholic provinces of Noord Brabant and Limburg, Catholic emigrants were underrepresented by only 5 percent and 1 percent, respectively. These regional differences in the propensity to emigrate are worthy of further study, but the salient fact remains that Catholics were less willing than Calvinists to leave the fatherland.

This Catholic-Seceder disparity in emigration raises the question of causation. Both were religious minorities and traditional culture groups with a strong sense of localism and large families. Yet Catholics were far more reluctant to emigrate. What factor(s) might explain this pattern?[21] The key is leadership. Seceder ministers organized and led the emigration while Catholic clerics generally resisted emigration because it threatened to disrupt religious supervision and instruction and might lead to the loss of social control. Only a few Catholic priests, notably Father Theodore van den Broek, actively recruited emigrants and this was done under the cloak of promoting missionary enterprise. Van den Broek had already established a mission outpost among the Menominee Indians near Green Bay, Wisconsin, and he sought to build a Christian community there.

Van den Broek was well aware of the risks to the faith. In an 1847 emigration pamphlet, he warned that in America the numerous Protestant sects may fight each other but they "stand side by side against the Catholics; . . . so it is desirable that all Catholic immigrants remain together and choose no other places except where they find their spiritual leaders."[22] Some 500 Catholics responded to Van den Broek's appeals, and in the following decades another 1,000–1,500 persons followed. By 1880, there were at least three Dutch parishes in northern Wisconsin—Green Bay, Little Chute, and DePere. But this was only a fraction of the more than ten thousand Dutch Catholic immigrants in these years. The rest scattered widely.[23]

The cultural and institutional forces discouraging Catholic emigration were reinforced by economic developments. The Catholic Netherlands was in the upland, sandy-soil region where traditional small-scale farming remained the norm. The introduction of commercial fertilizers and land reclamation projects in this region enabled fathers to subdivide their farms among their sons or to open new ones on reclaimed lands. However, in the diluvial sea-clay regions of the Protestant north and southwest, a different farming pattern developed. There the cash-grain farmers mechanized their operations, consolidated their holdings in the quest for efficient large-scale production, and cut their labor costs by laying off farm workers. These excess laborers had few alternatives but to leave farming and move to the large cities or emigrate to America where cheap land beckoned.

Another economic factor in the low Catholic emigration rate was that the sandy-soil farmers were heavily engaged in the home production of textiles as part of the textile industry in the region.[24] Home industry augmented their farm income and provided a greater measure of stability against fluctuating food prices. After 1865, when the textile industry modernized by shifting production from farm cottages to urban factory centers such as Eindhoven and Tilburg, sons and daughters of farmers could go to the nearby towns and cities for work and still remain within a predominantly Catholic culture. Many Catholics also found temporary work in nearby Germany. Catholic peasants thus had more attractive economic alternatives than did Protestant farm workers in the north and west.

In brief, the emerging industrial growth in the textile centers of southeastern Noord Brabant and Limburg in the third quarter of the nineteenth century served as urban magnets to attract families and single workers from the surrounding rural areas. The only major emigration from Noord Brabant, therefore, originated in the northeastern part of the province that was farthest removed from the new textile centers.

The timing of Protestant and Catholic emigration also differed. Both Catholic and Seceder emigration was heavier in the first wave from 1846 through 1856 and fell off in the decades after 1856. The pattern of the Hervormde emigration was the reverse—low in the early phase but gaining momentum over the decades, until the second half of the 1870s when 71 percent of all emigrants were Hervormde, but they numbered only 55 percent of the population.

The Seceders began to depart in large numbers in 1846, one year earlier than did the Catholics, and over 4,800 Seceders left by 1849. Once the Catholic outflow started in earnest in 1847, these too departed steadily, with the heaviest movement in 1850–1854 and 1865–1870, mainly originating in the provinces of Noord Brabant and Gelderland. In the interim years of 1857 to 1865, the adjoining province of Limburg first began contributing emigrants, sending out more than half of all Catholic emigrants during the Civil War era. In the postbellum decades (1865–1880), the overall Catholic proportion of the emigration declined to about 14 percent. Improved economic conditions at home and job opportunities across the border in Germany dampened the enthusiasm to emigrate. Thus Catholic emigration was more important before 1865 than in the postwar decade.[25]

On a minor note, a higher proportion of Catholic emigrants settled in the United States than did the majority of Protestants, many of whom—all non-Seceders—went to Dutch colonies in Southeast Asia and South America, or to South Africa. The Seceders, however, had the highest proportion settling in the United States—almost 99 percent, compared to 90 percent of the Catholic emigrants and 89 percent of the Reformed. Seceders and Catholics, the former a new religious minority and the latter a traditional minority, had suffered sufficiently as second-class citizens to dissuade them from emigrating *within* the empire, if equal opportunities beckoned elsewhere.

The settlement behavior of Protestants and Catholics in the United States likewise differed.[26] The Dutch Catholics established very few immigrant colonies, in distinction from the Calvinists, and especially the Seceders, who formed ethnic enclaves wherever they settled, whether in rural areas or major cities. Also, over one-third of the Catholic emigrants settled in cities and towns (above five thousand population), compared to only one-quarter of the Seceders. Thus, the Dutch Catholics and Calvinists in America distanced themselves from one another.

The only lasting Dutch Catholic colonies of the mid-nineteenth century were in the Green Bay area, at Little Chute, De Pere, and Hollandtown.[27] Many Dutch Catholic immigrants, however, went to the larger cities along the established transportation routes to the Midwest: Cincinnati and Saint Louis from the South, and from the East coast Rochester, Buffalo, Cleveland, Detroit, Grand Rapids, Chicago, and Milwaukee. All these places were Catholic centers with churches, schools, and social institutions in place. As a result, Dutch Catholics readily worshiped and intermarried with Catholics of other nationalities, especially Germans, Belgians, and Irish. As historian Henry S. Lucas says: "The common bond of faith made it possible for them to live happily with people who were not Dutch. . . . Dutch Catholics did not tend so markedly to settle in Dutch communities, but scattered, were speedily assimilated, and so left few distinctive traces."[28]

Cincinnati, Chicago, and Grand Rapids were notable exceptions. The Dutch Catholics in Cincinnati, 400 strong, had by 1854 established their own parish with a Dutch-speaking priest, Father Johannes van De Luijtelaar. In Chicago's Kensington district on the far south side, the only Dutch parish in the city, Saint Willebrord, was organized in the early 1890s and totaled 200 in the era of World War I, when a Dutch-born cleric, Father J.A. van Heertum, pastored the parish. Saint Joseph's parish on the near southwest side of Grand Rapids was founded in 1887 to serve some 70 Dutch families in the Furniture City. A Dutch-speaking priest, Henry Frencken, from 's Hertogenbosch, also served this parish from 1887 to 1906, and the church grew to 120 families by 1915. Dutch-language services ceased in 1906, however, when Father Frencken returned to the Netherlands, and the parish gradually lost its ethnic solidarity.

These Dutch Catholic urban churches were three of only twenty-five congregations nationwide that were primarily Dutch, but they had no mutual connections and all were short-lived. Even the concentrated Fox River Valley Catholic settlements failed to maintain a Dutch ethnic flavor after World War I, except for the small villages of Little Chute and Hollandtown that still celebrate their annual Schut (shooting) festival, which is of Brabantine origin.

By contrast, there were 500 Dutch Calvinist congregations in the 1920s and most continue to the present day.[29] "What held the colonists together," according to Van Hinte, "was the powerful bond of religion—a bond that showed itself to be stronger, in many aspects, than the one of ethnic identity. It was the power of religious conviction," Van Hinte continued, "that must be credited for the success of nearly all of these colonies and that made them into the foci of the Dutch presence in America."[30] In short, as Lucas succinctly summarized the matter, "religion encouraged dispersal" for Dutch Catholics, because the Catholic churches were everywhere, but religion cemented together Dutch Calvinists.[31]

Calvinists, especially Seceders, in contrast to Catholics, preferred settling in isolated rural colonies or forming Dutch neighborhoods in major cities where they could preserve their faith. As of 1870, more than three-fourths of the Protestants lived in colonies, whereas less than a third of the Catholics did so.[32]

In general, both groups favored the Great Lakes region, but the Protestants did so the most (63 percent), while 22 percent of the Protestants stayed in the East and 28 percent of the Catholics went west of the Mississippi River into Missouri and Minnesota. The primary colonies dotted the shoreline of Lake Michigan and the Mississippi River and its tributaries. In the East the colonies were on the Erie Canal–Great Lakes water route from New York City to the Midwest.[33]

In terms of the types of settlements, Protestant and Catholic Dutch both favored rural communities, but the Seceders, who had the highest rate of family migration, were most rural with 73 percent. Catholics were next in selecting rural locations (65 percent), and the Hervormde were the least rural (59 percent). Catholics and Reformed had the highest propensity to settle in large cities (over 25,000) at 17 percent, whereas only 9 percent of Seceders resided in large cities.

The reasons for these settlement patterns in the first colonies of the mid-nineteenth century are many. Leading individuals often directed immigrants to particular places for their own economic, religious, or cultural reasons. Dutch Catholics, for example, went to the Green Bay area because a Dutch priest had begun an Indian mission station there. Seceders followed their "dominies" to sparsely settled regions in order to establish homogeneous colonies. The Reformed sometimes sought out descendants of the Old Colonial Dutch in New York and New Jersey or they settled among the Old Dutch who had followed the frontier westward to the Great Lakes.

Given the historic Protestant-Catholic division in the Netherlands, it was to be expected that Protestants deliberately avoided Catholic-dominated areas such as northern Wisconsin and cities like Cincinnati and Saint Louis. But apart from the religious consideration, most Dutch in the mid-nineteenth century avoided hot climates and open prairies (both unknown in the Netherlands). The major exception was the Pella, Iowa, colony of the maverick Seceder cleric, Hendrik P. Scholte, who led some nine hundred followers to the prairies. Once the settlers adapted to the new environment, their sons and daughters in the 1870s and 1880s founded many other prairie settlements. The Dutch pioneers usually located near major waterways and markets, and they initially desired areas such as the forest lands of Michigan and Wisconsin that had exploitable natural resources for the cash-hungry settlers.

The geographical and institutional differences had a significant impact on marital assimilation. Already in the initial immigrant population (i.e., 1840–1870), Dutch Catholics had a higher intermarriage rate than did Protestants. The difference is apparent only a few years after emigration began. In 1850 32 percent of married Dutch-born Catholics had non-Dutch spouses, compared to only 5 percent among Protestant Dutch. By 1870 the Catholic "outmarriage" rate (i.e., those with non-Dutch spouses) had risen to 46 percent, whereas only 13 percent of Protestants had non-Dutch spouses. The Dutch Catholics in the United States were thus four to five times as likely as Protestants to have non-Dutch spouses (in order—German, Belgian, Irish, and French).

An even more dramatic picture of Catholic internationality marriages emerges when the 1870 census figures are differentiated by couples who married before or after immigration. Those marrying in the U.S. are mainly children of Dutch parents who were minors at the time of immigration. Among Protestants, 10 percent of the already-married immigrants had outmarried by 1870, compared to 24 percent of those marrying in the United States. But among Catholics, 37 percent of first generation couples married non-Dutch spouses and an overwhelming 70 percent of their unmarried children selected non-Dutch spouses. Clearly, the less isolated Catholic communities and the international nature of the Roman church broke down the ethnic identity of Dutch Catholics more rapidly than Protestants.

The explanation for the high Catholic outmarriage was the "mixed parish." In the Diocese of Green Bay between 1875 and 1900, where all the parishes were of mixed nationality, ten out of 58 parishes included a substantial number of Dutch. Four of the ten Dutch parishes were mixed English and German; two included English, German, and French: one English, German, and Bohemian; one was simply Dutch and Flemish; and two were Dutch and German.[34]

These mixed parishes, created out of needful compromise, were plagued with problems of language, customs, worship liturgies, and weak institutional loyalties. Most evolved into single nationality or territorial parishes. The immigrant groups, except those that resided in transplanted colonies, experienced a series of transformations. First they worshipped in an "alien" parish or became part of a mixed congregation, and finally when their numbers multiplied, they established their own parish. Over time, however, unless the congregation was nourished by a steady stream of new immigrants from the mother country, it reverted again to a mixed parish. The U.S. immigration restriction laws following World War I often caused such a reversion.

For millions of immigrant Catholics the nationality parish and parochial school were surrogate associations for the communal village they left behind. Ethnoreligious institutions relieved their emotional stress, protected them from the dominant Protestant world, and facilitated their transition to American life. As James Olson aptly noted: "Church newspapers, parish sodalities and confraternities, parochial schools, emigrant aid and mutual benefit societies, and religious associations dedicated to particular shrines and patron saints reconstructed the community that had died." In the decades before World War I, more than 80 percent of the children of East European immigrants attended parish schools using or teaching native languages. Church, school, and societies provided cultural continuity and became the social and emotional center of the neighborhood. In the minds of most inhabitants the parish and neighborhood melded together.[35]

However, a strong ethnic parish could retard but not prevent the slow movement toward a "Roman Catholic melting pot." Language was the first to go, even though its maintenance was the major function of the nationality parish. Then the immigrant press declined. Culturally, the patriarchal family and hierarchical church governance weakened and even national loyalties disappeared through intermarriage.[36]

The role of religion in promoting or retarding assimilation depended on modes of settlement, church institutional structures, and theological traditions. Transplanted churches and nationality parishes ensured the survival of European languages and cultures for three or more generations. Protestants, such as Dutch Calvinists, German Missouri Synod Lutherans, and Norwegian Haugean Lutherans, tended to establish homogeneous rural colonies more than did Roman Catholics, and the Protestant ethnics preserved their cultural ways longer. To what extent this was an artifact of settlement patterns rather than ecclesiastical structures is not always clear. William Petersen attributed the "imperfect integration" into American society of the Dutch Protestant colonies in Michigan and Wisconsin after more than one hundred years to the "efforts of the Orthodox Calvinist ministers to keep their flocks together," whereas Roman Catholics assimilated rapidly "principally because there was no separate Dutch Catholic Church." Lucas noted that "Reformed principles" gave the Calvinists their conception of life and "helped them to organize their social and economic activities."[37]

A group that assimilated even faster than Dutch Catholics were Dutch Protestants who settled away from the colonies and joined Presbyterian and other English-speaking churches. These persons deliberately chose the "fast track" to acculturation and quickly jettisoned their Dutchness. German Forty-Eighters, the so-called "secular-club" liberals, followed the same path. They deliberately abandoned German culture in favor of the American democratic system. Wherever the Forty-Eighter influence was greatest, they promoted rapid assimilation. By contrast, the so-called "church Germans," who were less cosmopolitan in their mental outlook and religiously conservative, formed "language islands" throughout the United States centered around church and creed. Lutherans clung to their various synods (Missouri, Wisconsin, etc.) and Catholics to their dioceses, priests, and bishops.[38]

Theological tenets also influenced the rate of assimilation. Churches with a prophetic (or pietistic) theology that stressed individual conversion and a life of benevolence ("good works") made it easier for members to shuck off old cultural patterns and to adopt new ones. The converts personally appropriated their faith and enlisted in the social reform crusades of the Second

Great Awakening, eventually appropriating the American individualistic success ethic. Churches with an orthodox theology or priestly hierarchy, on the other hand, stressed cultural maintenance and were therefore inherently countercultural and even anti-American.[39]

Dutch Calvinists even had a theological rationale for cultural separation, the doctrine of the "antithesis," which held that believers' religious value systems were squarely opposed to those of unbelievers. The power of resistance to Americanization inherent in this key doctrine of Calvinist orthodoxy proved to be the pioneers' most valuable asset. As Adriaan J. Barnouw remarked: "For, thanks to that same power, they were able to withstand the trials and hardships of the life that awaited the first settlers in the forests of Michigan and the prairies of Iowa. Calvinism, thanks to the fervor with which it inspires the faithful, is a great builder of colonies." A tight theological and ecclesiastical system certainly slowed the process of assimilation and sustained a secure fortress mentality. As Barnouw observed: "The stubbornest resistance to Americanization is offered by the most orthodox believers."[40]

Religious faith and theology, in short, were crucial to the existence of ethnic enclaves, led to resistance against nearby "out-groups," and strengthened commitments to the church community. The immigrant church also cushioned the shock for newcomers on a personal level and facilitated their gradual adjustment to the new society.[41]

The thrust of current immigration research is that religious affiliation significantly influenced the entire resettlement process—the decision to emigrate, the direction of the emigrant stream, and the subsequent adjustment and adaptation in the new homeland. But religious forces operated within a common context. Economic forces primarily spurred emigration among lower and middle classes in all religious communities, although with greater or lesser intensity. Immigrants of all religious affiliations overwhelmingly chose the United States as their destination, but dissenting religious minorities were the most America-centered because of the proffered freedoms. All immigrants relied on family resources and information networks in the first instance and created family migration chains. Catholic and Jewish immigrants likely experienced a greater uprooting than did Protestants and they assimilated more readily. The international character of Catholicism weakened national identities and ethnic feelings at the same time that Protestants transplanted their church-centered colonies and maintained their language and institutional life. Protestants even carved out new daughter colonies when expansion became necessary after the mother colony reached saturation.[42] Religion was truly the "bone and sinew" of immigrant group life and determined its form and character.

NOTES

* This essay is a slightly revised version of a chapter with the same title appearing in Philip Vander Meer and Robert P. Swierenga, eds., *Belief and Behavior: Essays in the New Religious History* (New Brunswick, NJ, 1991), pp. 164–188.

1. Randall M. Miller, "Introduction," in Randall M. Miller and Thomas D. Marzik, eds., *Immigrants and Religion in Urban America* (Philadelphia, 1977), p. xv; and John Bodnar, *The Transplanted: A History of Immigrants in Urban America* (Bloomington, 1985), pp. 144–168.

2. Oscar Handlin, *The Uprooted* (New York, 1951), p. 117. Sociologists and psychologists of the postwar decades assumed that faith was irrelevant to the successful adjustment of immigrants. See, for example, Abraham A. Weinberg, *Psychosociology of the Immigrant: An Investigation into the Problems of Adjustment of Jewish Immigrants into Palestine Based on Replies to an Enquiry among Immigrants from Holland* (Jerusalem, 1949), p. 20; and L.J. Menges, *Geschiktheid voor emigratie: een onderzoek naar enkele psychologische aspecten der emigrabiliteit* (The Hague, 1959), p. 104.

3. Henry S. Lucas, *Netherlanders in America: Dutch Immigration to the United States and Canada, 1789–1950* (Ann Arbor, 1955).

4. James D. Bratt, *Dutch Calvinism in Modern America: A History of a Conservative Subculture* (Grand Rapids, MI, 1984); Lawrence J. Taylor, *Dutchmen on the Bay: The Ethnohistory of a Contractual Community* (Philadelphia, 1983); Andrew T. Kopan, "Greek Survival in Chicago:

The Role of Ethnic Education 1890–1980," in Peter d'A. Jones and Melvin G. Holli, eds., *Ethnic Chicago* (Grand Rapids, MI, 1981), p. 95.

5. Lucas, *Netherlanders in America*, chapters 3–5. An example in the 1700s was the practice of Jewish synagogues in Amsterdam and The Hague to provide grants for paupers in their communities to emigrate to America. See Bertram Wallace Korn, *The Early Jews of New Orleans* (Waltham, MA, 1969), p. 13.

6. J. Stellingwerff, *Amsterdamse Emigranten: onbekende brieven uit de prairie van Iowa, 1846–1873* (Amsterdam, 1975), p. 15; Jacob van Hinte, *Netherlanders in America: A Study of Emigration and Settlement in the Nineteenth and Twentieth Centuries in the United States of America*, Robert P. Swierenga, general ed., Adrian de Wit, chief trans. (Grand Rapids, MI, 1985), pp. 729–730; and Mary Gilbert Kelly, *Catholic Immigrant Colonization Projects in the United States, 1815–1860* (New York, 1939).

7. Van Hinte, *Netherlanders in America*, pp. 131, 390.

8. Lucas, *Netherlanders in America*, pp. 473, 579, 315.

9. An example of this is Bastiaan Broere, a devout Calvinist in West Sayville, Long Island, who deliberately avoided any contact with two neighboring Dutch families because "they would offend us with their ungodly language." Van Hinte, *Netherlanders in America*, pp. 315.

10. Dennis J. Clark, "The Irish Catholics: A Postponed Perspective," in Miller and Marzik, eds., *Immigrants and Religion*, pp. 48–68; Henry B. Leonard, "Ethnic Conflict and Episcopal Power: The Diocese of Cleveland, 1847–1870," *Catholic Historical Review* 62 (1976):388–407; Timothy L. Smith, "Lay Initiative in the Religious Life of American Immigrants, 1880–1950," in Tamara K. Hareven, ed., *Anonymous Americans: Explorations in Nineteenth Century Social History* (Englewood Cliffs, NJ, 1971), pp. 214–249; and Jay P. Dolan, *The Immigrant Church: New York's Irish and German Catholics, 1815–1865* (Baltimore, 1975), p. 14.

11. Clark, "Irish Catholics"; Rudolph J. Vecoli, "Prelates and Peasants: Italian Immigrants and the Catholic Church," *Journal of Social History* 2 (1969):228–251; Jed Dannenbaum, "Immigrants and Temperance: Ethnocultural Conflict in Cincinnati, 1845–1860," *Ohio History* 87 (1978):125–139; and Nora Faires, "The Evolution of Ethnicity: The German Community in Pittsburgh and Allegheny City, Pennsylvania, 1845–1885" (Ph.D. diss., University of Pittsburgh, 1981). Faires argues for a dynamic concept of ethnicity, which suggests that churches played a greater role among immigrants in America than they did in the homeland (see pp. 66–68). See also Sylvia June Alexander, "The Immigrant Church and Community: The Formation of Pittsburgh's

Slovak Religious Institutions, 1870–1914" (Ph.D. diss., University of Pittsburgh, 1980), p. #11.

12. Rob Kroes, *The Persistence of Ethnicity: Dutch Calvinist Pioneers in Amsterdam, Montana* (Urbana, IL, 1992), pp. 101–103; Taylor, *Dutchmen on the Bay*, pp. 141, 152, 160. See also Bratt, *Dutch Calvinism;* John Gjerde, "Conflict and Community: A Case Study of the Immigrant Church in the United States," *Journal of Social History* 19 (1986):681–692; and Dolores Ann Liptak, *European Immigrants and the Catholic Church in Connecticut* (New York, 1987).

13. Miller, "Introduction," viii; Andrew M. Greeley, *The Catholic Experience* (New York, 1967), pp. 22–23; James S. Olson, *Catholic Immigrants in America* (Chicago, 1987), p. 186; Jay P. Dolan, "Philadelphia and the German Catholic Community," in Miller and Marzik, eds., *Immigrants and Religion*, p. 71.

14. Clark, "Irish Catholics"; Dolan, "German Catholic Community"; Olson, *Catholic Immigrants*, pp. 101–125.

15. Harry S. Stout, "Ethnicity: The Vital Center of Religion in America," *Ethnicity* 2 (1975):204–224; Martin E. Marty, "Ethnicity: The Skeleton of Religion in America," *Church History* 41 (1972):5–21; William J. Galush, "Faith and Fatherland: Dimensions of Polish-American Ethnoreligion, 1875–1975," in Miller and Marzik, eds., *Immigrants and Religion*, pp. 84–102; Timothy L. Smith, "Religion and Ethnicity in America," *American Historical Review* 83 (Dec. 1978):1155–85, esp. 1181; and James D. Bratt, "Religion and Ethnicity in America: A Critique of Timothy L. Smith," *Fides et Historia* 12 (1980):8–17.

16. Dolan, *Immigrant Church*, p. 44.

17. Robert P. Swierenga, comp., *Dutch Emigrants to the United States, South Africa, South America, and Southeast Asia, 1835–1880: An Alphabetical Listing by Household Heads and Independent Persons* (Wilmington, 1983). A thorough description of this source is in Robert P. Swierenga and Harry S. Stout, "Dutch Immigration in the Nineteenth Century, 1820–1877: A Quantitative Overview," *Indiana School Studies Quarterly* 28 (1975):7-34; Robert P. Swierenga, comp., *Dutch Households in U.S. Population Censuses, 1850, 1860, 1870. An Alphabetical Listing by Family Heads*, 3 vols. (Wilmington, DE, 1987).

18. Robert P. Swierenga, "Dutch Immigration Patterns in the Nineteenth and Twentieth Centuries," in Swierenga, ed., *The Dutch in America: Immigration, Settlement, and Cultural Change* (New Brunswick, NJ, 1985), pp. 27–32; Robert P. Swierenga, "Local-Cosmopolitan Theory and Immigrant Religion: The Social Bases of the Antebellum Dutch Reformed Schism," *Journal of Social History* 14 (1980):113–35. For more

details on Dutch immigration, see Robert P. Swierenga, "Dutch," in Stephen Thernstrom et al., eds., *Harvard Encyclopedia of American Ethnic Groups* (Cambridge, MA, 1980), pp. 284–295.

19. H. Blink, "Immigratie in Amerika en Emigratie uit Europe in Verband met de Economische Toestanden," *Vragen Van Den Dag* 30 (1910), p. 630; Henry van Stekelenburg, "Tracing the Dutch Roman Catholic Emigrants to North America in the Nineteenth and Twentieth Centuries," in Herman Ganzevoort and Mark Boekelman, eds., *Dutch Immigration to North America* (Toronto, 1983), p. 66. Lucas, *Netherlanders in America*, p. 213, contests this point unconvincingly and also greatly overestimates Catholic emigration.

20. *Verzint eer gij begint! Een hartelijk woord aan mijne landgenooten, over de in ons Vaderland heerschende ziekte ganaamd: Landverhuizing* (Hertogenbosch, 1846).

21. Roman Catholic emigration is described in greater detail in Robert P. Swierenga and Yda Schreuder, "Catholic and Protestant Emigration from the Netherlands in the 19th Century: A Comparative Social Structure Analysis," *Tijdschrift voor Economische en Sociale Geografie* 74 (1983):25–40.

22. Henry S. Lucas, "De Reize naar Noord-Amerika van Theodorus J. van den Broek, O. P.," *Nederlandsch Archief voor Kerkgeschiedenis* 41 (1955):96–123. An English translation by E.R. Post and D.F. Van Vliet, entitled "The Journey to North America of Theodouus J. van den Broek, O. P.," is in the Heritage Hall Archives, Calvin College, Grand Rapids, MI. The quote is on p. 115 of the Dutch version and p. 25 of the English version. Calvinist leaders likewise avoided Catholic regions. Van Raalte, the clerical founder of the Michigan colony, changed his original plan to settle in Wisconsin after he learned that the state was inhabited largely by "the mixed multitude from Europe," especially Germans. See A.C. van Raalte, *Holland in Amerika, of, de Hollandsche Kolonisatie in den Staat Michigan* (1847), English trans. by G. Vander Ziel, *Holland in America, or, The Holland Colonization in the State of Michigan* (1977), Heritage Hall Archives.

23. Lucas, *Netherlanders in America*, pp. 223–225.

24. Yda Schreuder, *Dutch Catholic Immigrant Settlement in Wisconsin, 1850–1905* (New York, 1990). See also by the same author "Emigration and the Decline of Traditional Industries in Mid-Nineteenth Century Europe," *Immigration History Newsletter* 17 (May 1985):8–10, and "Dutch Catholic Emigration in the Mid-Nineteenth Century: Noord-Brabant, 1847–1871," *Journal of Historical Geography* 11 (1985):48–69.

25. Yda Schreuder and Robert P. Swierenga, "Catholic Emigration from the Southern Provinces of the Netherlands in the Nineteenth Century," Working Paper No. 27, Netherlands Interuniversity Demographic Institute (Voorburg, 1982), pp. 15–17, 46.

26. H.A.V.M. van Stekelenburg, "Rooms Katholieke landverhuizers naar de Vereenigde Staten," *Spiegal Historiael* 12 (1977):681–689; idem, "Dutch Roman Catholics in the United States," Swierenga, ed., *Dutch in America*, pp. 64–75; Lucas, *Netherlanders in America*, pp. 213–225, 444–459; Van Hinte, *Netherlanders in America*, pp. 555–557; and Irene Hecht, "Kinship and Migration: The Making of an Oregon Isolate Community," *Journal of Interdisciplinary History* 8 (1977):45–67.

27. The role of family networks in the founding of Little Chute is documented in Yda Schreuder, "Dutch Catholic Immigrant Settlement in Wisconsin, 1850–1870," in Swierenga, ed., *Dutch in America*, pp. 105–124. For the role of the Dominican Order at Amsterdam in this settlement, see Kelly, *Catholic Immigrant Colonization Projects*, pp. 183–85, 270–272; and Frans H. Doppen, "Theodore J. van den Broek: Missionary and Emigration Leader: The History of the Dutch Catholic Settlement at Little Chute, Wisconsin," *U.S. Catholic Historian* 3 (1983):202–225.

28. Lucas, *Netherlanders in America*, p. 214. See also Van Stekelenburg, "Dutch Roman Catholics in the United States," pp. 73–74.

29. Van Stekelenburg, "Dutch Roman Catholics in the United States," p. 72; Van Hinte, *Netherlanders in America*, 856–857. The information on Saint Joseph's Parish was provided by Dr. Dennis W. Morrow of the Grand Rapids Diocesan Archives.

30. Van Hinte, *Netherlanders in America*, p. 579.

31. Lucas, *Netherlanders in America*, p. 459. For details see pp. 492–506.

32. This estimate is derived from Swierenga, *Dutch Households in U. S. Population Censuses.*

33. The religious variable is determined by classifying each township and city ward in the United States census file as to the "primary religious orientation" of its Dutch immigrant population according to one of five categories: Protestant, Catholic, Jewish, mixed, and unknown. The designation is based on several factors. The most reliable is the religion in the Netherlands of all families and individuals in the United States census that were linked with the Netherlands Emigration records. Secondary evidence was the family and given names common in the locality, the presence of ministers or priests, the nationality of marriage partners, occupation, and other social and cultural clues. The data only include the first two categories, Protestant

and Catholic. This information is available in tabular format in my chapter, "Religion and Immigration Behavior," in Vandermeer and Swierenga, eds., *Belief and Behavior*; see tables 8.1, 8.2, and 8.3.

34. Olson, *Catholic Immigrants*, p. 105.

35. Ibid., pp. 113–15, 117, 125.

36. Ibid., pp. 185–293, 203, 215–217. However, as late as the 1960s survey data showed that ethnicity was yet the strongest factor in differential church attendance rates and support for parochial schools among Catholics. See Harold J. Abramson, "Ethnic Diversity Within Catholicism: Comparative Analyses of Contemporary and Historical Religion," *Journal of Social History* 4 (1971):354–388, esp. 360–361.

37. William Petersen, *Some Factors Influencing Postwar Emigration from the Netherlands* (The Hague, 1952), pp. 65–66; Lucas, *Netherlanders in America*, p. 473.

38. Gunther Moltmann, "German Emigration to the United States During the First Half of the Nineteenth Century as a Social Protest Movement" in Hans L. Trefousse, ed., *Germany and America: Essays on Problems of International Relations and Immigration* (New York, 1980), pp. 104–136, esp. 126–127; Frederick Luebke, "The Immigrant Condition as a Factor Contributing to the Conservatism of the Lutheran Church— Missouri Synod," *Concordia Historical Institute Quarterly* 38 (1965):19–28; and Jon Gjerde, *From Peasants to Farmers: The Migration from Balestrand, Norway, to the Upper Middle West* (Cambridge, England, 1985), p. 157, 160–165.

39. J.J. Mol develops this intriguing line of argument in "Churches and Immigrants: (A Sociological Study of the Mutual Effect of Religion and Immigrant Adjustment)," *R. E. M. P. Bulletin* (Research Group for European Migration Problems) 9 (1961):11–15; Mol (pp. 54–55) also cites S.N. Eisenstadt, *The Absorption of Immigrants* (Glencoe, IL, 1955), 217–218, who notes that in the founding of Israel (1945–1948) the majority, who were strongly Zionist-oriented immigrants, assimilated more rapidly than the minority of secularists who emigrated for economic reasons. The Zionists readily discarded their former cultural traditions in favor of Zionist ideals and goals.

40. A.J. Baunouw, "Dutch Americans," in Frances J. Brown and Joseph Slabey Roucek, eds., *Our Racial and National Minorities: Their History, Contributions, and Present Problems* (New York, 1937), pp. 143–144. Cf. Mol, "Churches and Immigrants," p. 11, for whom I am indebted for the Barnouw article.

41. Mol, "Churches and Immigrants," p. 17.

42. This is also the conclusion of a study of the differential process of assimilation of Dutch Calvinists and Catholics in Canada in the twentieth century. See Joe Graumans, "The Role of Ethno-Religious Organizations in the Assimilation Process of Dutch Christian Reformed and Catholic Immigrants in Southwestern Ontario" (M.A. thesis, University of Windsor, 1973). Graumans found that "Calvinists build their own Church and Church-related organizational structures in Canada, whereas the Catholics join existing Canadian Catholic organizations" (p. ii). Unfortunately, Graumans did not investigate intermarriage rates by nativity or ethnicity between the two populations. He did, however, find that 88 percent of the Calvinists and 77 percent of Catholics preferred a marriage partner of the same religion for their children, so we can assume that the Calvinists would marry Dutch Reformed while the Catholics, as a minority group, would be unlikely to do so (p. 71).

CHAPTER 8

The Ethnic Dimension in American Catholic Parochial Education

Timothy Walch

The Catholic Church in the United States underwent a major transformation in the years from 1890 to 1930. Once a denomination of Irish laborers and German farmers, the American Church was to become a cosmopolitan, multi-national institution. It would become a church of Italians, Croatians, Bohemians, and Poles, most of whom flocked to the United States in the first decades of the twentieth century. This mass migration—the second in less than a century—added millions to the membership of the American Church, but it also created enormous problems for a denomination already fractured by inter-ethnic rivalries.[1]

Far from home, separated from loved ones, these new immigrants struggled to sustain their ties to the universal Church. "The more thorough the separation from other aspects of the old life," notes historian Oscar Handlin, "the greater the hold of the religion that survived the transfer. Struggling against heavy odds to save something of the old ways, the immigrants directed into their faith the whole weight of their longing to be connected with the past."[2] But the religion of these new immigrants was not the same as the religion of the Irish Americans or the German Americans. The religion of these newcomers was the transplanted Catholicism of their homelands.

Immigrant Catholicism was a conservative, intimate, rural religion. It was a religion that had not changed for hundreds of years and this continuity gave immigrant Catholics the strength to live in a new world of strangers. The key element in this religion was language, the language of home. Without their native language, their religion would not be the same. "The Church has made marvelous progress in this country," noted one immigrant priest, "by sustaining and keeping alive the languages and nationalities of the foreign elements."[3] In truth, American Church leaders had little choice but to accept these new immigrants on their own terms. The response of most bishops was to allow their new Catholics to form "national" parishes.

The national parish, that is, a parish where the liturgy was celebrated in a foreign language and occasionally in English, was very popular in the years from 1890 to 1916, particularly among the Germans, Poles, and Italians. Each of these groups established hundreds of national parishes during these years. The Bohemians, Lithuanians, Slovaks, and Croatians—who emigrated in smaller numbers—each established several dozen national parishes.

By 1916, there were over twelve hundred Catholic parishes in the United States using a foreign language exclusively and nearly three thousand more using a foreign language in addition to English. Concerned about the division and dissension precipitated by this growing number of national parishes, the Papacy ended the practice in 1918 through a revision of the Code of Canon Law. After that date, Rome would not allow any new national parishes without special "apostolic indult." The ban on new establishments notwithstanding, existing national parishes continued to be a vibrant part of the American Church for the next twenty years.[4]

As part of the national parish, immigrant Catholics established the foreign language parochial school. "The schools they set up," notes historian Philip Gleason, "performed the functions, in addition to intellectual and religious training, of transmitting the ancestral language, orienting the young to the national symbols of the group through successive generations."[5]

For many immigrant parents, religious faith and national heritage were treasures to be passed on to the next generation and measures had to be taken to insure that the treasure was not squandered in the new land. Unlike the local American public school, the ethnic Catholic school offered the promise of educating immigrant children without jeopardizing their spiritual salvation or cultural heritage. For this reason, many immigrant parents contributed their hard-earned dollars toward the establishment and support of parish schools.

Support for ethnic parish schools varied from one immigrant group to the next. The Germans had been the first to establish ethnic parish schools in the nineteenth century and were their most ardent supporters. But by the turn of the century, most German parish schools had felt the impact of Americanization and were using English as the main language of instruction. The Poles, who continued to arrive in this country in large numbers during the first two decades of the twentieth century, were enthusiastic supporters of ethnic parish schools. Other Slavic groups also established ethnic parish schools in proportion to their numbers.

The Italians took a different course, however, and turned away from the ethnic parish school. In spite of their large numbers and their willingness to build extraordinary churches, the Italians showed little interest in parish schools. This unique response to education—one so different from the Slavic response—perplexed the stolid, Irish-born bishops of the American Church.

Certainly the Italians posed the biggest challenge for these Church leaders. In fact, the unwillingness of the Italian immigrants to support the common goals of the hierarchy became known as the "Italian problem." The bishops' "solution" to this Italian streak of independence was to gain the allegiance of Italian children. "If we cannot get the adults," noted one bishop, "let us try for the children." The bishops focused their effort on capturing the hearts and minds of future generations.[6]

But this "solution" did not solve the Italian problem. In fact, it was but one aspect of the problem. "Experience has amply proved that the Italians will not send their children to parochial schools if they have to pay for them," noted one Italian priest.[7] Even when the bishops built and paid for Catholic schools in Italian parishes, the classrooms were not full.

Many Italian parents simply preferred a public education for their children. "Despite strenuous efforts to bring Italian children into parochial schools," adds historian Rudolph Vecoli, "only a small minority of them ever received a Catholic education. . . .Thus, as late as 1924, there was only one school for every six Italian churches."[8] It was a fact of American Catholic life that Italians would not support parochial education.

The story of Chicago's Italian Catholic community provides a case study of the passive resistance to parochial education. What took place in Chicago was also played out in New York, Boston, Philadelphia, San Francisco, and other cities with Italian communities. "With every other Catholic group," notes historian James Sanders, "ecclesiastical authorities struggled to keep enthusiasm within reasonable bounds. But with the Italians, the struggle went into providing churches and schools they would not build for themselves."[9] It was the same story in city after city.

The Italians came to Chicago in numbers as early as 1870, but they did little to establish a parish until a decade later and did not bother with a parochial school until the turn of the century. *The New World*, the archdiocesan newspaper, openly complained of Italian intransigence and implored other Catholic groups to contribute money for the establishment of churches and schools in the Italian community.

Help did arrive in the form of an energetic archbishop, James Quigley, who established eight Italian parishes in the years from 1903 to 1906. But Quigley also found that the Italians would do little on their own. By 1910, with an Italian community of 45,000 native-born Italians and 25,000 of Italian parentage, Chicago had only ten Italian Catholic parishes and just one Italian Catholic school. As late as 1930, after years of propaganda from the bishops, nothing had changed. The vast majority of Italian parents sent their children to public schools.[10]

What accounted for the Italian intransigence? The answer lies in the relationship between the Church and the laity in Italy and the economic circumstances faced by most Italians arriving in the United States at the turn of the century. These factors played a major part in the determination of Italians not to build or support parochial schools. This determination marked the Italians as unique among Catholic immigrants.[11]

Catholicism as a philosophy of life and as a world religion were unknown to the typical nineteenth-century peasant, known in their native land as "contadini." These peasants knew of the Church only through the personality of their local parish priests. Before the unification of Italy as a nation state in the 1870s, local priests came almost exclusively from the upper classes known as the "galantuomo." Not surprisingly, the contadini respected the galantuomo as leaders of a Church of immense wealth and power. Parish priests controlled local public lands, provided for the sick and destitute, and settled local disputes. Because of this power, the local priest was in constant contact with the people outside of Church services.[12]

But with the nationalization movement, known as the "Risorgimento," the Church and its priests lost control over temporal affairs in Italy. With nationalization, the priesthood was a less attractive career for the galantuomo and the Church was forced to recruit large numbers of new priests from among the middle classes and even from among the contadini. By the turn of the century, therefore, the relationship between Church and peasant had been turned upside down. The parish priest was no longer the leader of the local community. Indeed, the priest could not even count on the respect normally accorded to a representative of the Church.

More important, many priests were suspected of being traitors to their social classes. Because their material well-being was determined by the galantuomo, parish priests were often defenders of the privileges of the upper classes and opponents of change. Many of these priests were seen as sycophants at best and often seen as traitors to their people.[13]

It is not surprising, therefore, that the power of the Church over Catholic social and educational activities in these communities declined after the Risorgimento. Simply put, the Church lost its control over the lives of the contadini. "Religious education," notes educator Leonard Covello, "was almost entirely the prerogative of the older females within the family. It involved no Church tenets or Christian dogma, but included primarily the memorization of prayers and stories from the lives of the saints." Covello points out that this instruction usually lost its moral value and took on the semblance of folk tales.[14]

These Italian traditions of anticlericalism and religious self-education were transported to the United States by the contadini. In many Italian neighborhoods across the country, local ethnic newspapers attacked the Church generally and local priests in particular. Letters published in these papers indicated that many immigrants also were anti-Catholic. One reader castigated priests as among the "most dangerous men in the world." Another immigrant published an open letter to his sister in which he expressed his hope that "your child will not be contaminated by priestly waters." This tension was exacerbated by the presence of non-Italian priests in many Italian parishes. These Irishmen made Italian Catholics all the more wary of the American Church and its parochial schools.[15]

But anticlericalism was not the major reason for the low numbers of Italian-American children in parochial schools. In truth, the contadini were not inclined to enroll their children in any school—public or parochial. "From the immigrants' point of view," adds Covello, "there was no obvious need for more than a trifling amount of formal education. . . . In Italy, his knowledge, his various skills and work techniques had been comparatively static; they were simple and required no elaborate process of transmission from generation to generation. . . . School learning was, therefore, at a great distance from popular comprehension and consumption." To the contadini, there simply was no need for parish schools.[16]

More important, the contadini perceived the child as a useful, productive member of the family. Children were needed to support the family. Italian parents were shocked and amazed at the "imposed idleness" of the American children enrolled in school. Not surprisingly, Italian parents actively opposed any effort to have their children attend school. When school attendance became mandatory, the contadini grudgingly complied. But many turn of the century Italian Americans agreed with the New York Italian who noted that the attendance of his children at school "ruined all our hopes of a decent living, kept us poor, and destroyed the sanctity of the home."[17]

Skepticism about the value of education, particularly public education, was not peculiar to the Italians. Other immigrants—Eastern European Catholics—shared in this belief. Yet the concerns of Bohemian, Slovak, Ukrainian, and Polish Catholics were not the same as the Italians. Eastern Europeans saw a very specific and important purpose for education—to sustain cultural, linguistic, and religious values in the next generation. These Slavic Catholics embraced education for these purposes, but questioned the value of education for social advancement or social mobility. It is not surprising, therefore, that Slavic Catholics were willing to build their own parish schools and reluctant to send their children to public institutions.[18]

Cultural continuity and language loyalty were of central importance for Slavic Catholics because of the clash of native cultures in Europe. The Russians sought to subjugate the Poles and the Ukrainians; the Hungarians struggled to dominate the Bohemians and the Slovaks. Church schools quickly became the mechanism for protecting cultural and religious values against the onslaught of outsiders. Emigration to the United States did not allay the fears of Slavic Catholics. Efforts to sustain native languages, customs, and traditions put Eastern Europeans in conflict with the Americanization efforts of the native population.

Because of the close ties between language loyalty and religion, Slavic Catholics were almost unanimous in their support of parochial schools over public schools. "A Catholic education is the best education in the world," claimed *Jednota*, the newspaper of the First Catholic Slavic Union, "because it prepares for the main business of life: the saving of one's soul."[19]

The Poles were more forceful in their claims for maintaining their native tongue. "A Pole who says he is a Catholic but who is ashamed or neglects the Polish language," argued one writer, "is not a true Catholic."[20] The thought that a Slavic Catholic could send his children to an American public school, where instruction was in English and religious training was prohibited, was unthinkable.

Eastern European Catholics were also skeptical of public education for other reasons. Most Slavic Catholic parents were wary of the promises of public education. Public education would not only undermine cultural heritage and native language, it would also threaten family life and religious fealty. Slavic newspapers regularly condemned the atheistic, materialistic values of public education and warned their readers of the dire consequences of this education.

Even as late as 1929, Slavic Catholics continued to condemn public school values. "With a public school education," warned *Osadne Hlasy*, a Slovak paper, "[the children] go forth into the world, lost completely to the Slovaks. Their idea of life is a breezy, snappy novel, a blood curdling movie, and lots of money. But our duty to our people commands us to save our youth from the moral catastrophe that is confronting us."[21]

Like the Italians, Slavic Catholics were skeptical of the value of education beyond the elementary level. During the years from 1890 to 1930, most Eastern European Catholics removed their children from school after the sixth grade and sent them to work. "Slavic parents," notes historian John Bodnar, "not only influenced their children by the example of hard work and the demands of family survival, but also imparted definite views concerning education. A typical Slovak father stressed to his son that it was more important to learn a manual skill than attend school."[22] It is not surprising, therefore, that fewer than ten percent of Slavic children went on beyond elementary school. Like their fathers before them, second-generation Slavic American Catholics went to work at an early age.

There were, of course, differences between specific Slavic Catholic nationalities in their pattern of parochial school support. Among the Bohemians, parochial schooling was the logical extension of a European culture dominated by Catholicism. The Bohemian parish school in America was a mechanism to maintain a bond between parents and their children. "The school became something very intimate in the life of the Bohemian Catholic family," notes historian Joseph Cada. "They served as agents in closing the cultural gap between the old and the young generations."[23]

It is no wonder, then, that Bohemian Catholic school enrollments never declined in the years from 1895 to 1945. In the former year, the Bohemians maintained 42 schools with a total enrollment of 8,673; by 1915, the number of schools had increased to 68 and the enrollment was up to 13,790 and by 1925, there were 76 schools with 16,517 students. By 1945, long after the end of Bohemian emigration to the United States, Bohemians continued to support 94 parish schools with 16,809 students. Such statistics were a testament to the devotion of the Bohemians to their native culture and religion.

The Slovaks also were devoted to parochial schools as the major means of sustaining national identity and religious heritage. In Europe, the Slovaks had willingly established church schools in the 1870s and 1880s. But with the domination of Hungary over Slovakia at the turn of the century, the Slovak people were forced to send their children to public schools that emphasized Magyar culture and language.

Hungarian efforts to subjugate Slovak culture and language left a bitter impression among those Slovaks who emigrated to the United States. These emigrants vowed to fight all efforts to undermine their heritage. This viewpoint came through clearly in the American Slovak press and was expressed best by one writer who denounced public schools because "whether in Hungary or America, [these schools] denationalize our children."[24]

The Slovaks, therefore, went on to build their own schools to insure that the next generation would remain loyal to its native culture and religion. The unanimity of opinion on the school question is evidence of their determination. "Catholic leaders valued parochial schools above all else," adds historian Mark Stolarik, "they worried much more about their childrens' moral and national upbringing than about social mobility and they had no use for public schools."[25]

The statistics bear out Stolarik's generalization. By 1930, the Slovaks had built schools in over half of their 241 parishes in the United States and the majority of children in those parishes without schools attended parochial schools in other parishes. The Slovaks did everything possible to live up to the motto: "Our own church, our own school, and worship in our own language."[26]

The enthusiasm of the Slovaks for parish schools was exceeded only by the Poles, who were acknowledged leaders in the establishment of ethnic parochial schools from the time of their arrival in this country in the mid-nineteenth century. At first the number of schools was small, but as the number of Polish emigrants increased after 1890, so also did the number of schools. Their reasons for building the schools were the same as the Slovaks—parish schools would preserve ethnic identity and religious devotion—but their strength in numbers made the Poles far more visible than the Slovaks. By 1910, the Poles had established more than 350 parish schools in more than a dozen states.[27]

The dramatic growth of Polish Catholic education was fueled not only by the commitment of Polish parents, but also by the simultaneous establishment of several congregations of Polish-American sisters who devoted themselves to teaching. As early as 1874, Father Josef Dombrowski, considered by many to be the founder of the Polish-American school movement, convinced four sisters of St. Felix to migrate from Cracow to Wisconsin to staff his parish school. In 1882, these sisters became the founders of the Felician Sisters, a congregation they established in Detroit as the first order of Polish-American teaching nuns. The order grew very quickly, and by the turn of the century the Felicians numbered over 800 sisters.

The success of the Felicians sparked the establishment of other Polish-American orders. The Sisters of the Holy Family of Narazeth arrived in the United States in 1885, the Polish Sisters of St. Francis were established in 1893, the Sisters of the Resurrection arrived in 1900, and the Polish Sisters of St. Joseph were founded in 1901. Other orders quickly followed as the demand for Polish teaching sisters increased. The schools, in turn, generated vocations for their orders. In this manner, the growth of Polish Catholic education and the teaching orders proved mutually supportive. By 1914, there were 2,200 Polish-American nuns teaching in parish schools in two dozen states.[28]

The increasing demand for more sisters to staff new parish schools forced the superiors of Polish religious orders to cut corners on the education of their novices. It was not surprising for a parish pastor to discover that sisters in many of his classrooms were not much older than their students. One pastor in 1910 described the situation with a touch of humor: "A girl enters the convent; she is perhaps possessed of an elementary education and perhaps she is not. If she has advanced to the threshold of the high school, she has done well. Now she is coached as strenuously as possible and the degree work is given as quickly as possible. Three years later, little Wladislawa, whom you prepared for First Holy Communion four or five years ago, is hurried out to your neighbor's parish where . . . she is doing a work that will soon wear the life out of her, for it is beyond her power. There has been no time for training her along educational lines, certainly not along pedagogical lines."[29] It would not be until the 1920s, at a time of increasing pressure from the state, that Polish-American teaching orders upgraded their training programs to meet certification standards.

The conditions faced by these poorly trained sisters are primitive by contemporary standards. Parish schools were frequently located in cramped and unheated church basements. To make matters worse, students were literally crammed into classrooms. It was not unusual for a single sister to face 75 students at a time and some of these dedicated nuns had as many as 100 children in their charge. "So many of our young people were suffocating in cramped, poorly ventilated classrooms," remembered one parishioner in Chicago. "It was a pity to see them packed like herrings in a barrel during the hours of instruction pouring over their books."[30] Such conditions were typical of schools in Polish parishes across the country at the turn of the century.

The tools for teaching—books, maps, blackboards—were in short supply. "The lack of educational aids led to inventiveness," notes historian Anthony Kuzniewski. "At one school, children wrote with chalk on stone lids instead of slate tablets."[31] The Felician sisters did take the initiative in compiling texts for use in Polish-American parish schools, and between 1877 and 1904 the order published 45 titles on various subjects. The readers included prose and poetry from classic Polish authors and the history texts told the story of Polish-American heroes such as Thaddeus Kosciuszko and Casmir Pulaski. But the number of books was never sufficient to meet the demand.

The rapid growth of Polish Catholic schools in the first decade of the twentieth century caught the attention of the Catholic Educational Association. At the CEA's ninth annual meeting in 1912, Polish Catholic educators sat down to assess the future of their parish schools. The educators were pleased at the educational initiative of Polish parents. "They seem to realize perfectly," noted Father Francis Retka, "that there would be little use of raising magnificent churches to last for ages, if there were no schools to transmit Catholicity to future generations."[32]

The CEA group defended the use of the Polish language in the schools as an important tool in the campaign to preserve religious faith and they hotly contested critics who accused the Polish-American people of disloyalty. "I am not afraid to state here publicly," argued Father C. Tomaszewski, "that America is being served by none more truly than those who carry in their impetuous hearts, the memories and hopes of Poland."[33] Father Anthony Taskowski concluded "that the outlook for Polish schools is bright and with God's blessing and the continued efforts and sacrifices of our Sisters and pastors, the Polish parochial schools are bound to come up to the desired standard of efficiency and scholarship."[34]

Father Taskowski was correct; the future of Polish parochial schools over the next two decades would be bright. By 1930, the number of Polish parochial schools exceeded 500. This is not to imply that the Polish schools of 1930 were the same as those of 1912. The campaign for Americanization overwhelmed Polish Catholic schools in the years after World War I. The schools of the 1930s were Polish in name but not in curriculum or language. Father Taskowski and his colleagues must have been chagrined at the "success" of Polish parochial schools.

The Americanization campaign was waged on several different fronts. Certainly the most visible efforts originated outside the Polish-American community. State law in the early 1920s mandated that all instruction in private schools should be conducted in English and frequently required that private school teachers meet state standards in teacher training.

The Catholic hierarchy also joined in the campaign for Americanization through their instructions to pastors and diocesan school boards asserted the right to approve the languages and course of study used in parochial school classrooms. In fact, the hierarchy took a vocal and visible role in this process. Prelates such as James Gibbons, George Mundelein and John Ireland led the campaign. "Ours is the American Church," noted Ireland, "and not Irish, German, Italian, or Polish—and we will keep it American."[35]

As important as these external forces were, the most important force for Americanization came from within the Polish-American community itself. As the older generation of priests and laymen gave way to an American-born generation, the Old World ways were abandoned. Even as early as 1910, the signs of change were present. "Not two boys out of twenty employ Polish in their conversation with one another," noted one pastor in that year, "and in all probability the two boys, could they be found, would be immigrants."[36]

By the mid-1920s the number of Polish immigrants allowed in to the country was severely restricted and Polish-born nuns were being replaced in the classrooms by American-born sisters of Polish descent. Polish language and culture was less important to American-born Poles than it was to their parents. The new generation did not object to an Americanized curriculum; in fact, they welcomed it. A small minority of Polish Catholic educators tried to prevent "de-Polanization," but they had little effect. By the 1930s, Polish language and culture had become extra-curricular subjects in most parochial schools and dropped altogether at some of these institutions.[37]

The Americanization of Polish-American parochial schools during the years after World War I was not unique. All ethnic schools came in for the same treatment. Perhaps it was inevitable. The ethnic parochial school was tolerated as temporarily expedient by most Americans—both Catholic and non-Catholic. It was assumed by all that national parishes and foreign language usage would die out as the new immigrants acclimated themselves to American society. But many of these immigrants held on to their native languages and customs with a fierce determination that must have disheartened the American public.

But the war, with its propaganda campaign against all things foreign, ended the tolerance of the American public for ethnic parochial schools. The American public in general, and the Catholic hierarchy in particular, would no longer accept the argument of ethnic leaders that immigrants could maintain their native languages and cultures and still be loyal to their new nation. The American public rejected this argument as contradictory and pressured the foreign-born to openly pledge their total allegiance to the United States. Ethnic parochial schools were a casualty of this war-time loyalty campaign.[38]

The annual meetings of the Catholic Educational Association during and after the war reflected the growing concerns of Catholic educators about ethnic parochial schools. Flag-waving patriotism was interlaced throughout the programs during the war years and for many years after. Sensitive to public criticism of foreign nationalism, CEA speakers argued that Americanization was in the best interest of all Catholic children. Even after the war, with a world made safe for democracy, the CEA kept up the pressure on ethnic parochial schools.[39]

The CEA meeting held after the end of the war stressed this theme. At their meeting in June 1919, the Parish School Department formally and unanimously endorsed the proposal that "as thorough and consistent teaching of English" should be conducted in every parish school. Speakers at that meeting expressed similar arguments for the importance of Americanization. "It is hard to admit," noted Father Joseph M'Clancy of Brooklyn, "but the war made it evident that in all elementary schools of the land, Catholic, public, and private, patriotism was not instilled as a habit to the extent that the security of the nation demanded."[40] M'Clancy, a popular and frequent speaker at the CEA meetings, spoke for many when he urged all Catholic educators to work with public officials to instill patriotism in all school children.

Yet another speaker, William J. McAuliffe of Cathedral College in New York, attacked the immigrant claim that Americanization could be accomplished through the use of native languages. McAuliffe, like many Catholic educators, rejected this argument. In its place, he advocated a three-level approach. First, immigrant children were to receive a solid grounding in the English language. Second, the immigrant child should be in a thoroughly American classroom instructed by a teacher who had a thorough command of the English language and an unswerving devotion to American traditions. Finally, McAuliffe hoped that immigrant children would choose to extend their education beyond grade school. McAuliffe also advocated the establishment of a network of adult education classes to Americanize those immigrants beyond the influence of the parish school. The solution to the Americanization problem, noted McAuliffe, "will come by gathering the community around the Catholic Church and the Catholic school as the community centre."[41]

M'Clancy and McAuliffe were not alone in their views as educator after educator at CEA meetings throughout the 1920s spoke out in favor of Americanization. Additional momentum was provided by the National Catholic Welfare Conferences's Civic Education Bureau. Directed by John A. Lapp and Charles A. McMahon, the bureau promoted a variety of measures to Americanize Catholics of all ages. The bureau promoted the Boy Scouts of America because scouting formed boys into young men "who know one ism, who love one ism and who profess one ism—100% Americanism." More important, the bureau published and distributed *The Civics Catechism on the Rights and Duties of American Citizens* for use in the Catholic schools throughout the country. The pamphlet was translated into 14 languages and published in Catholic and foreign language newspapers. Within three years after the end of the war, the Church was putting substantial pressure on ethnic Catholic schools to conform to American ways.[42]

Perhaps the most articulate and certainly the most zealous spokeman for Americanization was Father M'Clancy. "In a word," M'Clancy wrote, "Americanization is the endeavor to make America a united people; to eliminate alienism and radicalism, to turn out of our lower school boys and girls the men and women of tomorrow, who will shed all foreign tastes and allegiance and come into the unity of a nation one in language, admiration, and action. It is a noble project, into which our Catholic schools are quick to enter." M'Clancy felt that he had the plan to Americanize the ethnic Catholic schools.[43]

How could national parishes improve their schools? "The classroom," M'Clancy argued, "should be in the charge of a teacher already a citizen or else on the way to the acquisition of that high honor. History and civics should be studied under the old idea of developing a burning love and admiration for America. The question of what language should be employed had definitely been decided in favor of English, the tongue of the land."[44] M'Clancy encouraged pastors to make the "atmosphere" of their schools "intensely American." This could be accomplished by having the children salute the flag and sing the national anthem each morning. Classroom walls should be decorated with pictures of national leaders and heroes. "When the public good so demands," M'Clancy concluded, "the use of our buildings should be placed at the disposal of the city, state, or nation."[45]

Even though some Catholic educators did not agree completely with M'Clancy, they did share his deeply-held commitment to the Americanization of Catholic education. As a Church, they pressured their foreign-born brethren to quickly abandon their Old World ways. "It is high time indeed," said M'Clancy, "that Catholics felt the impulse of life that beats in the real statesman as distinct from the mere politician. Duty demands that Catholics add their power of intellect and will to the similar power of other American citizens to help the commonwealth." Even though foreign language schools continued through the 1920s, it was clear that the ethnic dimensions of Catholic education had a limited future. "We are not aliens in this land," concluded M'Clancy, "not aliens by birth or principle."[46]

The ethnic Catholic school was a key element in the rapid growth of parochial education during the first three decades of the twentieth century. More important, these schools served as the bridge from the Old World to the new for many immigrant children. Yet these schools were destined to be temporary and transitional. With the pressure of American nationalism both during and after World War I and the end of mass immigration in 1924, the ethnic Catholic school gradually lost its value to the Catholic Church.

NOTES

1. The most recent account of the relationship between ethnicity and religion is Dolores Liptak, *Immigrants and their Church* (New York, 1989), pp. 57–191. See also, Thomas J. Archdeacon, *Becoming American*

(New York, 1983), pp. 101–111, 153–157; Dolores Liptak, ed., *A Church of Many Cultures* (New York, 1988), passim; and Roger Daniels, *Coming to America* (New York, 1990), pp. 197–198, 220–222, 261–269.

2. Oscar Handlin, *The Uprooted* (Boston, 1951), p. 117.

3. A.H. Walberg, "The American Nationality," republished in A.I. Abell, ed., *American Catholic Thought in Social Questions* (Indianapolis, 1968), pp. 44–45.

4. There has been no cross cultural study of the national parish. The story can be pieced together by consulting several essays in Jay P. Dolan, ed., *The American Catholic Parish*, 2 vols. (Mahwah, NJ, 1987). See also, Charles Shanabruch, *Chicago's Catholics* (Notre Dame, 1981), pp. 78–105; and Edward R. Kantowicz, *Corporation Sole: Cardinal Mundelien and Chicago Catholicism* (Notre Dame, 1983), pp. 65–84 for a detailed study of the rise and decline of the national parish in one of the most ethnic of American cities.

5. Philip Gleason, "Immigration and the American Catholic Intellectual Life," *Review of Politics* 26 (1964):147–173.

6. Rudolph J. Vecoli, "Prelates and Peasants: Italian Immigrants and the Catholic Church," *Journal of Social History* 2 (1969):248.

7. Ibid., p. 249.

8. Ibid., p. 251.

9. James Sanders, *Education of an Urban Minority: Catholics in Chicago, 1833–1965* (New York, 1977), p. 67.

10. Ibid., pp. 67–71; see also, Humbert Nelli, *Italians in Chicago, 1880–1930* (New York, 1970), pp. 67–73, 181–189.

11. Leonard Covello, *The Social Background of the Italo-American School Child* (Totowa, NJ, 1972), pp. 137–141, 287–315.

12. Ibid., pp. 137–139.

13. Ibid., p. 138.

14. Ibid., p. 139.

15. Virginia Y. McLaughlin, *Family and Community: Italian Immigrants in Buffalo, 1880–1930* (Ithaca, 1977), p. 225.

16. Covello, *Social Background of the Italo-American Child*, p. 287.

17. Ibid., p. 295.

18. John Bodnar, "Materialism and Morality: Slavic American Immigrants and Education, 1890–1940," *Journal of Ethnic Studies* 3 (1976):1–19; M. Mark Stolarik, "Immigration, Education, and the Social Mobility of Slovaks, 1870–1930," in R.M. White and T.D. Marzik, eds.,

Immigrants and Religion in Urban America (Philadelphia, 1977), pp. 103–115.

19. Bodnar, "Materialism and Morality," p. 2.

20. Ibid., p. 2.

21. Quoted in Ibid., p. 9.

22. Ibid., p. 6.

23. Joseph Cada, *Czech-American Catholics, 1850–1920* (Lisle, IL, 1964), p. 54.

24. Quoted in M. Mark Stolarik, "Immigration, Education, and the Social Mobility of Slovaks, 1870–1930," in Miller and Marzik, *Immigrants and Religion in Urban America*, p. 106.

25. Ibid., p. 107.

26. Ibid., p. 108. See also, Josef J. Barton, *Peasants and Strangers: Italians, Rumanians, and Slovaks in an American City* (Cambridge, MA, 1975), p. 147.

27. William J. Gallush, "Faith and Fatherland: Dimensions of Polish-American Ethno Religion, 1875–1975," in Miller and Marzik, *Immigrants and Religion in Urban America*, p. 93.

28. Ellen Marie Kuznicki, "The Polish American Parochial Schools," in Frank Mocha, ed., *Poles in America* (Stevens Point, WI, 1978), pp. 435–460.

29. James A. Burns, *The Growth and Development of Catholic Schools* (New York, 1912), pp. 322–323.

30. Quoted in Anthony J. Kuzniewski, "The Catholic Church in the Life of Polish Americans," in Mocha, ed., *Poles in America*, p. 410.

31. Ibid.

32. Francis Retka, "Catholic Schools in Polish Parishes," *Catholic Educational Bulletin* 11 (1914):419.

33. Commentary on Retka's remarks in Ibid., p. 426.

34. Commentary on Retka's remarks in Ibid., p. 428–429.

35. Quoted in Daniel S. Buczek, "The Polish American Parish as an Americanizing Factor," in C.A. Ward, P. Shashko, and D.E. Pienkos, eds., *Studies in Ethnicity: The East European Experience in America* (New York, 1980), p. 157.

36. Quoted in Burns, *Growth and Development*, p. 327.

37. Kuzniewski, "Catholic Church and Polish Americans," p. 415; Buczek, "Polish American Parish," pp. 159–163; Kuznicki, "Polish American Parochial Schools," pp. 454–455.

38. Kuznecki, "Polish American Parochial Schools," p. 454; Kantowicz, *Corporation Sole,* pp. 77–82; Gallush, "Faith and Fatherland," pp. 95–97.

39. See Fayette Veverka, *For God and Country: Catholic Schooling in the 1920s* (New York, 1988), pp. 52–90.

40. Joseph V.S. M'Clancy, "Americanization and Catholic Elementary Schools," *Catholic Educational Bulletin* 16 (1919):253.

41. William J. McAuliffe, "The Problem of Americanization," *Catholic Educational Bulletin* 16 (1919):190.

42. Veverka, *For God and Country,* pp. 79–90.

43. M'Clancy, "Americanization," p. 253.

44. Ibid., p. 256.

45. Ibid., p. 257.

46. Ibid., p. 259.

CHAPTER 9

The World of Work
The Croations of Whiting, Indiana

Edward A. Zivich

The most remarkable human migration in history took place from the 1880s until the outbreak of World War I in 1914. Traditionally designated as the "new immigration," it brought millions of people from the south and east of Europe to the mines, mills, and factories of America. While the so-called "old immigration" from Europe's northern and western countries continued, the eastern European "stream" clearly predominated. The great industrial centers in the northeastern and midwestern regions of the United States were teeming with new ethnic neighborhoods complete with a myriad of languages, food, music, and cultures that often seemed exotic to native-born Americans.

Displaced peasants from the various Slavic nationalities formed a key component of the new immigration. From mountainous Slovenia on the west to the wheat belts of the Ukraine on the east, village after village of the different Slavic peoples sent sons and daughters to far away American industrial communities. It was no promised land; the Slavs in America encountered hard, very dangerous industrial work in America's burgeoning post-Civil War factories.

This essay will examine the work experiences of one Slavic immigrant group—the Croatians—in one industrial city—Whiting, Indiana. Whiting was chosen for four major reasons. The site of one of the biggest refineries in the history of the Standard Oil Company, Whiting provided typical industrial employment for the Eastern European immigrants. Second, the population of Whiting was relatively small throughout the city's history, making the study of one representative immigrant group much more thorough than surveys based on experiences in large urban settings. Third, Whiting's Croatian community was unaugmented by any major post-World War II immigration of displaced persons, permitting the Americanization of the group to proceed without hindrance. Finally, the author has his own ethnic roots in the community, thereby facilitating contact with individual Croatian Americans as well as their organizations.

In the aftermath of this migration to Whiting, Croatian immigrants traded the role of peasant cultivator for that of industrial worker. And in Whiting, especially after 1890, industrial work was most often found at the local Standard Oil Refinery. In fact, during the 1890s Whiting was little more than a frontier town dominated by the refinery—an isolated outpost of industrialism in a world of rolling sand dunes. The steel mills of neighboring East Chicago and Gary emerged in the years after 1906 and attracted some of Whiting's Croatian workers, but the permanent Croatian American population of Whiting was closely tied to Standard Oil from the 1890s to well into the twentieth century.[1]

This is not to say that every Croatian in Whiting worked for Standard Oil. The Union Tank Car Company had a plant on the grounds of the refinery and employed Croatians in the manufacture of rail tank cars used to ship the oil. Sinclair Oil also operated a small refinery on the southern edge of town; Union Carbide later constructed a chemical factory on the lakefront between Whiting and East Chicago; American Maize processed corn oil in nearby Robertsdale. All three of these corporations employed a few Croatians. There also were two Croatians who worked for the City of Whiting and a number who maintained saloons and boarding houses. But the vast majority of Croatian Americans in Whiting could be found at the Standard refinery.[2]

Despite dramatic changes in technology and in the finished products of the Whiting Refinery, the nature of the unskilled jobs at the plant remained relatively consistent during the major years of immigrant employment, roughly from 1890 to

1950. The basic refinery process involved distilling crude oils into finished products and by-products. These finished petroleum products and materials would then be packaged and shipped out by rail to Standard Oil distributors throughout the Middle West and West.

The actual production process centered around a variety of distillation units, known as "stills." As the refinery entered the twentieth century and the demand for petroleum products increased, the stills grew in size and complexity. But no mater how large or complex, the principles of operation remained the same and workers performed the same general tasks.

The process was as follows. First the crude oil was pumped into a cylindrical still where it was heated by fire outside and beneath the cylinder. Subjected to intense heat, the impurities in the crude oil would vaporize into a condenser on the roof of the still, undergo treatment, and be discharged. The purified product at the bottom of the still would be pumped into barrels and tank cars for shipment. By varying the intensity of the heat applied to the crude, different products resulted. Low heat produced "heavy" oil products while high heat resulted in "light" products.

Three major types of stills evolved during the immigrant era in Whiting. The first of these was the "vapor-brush" still, the first unit to successfully purify Lima crude in the early 1890s. Vapor-brush stills used a cylinder thirty feet long and eight feet in diameter, resting on one side, with ten of these stills comprising a battery. The sulphur content of the Lima crude was absorbed by a black copper oxide powder in the condenser. The stills were cleaned on the inside following each change of crude oil. The copper sulfide powder was purified by heat and then was milled for reuse as copper oxide powder.[3]

The skilled worker on the vapor brush still was called simply the "stillman." In the 1890s, the stillmen at Standard Oil in Whiting were exclusively native-born Americans or northern European immigrants.[4] On the primitive vapor-brush stills, each stillman was in charge of two complete batteries, a total of twenty stills. Each stillman received his orders from a native-born supervisor or foreman.

The task of the stillman was something of an artform. He had to regulate precisely the temperature of the crude in the stills without the benefit of modern control panels or valves. A mistake in the temperature and the result was the wrong by-product. Thus the stillman became a master at regulating fire; he came to know temperature almost from looking at the flames.

There were no Croatians among the stillmen at Standard Oil in the 1890s. In fact, Croatians would not become stillmen in Whiting until the 1930s and 1940s. For the most part, Croatians filled three jobs. Many were stillman's helpers, following the direction of the stillman in making physical adjustments during operation. Others were firemen, shoveling coal into the still fires to the level set by the stillman. Finally, there were the still cleaners who scrubbed out the murky, fume-filled interiors of the stills prior to each new change of crude oil.[5] All of these unskilled jobs were dirty, sweaty, and dangerous. Accidents and explosions were frequent and often fatal.[6]

A number of Croatians manned other unskilled positions at the refinery. Some worked in the millhouse where the copper sulfide powder was heated and reground as copper oxide. The heat produced during this process was the hottest in the refinery and respirators were required to prevent the inhalation of poisonous sulphur. Overexposure to the deadly powder turned a worker's hair green and burned exposed flesh. The dangers in the millhouse were so great that workers were assigned to the millhouse on a rotational basis to avoid permanent disability.[7]

Additional Croatians worked in the barrelhouse as packers working on an assembly line and as laborers loading the barrels of kerosene and naphtha on to teamster wagons and railroad cars. Still other Croatians worked on the refinery's production of by-products, most notably in the refinery's paraffin works which produced commercial and industrial wax products.[8] Other Croatians did general yard work.[9]

A second type of still called a "cheese-box" still was introduced in the refinery in the mid-1890s. The cylinder of the still rested on its bottom instead of its side and the condenser was contained in a domed top. This type of still predominated in the production of kerosene. Although the technology was different, the unskilled jobs were the same on the cheese box still as on the vapor brush still. The major change in work in the 1890s was improved safety in the millhouse.[10]

The Whiting refinery had no employment office in the 1890s. Foremen and supervisors chose Croatian and other immigrant workmen using a "shape-up" system. As the refinery began work each day, a crowd of Croatians and other immigrants would mass at the plant gate. Supervisors from each department hired workers by pointing at faces in the crowd and asking them to step forward.

Not surprisingly, the supervisors favored Croatians who had at least a rudimentary knowledge of the English language.[11] This was done for two major reasons. First, supervisors believed that a quick grasp of the stillman's commands by the workers prevented accidents. Second, the supervisors employed mixed ethnic crews in all refinery operations. With a range of eastern Europeans working side by side at various tasks, English was the only possible common language. Thus in the roughest way possible Croatians were forced to abandon their mother tongue in the workplace and use the language of their adopted land.

Throughout the 1890s, wages for unskilled work at Whiting averaged fifteen cents per hour and the refinery operated on a twelve-hour workday, seven days a week. As hard as it is to believe by today's standards, jobs at Standard were highly prized. The wages were a bit higher than for similar jobs in other Chicago area industries and the length of the work day and week was fairly common for the decade.[12]

Because they were on the bottom of the occupational ladder in the 1890s, the Croatians of Whiting were uncertain how long they would keep their jobs. The abundant surplus of immigrant labor in northern Indiana allowed Standard Oil to hire and fire at will. Not surprisingly, there was no worker resistance to any task or requirement, no matter how dangerous. Immigrant workers were subject to the whims of their foremen, some of whom used their authority to coerce gifts or favors from their subordinates. Since the Croatians employed at the refinery were always subject to immediate dismissal and replacement by other eager immigrants, it is not surprising that the Croatians accepted their lot in life without complaint.

The 1890s was a decade of only limited geographic mobility among Whiting's Croatian immigrants. Many were arriving directly from Croatia, but most arrived in Whiting after an intermediate stop in some other community. Most settled permanently in Whiting, but there were a number that chose to push on after a stint in the refinery.

In the early years of the decade, the Croatian community in Whiting was virtually all male and the most successful social institution was the saloon. In fact, the earliest Croatian saloon in Whiting was constructed simultaneous with the refinery.[13] By the middle of the decade there were several more saloons catering to the thirsts and tastes of the growing body of Croatian workmen.

It is important to note that these saloons were more than bars or restaurants. They were social centers and boarding houses for many Croatians. Saloon keepers acted as immigrant bankers by cashing paychecks and selling money orders for the remission of money to parents and wives back in Croatia. In fact, one could argue that these saloons were the first American home for the first generation of Croatian Americans in Whiting.[14]

It was on payday that Croatian saloons came to life. The factories ended their workday an hour early and the workmen celebrated at the saloon of their choice. Piles of workers' lunch tins were deposited on the saloon porches while their owners quaffed beer and whiskey inside. Singing and tamburica music punctuated these payday celebrations.

By 1900, the frontier feeling of Whiting's immigrant settlement began to change. Croatian fiancées and wives began arriving in the city and marked a shift away from a community of single men toward a community of couples and children.[15] Coming directly to join husbands or relatives, the young women had lower rates of geographic mobility than the men.

Life for Croatian women in Whiting was narrowly defined. There was little for the women to do other than keep house, raise children, and pray to God for a better life. Unlike some other industrial communities, Whiting provided few opportunities for women to work, yet there was no objection from Croatian men. They were proud of the fact that they could support their families on their own income. Their wives raised large families and perhaps took in a few boarders.[16] Not surprisingly, with the appearance of women also came the first efforts to establish a Catholic parish in Whiting.[17]

The Croatians of Whiting were a stable, dependable work force. The only labor strike that involved the Croatians erupted at the end of the kerosene era in 1906. Stillmen in the plant had joined the American Federation of Labor as far back as 1890, but Standard Oil refused to recognize the union. In July and September of 1906, two craft organizations went on strike for higher wages. The company fired seven craft workers associated with the union in mid-September. A handful of Croatian radicals led a sympathy strike of 150 still cleaners. It was an unprecedented action.

The company proceeded to break the strike on a number of fronts. Following the walkout by the still cleaners, with the strike threatening to spread to other departments, Standard Oil obtained an injunction to jail the strike leader. Rumors spread throughout the refinery that the company intended to evict strikers from homes rented or mortgaged to Standard Oil. The company further isolated the immigrant strikers by negotiating a separate agreement with the craft union. By the end of the month the immigrant strike was over with some workers capitulating to management and others being replaced.[18]

In the wake of the 1906 strike, many Croatians had to leave the community; known strikers were not welcome in local plants. These strikers and their families migrated to Gary and East Chicago where anonymity assisted the men in finding jobs in the steel mills.[19] This migration out of Whiting was the last significant alteration to Whiting's Croatian community. The following year would mark the high point of Croatian immigration to the United States, but only a few of these new arrivals chose Whiting.[20] When the U.S. Immigration Commission produced its detailed report on various immigrant groups in the United States it reported 125 Croatian-American families in Whiting, a total of some 500 individuals.[21]

In many ways the practices used by Standard Oil to break the strike were not typical of the company. In fact, what prevailed at Standard was a system that can only be called corporate paternalism. The tradition of "good treatment" was generally considered to be responsible for retarding unionism among the refinery's unskilled workers. The company consistently paid wages that were marginally higher than those paid in other area industries. Promotion was on merit with Croatians allowed to advance as they showed the necessary skills. The company also provided free medical care and hospitalization for those injured in industrial accidents not caused by "negligence."[22]

After 1910 the petroleum industry shifted to the mass production of gasoline. The importance of kerosene declined at Standard in Whiting as the refinery devoted almost all of its production capacity to "gas oil" as it was then called. This transformation was not simple, however. Heating of crude oil did not remove all the impurities necessary for gasoline and until chemist William Burton devised a new "cracking still" that combined heat and pressure, all the impurities could not be removed from crude oil.

The new cracking stills frightened all of the still workers in the first few years of use. The stills were mammoth in size rising several stories and surrounded by a maze of platforms and pipes. In addition, the pressure used in the Burton process was so great that the steel that made the stills would swell and expand. Leaks and split seams were common and the threat of explosion was real on every shift. A rigid safety program, redoubling old refinery rules against drinking and smoking on the job, prevented many certain disasters.[23] It was on these stills—largely devoid of instruments—that the Croatian immigrants would advance into the ranks of the stillmen.

World War I brought years of steady work at the refinery. Military demand for a wide variety of petroleum products coupled with a decline in immigration kept the demand for labor high. Standard Oil increased benefits to hold onto its experienced Croatian workforce.[24]

Perhaps the most significant benefit introduced during the war years was the eight-hour workday. On September 1, 1915, Standard took the lead in establishing the eight-hour day without any loss of pay or benefits. Another wartime benefit was the establishment of an employment office and the elimination of the abuses of the shape-up system. Arbitrary hiring and firing came to an end along with the graft required of immigrant workers. In July 1918, Standard added a safety department complete with a first aid office staffed by a physician. Also that same month, the company established a company annuity system that included death benefits among its provisions.[25]

A cornerstone of the company's paternalism proved to be an industrial relations plan developed in 1919. In this effort Standard was more than a decade ahead of other industries. Representatives of the plant workers were elected in plant-wide elections and served for a year at company expense. The representatives tended to come from the ranks of the skilled workers. The Joint General Committee, as it was called, remained the refinery workers' forum until 1937.[26]

This generous benefit package shielded the Whiting refinery from the labor disputes and disorders that so plagued other plants in 1919. By actively involving the skilled American workers in plant procedures through the employee representation process, Standard in Whiting checked the influence of the American Federation of Labor at the refinery. It also involved Croatians and other immigrant workmen who had no alternatives in labor representation.

But the company also ensured labor peace through deception. Beginning in 1918, Standard Oil paid informants to work in the plant and report on suspected radicals and union agitators among the refinery workers. Agents from the notorious Corporation Auxiliary Company submitted daily reports on the activities of all refinery employees. This spy system continued in operation until 1923.[27]

Standard introduced yet another employee benefit in the 1920s—an employee stock purchase plan. Inaugurated in 1921, the plan allowed employees to purchase company stock through payroll deductions. It was an immediate success and especially popular among the Croatians.[28]

Standard also made an effort to be a good neighbor. In November 1923, company and community officials dedicated the Whiting Community House, a magnificent Italian-style structure built by Standard and donated to the city of Whiting and its citizens. The center contained an auditorium, a swimming pool, a gymnasium, and a variety of game and meeting rooms. The

House immediately became a center for all types of Croatian-American activity.[29]

The coming of the Great Depression in the 1930s did not have any immediate effect on workforce in the Whiting refinery. Through 1930 Standard transferred oil production workers to construction and maintenance work. But as the demand for gasoline declined and the Depression worsened, many Croatian workmen were cut back to part-time work. A ten percent pay cut was instituted in 1931 and 1932 and more than one third of the workforce was laid off by the end of 1932.[30] Those remaining on the job worked a short week, thereby spreading the available work among many employees. Not surprisingly, employee participation in the stock purchasing plan declined rapidly.[31]

The Depression forced Standard to make a number of tough decisions—some benefiting workers and others hurting them. For example, in 1933, Standard established the State Bank of Whiting and absorbed two smaller banks that were failing. In doing so, the company preserved the hard-earned savings of thousands of immigrants.[32] At the same time, the decline in benefits forced the company to reduce annuity benefits.[33]

In spite of the severe work shortages of the Depression, few Croatians chose to leave Whiting. In fact, some saw the Great Depression as the last test of the fateful decision to remain permanently in America. Beginning in the 1920s, Croatian immigrants were forced to make a final decision—either Europe or America. If immigrants returned to the land of their birth, they could no longer return to America without starting the immigration process all over. To leave America after 1924 was to leave it forever.

For most Croatians, there was not much reason to return across the Atlantic. Croatia had become a province of the new nation of Yugoslavia, which was largely dominated by Serbia. Making matters worse, Croatia of the 1930s also suffered from the same worldwide depression that had so gripped the United States and the economic distress was compounded by a rising fascist and terrorist movement. The Croatian Americans of Whiting followed these events through the Croatian American press.[34] Depression-era Whiting, even with all its economic difficulties, seemed a better place to live and work than the motherland.

The Joint General Committee continued to function as the key labor representation in the refinery even after the passage of the National Industrial Recovery Act of 1933. But the news of labor unrest elsewhere soon reached Whiting and the message was not lost on the rank and file. Following the Supreme Court's affirmation of the National Labor Relations Act in 1937, Standard Oil disbanded its Joint General Committee and it was replaced by an independent union, the Standard Oil Employees Association. This new union lasted into the 1960s, well after the retirement of most Croatian workers.[35]

As they approached retirement, the Croatian immigrant workers in the Whiting refinery became increasingly active in the new union. This activism was the result of two factors. First, the establishment of the Congress of Industrial Organizations gave these workers confidence that they could stand up to management and clearly articulate their grievances. Second, by 1940 most Croatian workers had become stillmen or members of other skilled trades. They felt individually and collectively that they had real bargaining power.

The Croatians of Whiting had been patient in their effort to move up the occupational ladder. Eventually their patience was rewarded with modest success. From the ranks of the unskilled jobs like fireman and still cleaner, they became stillmen late in their working lives. They were proud of their achievement if only because it was so long in coming.

The Croatians of Whiting never left the world of blue collar work. There was no significant escape from industrial employment. The Croatians "made it" in Whiting and America but only on the first few rungs of the economic ladder. The fragmentary record that exists documents the progress and decline of these workers as the oil industry in general and Standard Oil in particular suffered through technological and economic change. Through it all the Croatian oil workers of Whiting persisted.[36]

NOTES

1. St. Peter and Paul Catholic Church, "Marriage Ledger, 1910–," hereafter cited as "Marriage Ledger."

2. Edward A. Zivich, comp. "Immigrant Family Notebook" [A compilation of interviews done by the author with members of the Croatian-American community in Whiting.] The notebook is in the possession of the author.

3. Paul H. Giddens, *Standard Oil Company* (Indiana) (New York, 1955), p. 26.

4. U.S. Immigration Commission, *Immigrants in Industries*, Vol. 16 (Washington, 1910), pp. 745–806.

5. Standard Oil, "Whiting Refinery Employment Records," hereinafter cited as Employment Records.

6. Giddens, *Standard Oil*, p. 27.

7. Ibid, p. 28, and Employment Records.

8. Employment Records.

9. Ibid.

10. Giddens, *Standard Oil*, p. 28.

11. Employment Records.

12. Ibid.

13. Croatian Fraternal Union, Lodge 57, Membership List, 1894 [Handwritten Ledger in the possession of the Lodge].

14. *Immigrants in Industries*, Vol. 16, pp. 745–806.

15. Ibid.

16. Ibid.

17. "History of S.S. Peter and Paul Church of Whiting, Indiana," *In Souvenir of the 50th Anniversary of S.S. Peter and Paul Parish* (Whiting, 1960), p. 9.

18. *Whiting Call* (September 27, 1906).

19. S.S. Peter and Paul Catholic Church, Baptismal Register, 1910–.

20. George J. Prpic, *The Croatian Immigrants in America* (New York, 1971), p. 103.

21. *Immigrants in Industries*, Vol. 16, pp. 745–806.

22. *Whiting Democrat* (July 18, 1895).

23. Giddens, *Standard Oil*, p. 204.

24. Ibid., p. 202.

25. Employment Records.

26. Standard Oil Employees Association, "Whiting Cases, 1937–1959," p. 1 [Ledger in the possession of the Oil, Chemical and Atomic Workers Union, Local 7–1] .

27. Giddens, *Standard Oil*, p. 207.

28. Employment Records.

29. Arthur F. Endres, Refinery Supervisor's Handbook (Whiting, 1953), pp. 1–4.

30. Employment Records.

31. Ibid.

32. Giddens, *Standard Oil*, p. 470.

33. Employment Records.

34. Stephen Gazi, *A History of Croatia* (New York, 1973), pp. 293–330.

35. Whiting Cases, loc cit.

36. A detailed account of the Croatians in Whiting can be found in Edward A. Zivich, *From Zadruga to Oil Refinery: Croatian Immigrants and Croatian Americans in Whiting, Indiana, 1890–1950* (New York, 1990).

PART IV

The Contours of Ethnic Community

Introduction

A sense of community is a very personal feeling. In fact, most Americans include community as a component of their sense of identity. This certainly was the case with European immigrants arriving in this country. Living in a new land far from their country of origin, these immigrants looked for ways to reconnect and maintain their ties with their past.

The most elemental action taken by these immigrants was to establish ethnic "islands" throughout the United States. In some cases these enclaves were rural farming communities. The Germans and the Scandinavians, for example, dominated scores of small towns across the upper Midwest. Taking names such as "Rhinelander" and "New Ulm," these communities were Americanized versions of the hamlets these immigrants had left behind in Europe.

But most European immigrants did not become farmers or small town merchants. Underskilled and impoverished, most immigrants settled where the jobs were—in the emerging industrial cities of the Northeast and Midwest. It was within these cities that various ethnic groups established their own distinct neighborhoods. By the turn of the twentieth century, most American cities were patchworks of ethnic ghettos.

These neighborhoods were grids of narrow streets filled with small shops and crowded, substandard housing—hardly the streets filled with gold that the immigrants had been promised. For most Americans, this pattern of settlement, notes historian David Ward, "was viewed as a failure of the American dream, not only in regard to material conditions and opportunities, but also because it spawned political corruption and threatened democracy." Many Americans were concerned that ghettoization would slow or perhaps stop the process of transforming these foreigners into Americans.

To be sure, the large concentration of foreigners linked by common concerns became a potent political force in opposition to Republican reformist ideals in the last quarter of the nineteenth century. The ethnic political boss and his "machine" organized ethnic voters and changed the nature of American politics. Just as important, the boss and his machine defined the quality of life in these ethnic communities.

Yet it would be wrong to perceive the political machine as a disruptive force in American life. "Immigrants and their children," noted Edward Kantowicz, "had special needs that political machines were suited to fill. The boss found jobs for the men, accompanied them to their naturalization hearings, distributed food baskets at Christmas and buckets of coal in the winter. They deferred to each other's ethnic groups' customs and attended festivals and holy days. For all its centralization, a machine was government with a human face." Appeals from Republican reformers for "good government" seemed remote and unfriendly at best.

Depending on the ethnic group, machine politics and bosses were variations on a theme of service for votes. Certainly the group that orchestrated this theme was the Irish. Kantowicz notes that the Irish success in ethnic politics was "the product of both their old country heritage and the circumstances in which they found themselves after immigration."

This is not to say that other immigrant groups merely followed the dictates of the Irish. The Irish may have been the most visible ethnic leaders, but they were not necessarily the most important to specific ethnic communities. Each immigrant group had its own leaders who served as prisms for American culture. These ethnic leaders filtered American culture and encouraged their fellow countrymen to embrace the best of America without abandoning their ties to the old country.

The historian John Higham has articulated four elements that define ethnic community leadership. The first was security and service. Some services were provided by the Irish, but by no means all. The local priest or rabbi was a leader because he provided for immigrant spiritual welfare. Other immigrants became leaders by establishing mutual benefit societies and fraternal lodges. Assistance in finding a job came from labor bosses. All of these men became ethnic leaders because of the services they provided.

The second element was group solidarity. To be sure, group solidarity was the preoccupation of a wide array of potential leaders. It was important to the clergy because it kept the congregation loyal to the Faith. It was important to the mutual benefit society because it kept the premiums coming in. It was important to the labor boss because it kept his workers diligent, deferential, and ambitious.

Yet the group leaders who most benefited from group solidarity were the owners and editors of ethnic newspapers. The ethnic newspapers simultaneously reflected the past, present, and future of their respective ethnic groups. Past events were recorded for posterity; present views of a whole range of issues were articulated and discussed; and future events were highlighted to prepare the group for what was to come. Because they were the voices of these ethnic groups, ethnic publishers were prominent leaders.

The third element was foreign nationalism. Here again, many aspiring ethnic leaders embraced the issue because it promised group cohesion. The groups most successful in using ethnic nationalism were the Irish, the Germans, the Poles, and the Jews—groups from nations that were still struggling for independence or national identity. For the Germans, ethnic nationalism became a nightmare when the United States and Germany were on opposite sides during World War I. Ethnic nationalism was a useful organizing tool so long as the message was a compliment to American ideals.

The final element of ethnic leadership was group involvement. Ethnic leaders pointed to the progress made by members of the group in politics, business, religion, the military, the arts, entertainment, and even in sports. Those immigrants who succeeded in those arenas on both the local and the national levels became role models and indeed leaders for their ethnic groups.

John Higham has compared ethnicity to a magnetic field because it fades in and out depending on the state of acculturation of any one ethnic group. The analogy is apt; in fact, it could be expanded to the concept of ethnic community as a whole. As Edward Kantowicz, LaVern Rippley, and Margaret Sullivan indicate, the contours of ethnic community are always changing.

CHAPTER 10

The Changing Face of Ethnic Politics
From Political Machine to Community Organization

Edward R. Kantowicz

When immigration from Europe was swelling to its crest in the early years of the twentieth century, political machines ruled the big cities where most of the immigrants settled. The bosses of these machines, both Democrats and Republicans, welcomed the newcomers, exchanging jobs and favors for their votes.

The bosses, of course, only wanted to gain and hold power for themselves; but in the process, they also performed many useful functions for immigrants. The machine was not a dictatorship, as many believed. It was, in its own way, a service organization and an expression of small-scale democracy.

The boss and his ward-heelers performed favors and asked for votes personally. They knew their turf extremely well, and the people identified with them and their party. Bosses found jobs for their constituents, accompanied them to naturalization hearings, distributed food baskets at Christmas and buckets of coal in the winter. They deferred to each ethnic group's customs, faithfully attending wakes and weddings and religious festivals. For all its centralization of political power, the machine represented government with a human face. A greenhorn, freshly escaped from the terrors of European police, the wiles of steamship agents, and the rigors of Ellis Island bureaucrats, must have breathed a sigh of relief when the machine's ward-heeler greeted him with a smile and an outstretched hand.[1]

Besides the material assistance they doled out to individual immigrants, the political machines furnished three intangible benefits to ethnic communities—recognition, protection, and leverage.

When a machine boss gave an immigrant a job at City Hall or slated one of his bright, ambitious sons for an elective office, the whole ethnic group—be it Irish, Polish, or Italian—basked in reflected glory. Political patronage, therefore, had psychological ramifications as well as economic significance. If an immigrant fell afoul of the law, the boss or his precinct captain would accompany him to court and put in a timely word with the judge. Such personal protection seemed only natural to an immigrant unaccustomed to the impersonal ways of Anglo-Saxon justice. Finally, the political machine gave immigrant communities a certain amount of leverage in the American city. It would be an overstatement to say that machines "empowered" immigrant communities. The bosses were only interested in perpetuating their own power. Yet the boss's self-interest gave the immigrant leverage. As he learned the system, he could play one party boss against another, and sometimes a whole community could mobilize around an issue that mattered to them. If the machine didn't respond, its gears could foul and it might grind to a halt.

It has become commonplace to say that political machines began eroding at the time of the New Deal, and that the last of the big city machines died with Boss Richard J. Daley of Chicago in 1976. The increasing largesse of big government in Washington overshadowed the jobs and favors that city machines doled out, and constant legal assaults on the patronage system finally dried up the bosses' main source of power. Above all, television hastened the demise of political machines. Voters today identify with politicians who look glamorous and decisive on the tube. They ingest their political information in 30-second sound bites rather than chats with the precinct captain. What is not so widely recognized is that other small-scale institutions have cropped up to replace the personal contact of the old-style machine.

The best place to begin exploring this idea is in suburban town halls. Political scientists have long decried the proliferation of governmental units in metropolitan areas. Hundreds of suburbs around each big city elect their own town or village councils, and numerous county boards, park districts, sanitary districts, and other special purpose agencies swell the number of governmental bodies. The state of Illinois alone has 6,627 units of local government.

Though academics have long proposed the consolidation of these superfluous units into one big metropolitan government, suburban citizens, many of them descendants of the European immigrants, still fear absorption by the big city and annihilation by impersonal bureaucracies. Thus they cling to their small-scale governments. They may not vote in impressive numbers for suburban municipal officers or school board members, but they like to know they are there if they need to complain.[2]

Condominium apartments, both in cities and suburbs, are another hotbed of small-scale democracy. Young professionals who would never think of engaging in "politics" or running for government office, battle fiercely for spots on their own condo boards. They enjoy socializing with their neighbors and voicing an opinion on decisions that affect their lifestyle. Sometimes too, condo politics directly resembles the old-style machine politics, with construction contracts for friends or in-laws at stake.

If middle-class professionals are active in suburban politics and condo board meetings, it should come as no surprise that the newest migrants to the cities—Asians, Latinos, and African Americans—still feel the need to form personal bonds with powerful people and engage in small-scale politics. Increasingly, the newcomers in American cities are turning to community organizations for recognition, protection, and leverage.

Community organizations of many types are experiencing a renaissance.[3] Middle- and upper-class homeowners often form neighborhood improvement or booster associations. These associations sometimes hire professional planners to deal with City Hall and direct the shape of urban renewal plans. Usually, such bourgeois community organizations adopt the acronym N.I.M.B.Y. (Not In My Back Yard) as their war cry. They are primarily concerned with protecting and increasing property values, and they have proven most vigorous and effective in attacking any perceived threats to their real estate.

Recent migrants do not generally own much property and they have little to lose, so they often turn to the more confrontational community organizations that follow the tradition of Saul Alinsky. A tough criminologist from the University of Chicago, Alinsky organized the stockyards neighborhood of Chicago in the late 1930s according to the principle that "power is never given, it can only be taken." He later founded the Industrial Areas Foundation to teach his organizing principles to others. Over the past fifty years, scores of neighborhoods across the country, comprising many different ethnic groups, have started Alinsky-style organizations. They always build on existing local power centers, such as churches, adopt confrontational tactics, and personalize the issues facing communities.[4]

In order to illustrate the changing face of ethnic politics in American cities over the course of the twentieth century, I will focus on two groups of immigrants in the city of Chicago. A hundred years ago, Polish peasants poured into industrial Chicago, transforming it into the second largest Polish city in the world, after Warsaw. Poles entered politics at a time when the city's Democratic machine was just consolidating its power, and the Polish community became a trusty cog in that machine.[5]

After the Second World War, immigrants from Mexico and Spanish-speaking migrants from the Commonwealth of Puerto Rico began to settle in Chicago. Mexicans, Puerto Ricans, and other Spanish-speakers from Central and South America, collectively known as Latinos, have displaced Poles and other Slavs as the largest white ethnic group in Chicago.[6] The decaying political machine ignored them until the day it died, so political bosses proved of little help in fulfilling Latino aspirations. In the last two decades of the century, however, community organizations have appeared in both the Mexican and Puerto Rican barrios which perform some of the same functions that the machine did for Polish immigrants one hundred years ago.

Chicago is an apt choice for this case study. The city was home to the last of the big city bosses, Richard J. Daley; and currently Richard M. Daley, the "son of Boss," presides over the remnants of his father's Democratic machine. Likewise Chicago was home to the legendary organizer, Saul Alinsky, and Chicagoans have been his best pupils. One veteran activist, John McDermott, has called Chicago "the Harvard of community organizing, or maybe the Notre Dame of organizing since the Catholic Church has played such an integral role."[7] Fighting City Hall is as typically Chicagoan as patronage or Polish sausage.

Boss Politics in Polonia

Polish immigrants settled in five Chicago industrial areas on the northwest, southwest, and southeast sides of the city; and smaller Slavic ethnic groups, such as the Bohemians, Slovaks, Serbs, and Croats, also clustered near the steel mills, stockyards, foundries, and tanneries. By 1930 Poles numbered 401,316, roughly 12 percent of the city's population. Other Slavs added another 5 percent to the total.[8]

Politics was not a high priority for Slavic immigrants. Many intended to return to Europe eventually, so they took a long time becoming naturalized. Economic and cultural survival came first. Newcomers found jobs in the factories through networks of friends and relatives, and they also gathered together with their countrymen to start up mutual benefit societies, fraternal organizations, and Catholic parishes. These Polish-American institutions conferred an identity on the industrial neighborhoods where Polish immigrants settled. They called them all, collectively, *Polonia*.

Politics intruded upon Polonia in three different ways. First of all, there was the politics of Poland, aimed at the liberation of the fatherland from the partitioning powers. The Polish National Alliance, the largest fraternal order, considered Polonia merely a "fourth province of Poland" and bent all its lobbying efforts towards a sort of Polish Zionism. This work came to fruition when Woodrow Wilson played an active role in the restoration of Polish independence after World War I.

A second form of politics played out within Polonia itself. No immigrant institution, from the smallest parish social group to the powerful Resurrectionist religious order, was without its internal political struggles. And the two largest fraternal orders, the Polish National Alliance and the Polish Roman Catholic Union, were federated national bodies organized on representative lines. The members of local associations elected delegates to a national congress, which in turn elected officers and standing committees. For peasant immigrants, this fraternal politics provided useful lessons in democracy.

Finally, American politics beckoned; or to be more precise, an American politician beckoned. The genius of the boss system was its personalism. The political boss resembled the lord of the manor back in Poland, a man of importance who wielded power and lived well. He provided jobs and afforded protection from hostile forces and unfamiliar processes. Yet unlike the old country lord, the boss was a man very like the immigrants themselves. Most likely his parents had been immigrants, and he himself had worked as a common laborer in his younger days. Thus an ambitious Polish-American could aspire to be a boss, or at least one of his subalterns, in his own right. The boss system, therefore, provided jobs, ethnic recognition, protection, and some leverage as immigrants struggled up the ladder of social mobility.

Both political parties remained competitive in Chicago when the Poles first arrived. Republicans and Democrats alike had their bosses, and no one machine dominated the city. American-born Protestants, most of the Germans, and nearly all Scandinavians gravitated to the Republicans, whereas Irish and Slavic Catholics and the Eastern European Jews usually voted Democratic. Democrats were the party of outsiders. Those ethnic groups that were farthest outside the Anglo-Saxon, Protestant mainstream looked to the Democrats to protect them from intrusive Protestant meddling with their culture and religion. The most threatening form of meddling came in the form of prohibition of alcoholic beverages. Chicago Democrats fought prohibition vociferously and ensured that it was not enforced vigorously when it became the law of the land.

Early in the century, two kinds of Democratic politicians, bosses and respectables, emerged in Chicago's Polonia. The latter were well-educated, middle-class businessmen who entered politics as a civic duty, served a term or two in the city council or some appointed position, but soon wearied of the political wars. Bosses and their subordinates, on the other hand, emerged from the most humble origins and made politics a lifelong career.

The most important of the early Polish bosses in Chicago was Stanley Kunz. Though born in the mining district of Pennsylvania, he came to Chicago as a child and represented the "Polish Downtown" area as an alderman for over thirty years. This neighborhood on the near northwest side, surrounding St. Stanislaus Kostka church, was not only a place of residence for immigrants, but a commercial district where the various Polish fraternal organizations and ethnic newspapers made their headquarters. It functioned as an alternate downtown for Polish-Americans. So Kunz was a figure of city-wide importance, as well as a local ward boss.

Kunz suffered from an unsavory reputation outside Polonia. Newspapers often commented on his addiction to horseracing and inquired sharply where he got the money to own a stable of racehorses in Tennessee. He carried a heavy cane at all times, often rapping on tables, or opponents' skulls, for emphasis; and thus he earned the nickname, "Stanley the Slugger." Polish immigrants didn't care. Stanley Kunz was, as Jane Addams termed it, "the Little Father of the Community, who is always there and ready to help as best he can." In 1920, he capped his long career by winning election as the first Polish-American congressman from Chicago, serving six successive terms.[9]

Beginning in the 1920s, the Democratic party began to put together a winning ethnic coalition that kept getting larger. This resulted in a dominant machine that ran the city from the 1930s to the 1980s. Stanley Kunz sat in the inner circle of the emerging machine, but he never ran for mayor and no other Polish American rose to the top rank of power. However, Anton Cermak, a Bohemian politician, did play a central role in the forging of the Democratic machine and was elected mayor in 1931.[10]

Historian John Allswang has aptly characterized the Chicago machine as "a house for all peoples."[11] Poles and other new immigrants felt at home within it. The bosses doled out jobs and favors, slated enough of their countrymen to give them recognition and instill pride, protected them from rigorous enforcement of prohibition and other bothersome laws, and gave them a certain amount of leverage for their own economic progress.

If all the Polish Democrats had resembled Stanley Kunz, however, the Democratic party might have reached a point of diminishing returns in Polonia. As the ethnic group gained a foothold in the United States, it became more self-conscious. Particularly in the period between the two world wars, the children of the immigrants were delicately working out their identities as hyphenated individuals, no longer Poles living temporarily in America but Polish Americans. The more upwardly mobile felt embarrassed at the "Stanley the Slugger" image of their countrymen. Fortunately for them, one of the Polish respectables, Edmund K. Jarecki, carved out a remarkable political career for himself, thus counterbalancing the Stanley image.

Jarecki was born in Poland, but was brought to Chicago as a youth. His father worked briefly in the stockyards but soon opened his own butcher shop in the Polish Downtown neighborhood. Young Edmund entered law school and passed the bar in 1908. Boss Kunz and the pastor of St. Stanislaus Kostka parish jointly convinced Jarecki to fill an aldermanic vacancy in 1911. Kunz found his new protégé too independent-minded so he didn't slate him for reelection; but as Jarecki himself phrased it, he "got stubborn and ran independent." This time he lost, but his actions set a pattern Jarecki followed the rest of his life. He would use the leverage of boss politics to get slated, then build up a reputation for honesty and independence, bucking the machine whenever necessary to survive.[12]

A decade later, in 1922, Stanley Kunz again tapped Jarecki and convinced the Democratic Central Committee to slate him for county judge. Jarecki won and held the office for over twenty years. The county judgeship, a curious political hybrid that no longer exists, enjoyed enormous political significance. The county judge exercised sweeping, nearly autocratic, power over the election machinery of the city, appointing a three-man Board of Election Commissioners and monitoring the conduct of every election. Legally, all the poll judges in every precinct were officers of the county court, and the judge could summarily hold them in contempt for any irregularities. Obviously, it was vital for the Democratic machine to control the county judgeship and thus be able to manipulate elections.

Once elected, Judge Jarecki avoided Boss Kunz. He turned his office into a Polish patronage haven, but he made the appointments himself and did not clear them with Kunz. At the same time, however, he earned a reputation for scrupulous honesty and he watched the electoral process like a hawk for any hints of voting fraud. Kunz and the other bosses of the party realized too late they had created a monster they could not control.

Jarecki's image as a "professional honest man" made him a fixture on the ticket every four years. The bosses felt they had little choice but to retain him. In 1934, he even led the whole ticket, garnering more votes than any other Democrat. Then in 1938, the Kelly-Nash machine (Edward J. Kelly and Patrick Nash had succeeded Anton Cermak at the head of the machine) finally decided to dump Jarecki from the ticket. The judge refused to go quietly, however, and defeated the machine candidate. In a very close race, the united Polish vote made the difference. Thereafter the machine left Jarecki alone until he retired in the 1950s.

Though Polish Americans in Chicago have often lamented the fact that they never elected one of their own group as mayor, they have in many ways enjoyed the best of both worlds in local politics. Bosses such as Stanley Kunz and his successor Joseph Rostenkowski (father of the present Congressman Daniel Rostenkowski) provided tangible rewards and the intangible benefits of recognition, protection, and leverage. Then, Judge Jarecki's reputation for uncompromising honesty furnished the perfect counterpoint to the bosses, an image of respectability and the additional political leverage it provided. Jarecki milked the boss system for all it was worth, then opposed it when he needed to. The Democratic political machine served Polonia well.

Latino Community Organizations

Latino migrants settled in roughly the same industrial neighborhoods on the northwest, southwest, and southeast sides of Chicago that Slavic immigrants had populated fifty years before. Some Mexican Americans, indeed, shared the industrial labor of steel mills and stockyards with Poles as early as the 1920s, but their numbers did not become very large until after World War II. Many Puerto Ricans also moved to the city from New York after the second war. By 1980 Latinos had reached about the same stage of emigration as the Poles and other Slavs in 1930. The 1980 census counted 255,802 Mexicans, 112,074 Puerto Ricans, 11,513 Cubans, and 42,674 "other" Spanish-speaking people. Altogether they numbered 422,063; that is, 14 percent of the city's population, or about the same percentage as the Poles in 1930.[13]

By the time Latinos became numerous in Chicago, the city's vaunted industrial might had waned and good-paying, unskilled jobs in heavy industry were becoming scarce. Puerto Ricans, in particular, arrived too late to share the industrial labor of earlier immigrants and found mainly minimum-wage service jobs.

Nor did the aging Democratic political machine welcome Latinos with the same enthusiasm it had showed in its "house for all peoples" phase fifty years before. The Spanish-speaking migrants confronted a machine that had been entrenched for decades and enjoyed a monopoly of political power, and they settled in neighborhoods where some of the most intransigent political bosses, such as Vito Marzullo, Thomas Keane, and Edward Vrdolyak held sway. Keane, in particular, the number two man in Mayor Richard J. Daley's organization, kept the Latinos powerless by manipulating the ward maps every ten years so that the newcomers never held a majority in any district. Furthermore, the extreme youth and low rate of naturalization among Latinos meant that a small proportion of them were registered voters. In the early 1980s, they accounted for about 14 percent of the city's population but they comprised only 5 percent of the electorate. As a result, Latinos were virtually shut out of Cook County politics as the 1980s began, without a single alderman, Democratic committeeman, or state legislator. By way of contrast, Poles had elected five aldermen and four ward committeemen in 1930.[14]

Fortunately for the Latinos, they enjoyed a political re-source that was unavailable to earlier immigrants, the federal government's civil rights laws. The Voting Rights Act of 1965 and its various amendments mandated that minorities be given every opportunity to win political representation, so in 1985 a federal judge threw out Chicago's ward map and approved a new redistricting plan creating Latino "super-majorities" of 65 or 70 percent in four wards. Luis Guiterriez and Miguel del Valle won election to the city council and the state senate, respectively, and other Latino politicians followed swiftly.[15]

None of this happened automatically, of course. As Saul Alinsky always said, "Power is never given, it is always taken." Latino civil rights organizations, led by the Mexican American Legal Defense Fund, roughly modeled on the NAACP, litigated for years before they succeeded in overturning the city's gerrymandered ward map.

Latinos, therefore, enjoyed at least a modicum of political recognition in Chicago by the mid-1980s. But legal attacks on the patronage system had dried up the machine's source of city jobs by then, just as the rusting of heavy industry had eroded good-paying private sector employment. No one could do much about the lack of jobs; but community organizations did spring up to earn further recognition for Latinos, win protection from various neighborhood ills, and attain some important leverage for the community.

The most important Latino community organization in Chicago is the United Neighborhood Organization (UNO).[16] Mary Gonzalez, a Chicago-born Mexican American, and her husband Gregory Galluzzo, a former Jesuit priest, founded UNO in 1980 in southeast Chicago, the former steel mill district. Wisconsin Steel had just closed its plant in the neighborhood a few weeks previously, but Gonzalez and Galluzzo knew they could do nothing about that so they didn't try. Instead they built a church-based community organization that pursued more readily attainable goals, such as building a new elementary school and a public health clinic for the neighborhood. Gonzalez and Galluzzo, however, harbored more ambitious long-range plans. Drawing on the model of Communities Organized for Public Service (COPS) in San Antonio, they intended to build a city-wide organization that could have an impact on major issues affecting the Latino community.[17]

Over the next few years, Gonzalez and Galluzzo, with the help of Danny Solis and other organizers, extended their organization to three other Mexican American barrios, the Back of the Yards, Pilsen, and Little Village. Following Saul Alinsky's model, they built their organization on the resources of local Catholic parishes. They followed Alinsky's example in three other particulars as well: local leadership, confrontational tactics, and personalizing the issues.[18]

By the mid-1980s, UNO had developed a corps of about 300 local leaders and a membership of about 700; but they could turn out many hundreds more for confrontational tactics. They became famous for personalizing the issues at their "accountability forums." Especially at election times, they would invite politicians to a meeting at a church hall, pack the hall with hundreds of screaming people, and grill the unfortunate politicos about services for the neighborhood. In 1985, UNO followed Governor James Thompson around in school buses, both in Springfield and Chicago, until he released $24 million in state funding for new schools in overcrowded districts.

Ironically, UNO almost missed out on the most important issue facing Latinos in Chicago, education reform. As the decade of the 1980s began, Latino students outnumbered whites in the Chicago public schools for the first time. African Americans still formed an overwhelming majority of the system (60 percent in 1980) but Latinos now took over second place with about 20 percent of the enrollment. Overcrowding and language difficulties were the most obvious problems facing Spanish-speaking students and UNO attacked both of them head on, demanding the building of more schools and the entrenchment of bilingual programs. Yet it was another Latino organization, the Network for Youth Services, that exposed the biggest problem in the public schools and ignited a city-wide movement for school reform.

Network for Youth Services (NYS) was not an Alinsky-style, confrontational organization, but a loose federation of youth-oriented social service agencies on the largely Puerto Rican near-northwest side of Chicago. Yet in 1983 a Catholic priest, Charles L. Kyle, brought some astounding research to the attention of NYS's education director, Roberto Rivera. Kyle had just completed a study of two public high schools in NYS's territory that revealed a dropout rate of 75 percent. The Chicago Board of Education used a calculation formula that masked this reality. The school board only reported the yearly dropout rate: just over ten percent for the whole system, with a high of 17 percent at Roberto Clemente, one of the two schools that Kyle studied. When these figures were compounded over the ordinary four-year student career in high school, however, they indicated that three-quarters of the Latino youth who entered high school did not complete their education. Just as shocking as the dropout numbers were the reasons for youths leaving school. Kyle's study determined through interviews that a pervasive fear of gangs was the major cause of the dropout problem. Latinos were lacking both education and basic physical protection in the public school system.[19]

Kyle, Rivera, and other leaders at NYS mounted a protest march at Roberto Clemente High School on March 26, 1984, that highlighted the dropout problem and led to the firing of Schools Superintendent Ruth Love. This, in turn, eventually resulted in a movement of radical school reform for the whole Chicago public school system. Enraged by low test scores, constant teacher strikes, gang violence in the schools, and the shocking dropout statistics, Latino, white, and African-American parents joined with education advocacy agencies, community organizations, and business leaders to pass a milestone School Reform Act in 1988. The reform bill decentralized the governance of the school system to the local level, authorizing elective local school councils with a parent majority at each elementary and high school in the city. These councils are not merely advisory. Council members have the power to hire and fire the school principal and the authority to spend significant amounts of discretionary funds at each school.[20]

The movement for school reform that unfolded in the 1980s was multi-racial and multi-ethnic, but it held special meaning for Latinos. Their protests over the dropout problem initiated the movement and this marked the first time that Latinos made an impact on an important city-wide issue. Truly, the Latino community found its voice in the school reform movement.

UNO had originally held back from joining the movement because the issue seemed unwinnable, and Alinsky-style organizations always shy away from quixotic quests and concentrate on winning tangible victories. Yet shortly before the passage of the school reform act in 1988, UNO executive director Danny Solis signed on to the movement and his organization made a notable contribution to the lobbying effort.[21] UNO chartered hundreds of yellow school buses and sent them rolling down to Springfield day after day to lobby the legislators. When the law was passed, UNO and the Network for Youth Services tried to outdo each other in turning out voters for the local school council elections. As a result, the Latino neighborhoods produced the largest turnout of parents in the city.

Cogwheels of Democracy

Neither the Polish immigrants fifty years ago nor the Mexican and Puerto Rican migrants of today have dominated Chicago politics. There has never been a Polish or Latino mayor. Yet both groups earned significant political recognition in the Democratic party and they have successfully protected their communities' interests and enjoyed some leverage over the powers-that-be. The tactics of ethnic politics employed by the two groups, however, have been strikingly different.

Fifty years ago the Democratic political machine was still vigorous and adaptable and it furnished an avenue of progress for individual Polish politicians and a malleable vehicle for advancing Polonia's self-interest. By the time Spanish-speaking people became numerous in Chicago, the machine had reached old age and the system was no longer open to new groups. Latinos, therefore, employed Alinsky-style community organizations, civil rights groups, and social service agencies as levers of power.

Both the political machine and the community organization satisfied the basic need of immigrants for a small-scale, personal approach to politics. They gave the voters a sense of identification with a larger community, offered them a chance to have a voice in issues affecting them, and humanized the impersonal workings of government bureaucracies. They both furnished recognition, protection, and leverage to immigrants.

Fifty years ago, a Polish immigrant asked his precinct captain to fix a pothole in the street or get an abusive policeman off his beat. Nowadays, a Mexican or Puerto Rican with a similar problem is more likely to ask Danny Solis's UNO or some other community group to pressure the city government. Over the years, community organizations have replaced political bosses as the "cogwheels of democracy."[22]

NOTES

1. The best introduction to the lost world of the political machine is the "memoir" of Tammany Hall boss George Washington Plunkitt, *Plunkitt of Tammany Hall*, William L. Riordon, ed. (New York, 1963), and the insightful introduction to that volume by Arthur Mann. See also, Edward R. Kantowicz, "Politics," in the *Harvard Encyclopedia of American Ethnic Groups*, Stephan Thernstrom et al., eds. (Cambridge, MA, 1980).

2. Robert C. Wood made this point long ago in *Suburbia: Its People and Their Politics* (Boston, 1958).

3. Robert Fisher and Peter Romanofsky, *Community Organization for Urban Social Change: A Historical Perspective* (Westport, CT, 1981), and Robert Fisher, *Let the People Decide: Neighborhood Organizing in America* (New York, 1984), provide historical overviews; and Patricia Mooney Melvin, ed., *Community Organizations: A Historical Dictionary* (Westport, 1986), gives a selective listing of some important community organizations.

4. Saul D. Alinsky, *Reveille for Radicals* (New York, 1946), and *Rules for Radicals* (New York, 1972); Sanford D. Horwitt, *Let Them Call Me Rebel: Saul Alinsky, His Life and Legacy* (New York, 1989); Ben Joravsky, "Alinsky's Legacy," in Peg Knoepfle, ed., *After Alinsky: Community Organizing in Illinois* (Springfield, IL, 1990); Joan E. Lancourt, *Confront or Concede: The Alinsky Citizen-Action Organizations* (Lexington, MA, 1979).

5. Edward R. Kantowicz, *Polish-American Politics in Chicago, 1888–1940* (Chicago, 1975).

6. Louise Ano Nuevo Kerr, "Mexican Chicago," in Melvin G. Holli and Peter D'A. Jones, eds., *Ethnic Chicago* (Grand Rapids, MI, 1984); Felix Padilla, *Puerto Rican Chicago* (Notre Dame, 1987).

7. Joravsky, "Alinsky's Legacy," p. 3.

8. Kantowicz, *Polish-American Politics*, pp. 12–27, 165–172. See also, Edward R. Kantowicz, "Polish Chicago: Survival Through Solidarity," in *Ethnic Chicago*; and Dominic A. Pacyga, *Polish Immigrants and Industrial Chicago: Workers on the South Side, 1888–1922* (Columbus, OH, 1991).

9. Kantowicz, *Polish-American Politics*, pp. 57–71, 175–79.

10. Alex Gottfried, *Boss Cermak of Chicago* (Seattle, 1962); Paul M. Green, "Anton J. Cermak: The Man and his Machine," in Paul M. Green and Melvin G. Holli, eds., *The Mayors: The Chicago Political Tradition* (Carbondale, IL, 1987).

11. John M. Allswang, *A House for All Peoples: Ethnic Politics in Chicago, 1890–1936* (Lexington, KY, 1971).

12. Kantowicz, *Polish-American Politics*, pp. 196–207; Douglas Bukowski, "Judge Edmund K. Jarecki: A Rather Regular Independent," *Chicago History* (Winter 1979–80).

13. By 1990, the total number of Latinos had swollen to 545,852, including 352,560 Mexicans, 119,866 Puerto Ricans, 10,044 Cubans, and 63,382 others.

14. Luis W. Salces and Peter W. Colby, "Manana Will be Better: Spanish-American Politics in Chicago," *Illinois Issues* 6 (1980); David K. Fremon, "Chicago's Spanish-American Politics in the '80s," *Illinois Issues* 16 (1990).

15. Fremon, "Chicago's Spanish-American Politics."

16. UNO should not be confused with a similarly-named organization in East Los Angeles. The Chicago UNO sprang up independently and its organizers apparently did not even know of the West Coast group's existence.

17. Wilfredo Cruz, "United Neighborhood Organization," in *After Alinsky*, pp. 12–21; Cruz, "The Nature of Alinsky-Style Community Organizing in the Mexican-American Community of Chicago: United Neighborhood Organization" (Ph.D. diss., University of Chicago, 1987); personal interviews by the author and Charles L. Kyle with Mary Gonzalez and Danny Solis, October 12, 1990 and October 17, 1990, respectively.

18. Ben Joravsky isolates these three factors as the essence of the Alinsky method in "Alinsky's Legacy," *After Alinsky*, p. 2.

19. Charles L. Kyle and Edward R. Kantowicz, "Bogus Statistics: Chicago's Latino Community Exposes the Dropout Problem," *Latino Studies Journal* 2 (1991).

20. Charles L. Kyle and Edward R. Kantowicz, *Kids First—Primero Los Ninos: Chicago School Reform in the 1980s* (Springfield, IL, 1992).

21. Gregory Galluzzo had previously left UNO to found the Gamaliel Foundation, a training school for community organizers. Mary Gonzalez also left the organization shortly after passage of the 1988 school reform act, due to strategic and philosophical disagreements with Danny Solis.

22. Sonya Forthal coined this phrase as the title of her classic study of the precinct captain, *Cogwheels of Democracy* (New York, 1946).

CHAPTER 11

The Ethnic Frontier
Rural Germans and the Settlement of America

La Vern J. Rippley

To the American historian, the Frederick Jackson Turner theory that the frontier was the all-critical element in the formation of an American character, even today, remains the cornerstone for an understanding of the melting pot metaphor and its capability for assimilating the newcomer. Inevitably the frontier suggests rural America. If the frontier is key to understanding American history and culture, then an interpretation of the immigrant experience in the rural setting, often being synonymous with the frontier itself, is essential to an understanding of America. In the words of Turner, "In the crucible of the frontier, immigrants were Americanized, liberated, and fused into a mixed race, English in neither nationality nor characteristics."[1]

Turner suggests that in the "steady movement away from the influence of Europe," the immigrants melded together characteristics and cultures that, though different in origin, were consolidated together into a new and distinct national stock. The outcome was both a biological and a cultural amalgamation—a distinctly American, democratic, individualistic and self-sufficient spirit—that "held the promise of world brotherhood." It offered the possibility of a richer civilization that would eschew ethnocultural particularism for an exuberant new form of nationalism that would overarch first the new nation and eventually the world.[2]

The Turner thesis has been as tenacious as it was brilliant in its conception. And to question its application to rural settlements of Americans from Germany in many respects is unfair to its founder. However, it is doubtful that Turner ever conceived that his treatise would gain as wide and universal an applicability as it has generally been accorded. What follows, then, is not intended as any outright rejection of his argument, but rather as a refinement of its application.

The vast bulk of immigrants from Germany were peasants. They were people who resisted industrialization and the urbanization that manufacturing demanded. As an alternative to moving into crowded European cities to work in factories, they preferred to emigrate. Thus recent researchers have begun to concatenate the links between rural or otherwise tightly defined regional neighborhoods of Germany and the equally rural or precisely definable urban wards to which they migrated in the United States.[3] Thus a new term—"chain migration"[4]—is used to reject the Handlin thesis which asserted that the immigrants were poor, abandoned and "uprooted" wanderers in favor of a concept of homogeneous clusters of rural, or for that matter, of ward and precinct-confined urban settlers who share a heritage that is well rooted in the European past.[5] Once an immigrant group had sunk roots into an emerging American locality, it was likely that newcomers from the same original social units were going to join the pioneers quickly, thus explaining the ethnic concentrations that have far outlasted the ability of the frontier, in the belief of Frederick Jackson Turner, to thoroughly alter or radically amalgamate the neophytes.

This broad principle in many respects is not very new for it has been embedded in the very bricks and steel of American industrialization. In antebellum Massachusetts, for example, a pattern emerged according to which factories, spun by ensuing industrialization, attracted clusters of immigrants who coalesced into neighborhoods in which European cultures were replicated in America.

Importantly, these factories did not develop first in the coastline Yankee-dominated harbor cities, but rather on the inland frontier where there was water power to energize flour and textile mills. A lack of available water and wind power was a factor in retarding rapid industrialization in the large Yankee cities on the waterfronts. The inland economic system that resulted created a "boardinghouse" lifestyle that appealed to immigrants not driven by their instincts for land, in particular the Irish and Italians. In the later nineteenth century this "boardinghouse syndrome" appealed alike to the immigrants as it did to reform-minded social theorists who railed against the "horrors" of the shelter houses as they sought alternatives for these ghetto poor somewhere on midwestern land.[6]

Frequently the social reformers proved as inept with their solutions as were the tenement conditions they sought to mitigate. When Minnesota's Archbishop John Ireland of St. Paul attempted to position the shanty Irish on their own frontier farms in the western part of the state he quickly learned that you can put the poor out in the country but you can seldom put the "country" into the lifestyle of the poor. Soon officials of the colony were chiding the Irish settlers for spurning the means of existence offered them by Bishop Ireland, to which the offenders replied, "the Bishop brought us here and he must care for us." Since these unfortunate people lacked the foresight needed to succeed in farming but had shown at least some willingness to work for daily wages, and since the city of St. Paul was growing rapidly, it was agreed that they would give up their farms and seek employment in the city. The bishop paid for their transportation to St. Paul and secured them day laboring jobs.[7] The Irish could not be re-shaped and re-conditioned for life on the rural frontier simply by being transplanted into the geographic molds that Turner thought were all embracing.

Frederick Jackson Turner, by his thesis that laid emphasis on the *geographic* frontier rather than on the various cultural pockets that pervaded the frontier, neglected to differentiate between those immigrants who were culturally prepared—and therefore inclined to benefit by the rural experience—and those whom the frontier by its harsh realities would all too readily destroy.

To be sure, in fairness to Turner, it must be admitted that when he formulated his frontier theory our perspective on the immigrant farmer stood in almost total eclipse from research into the settlement of rural immigrants. Scholarship has advanced a goodly distance since the 1929 comment of Edmund de S. Brunner that in "the immense volume of literature dealing with the question of immigration, hardly any consideration has been paid to those of the foreign-born that live in rural America."[8]

If, as is maintained in this essay, the Germans were immigrants who traditionally were land-based, day laborers and small-parcel-holding peasants in Europe, and who continued their farming life style on the American frontier, then a synthesis between the Turner thesis and Oscar Handlin's view about the "uprooted" must be granted. Rather than a compelling force wrought upon people by their being in a geographic location at the edge of expanding civilization, and rather than representatives of the huddled masses dislocated from European poorhouses who came to America as "the uprooted," the Germans were most frequently immigrants from small, rural, peasant villages.

In America they settled in partially replicated enclaves where they perpetuated their language, their ethnicity and their culture with the result that for them, unlike many of their Irish co-settlers, disorientation and isolation were minimized. It was their traditions from the Old World community that, maximized and maintained for several generations, enabled them to enjoy a natural, almost evolutionary transition to the New World with its new language, tradition, and heritage.[9] Not that the process of assimilation was voluntary, rather it was often difficult and during World War I, in particular, it was frequently violent and repeatedly unfair.[10] Nevertheless, German immigrants formed New World communities based on their Old World village life patterns that have persisted with remarkable resilience to this day.

Often the German enclaves were strengthened by an added force which had little to do with nationalism in the pejorative nineteenth-century European sense of the word, but which had much to do with a drive for separateness that was based in nineteenth-century European nationhood. This was the phenomenon of religion. Of all the nations in Europe that formed the primary wellsprings of immigration for the United States, only Germany, and to a limited degree also Holland and Switzerland, was rigidly divided into religious regions based historically on the treaty that concluded the Lutheran and Peasant Wars in the first half of the 16th century, namely, the 1555 Treaty of Augsburg which provided for *"cuius regio, eius religio* [whatever is the religion of the prince, that is the religion of the region]." Believers in the Augsburg Confession [Lutherans] and Catholics were guaranteed religious freedom in regions as determined by their rulers, and were guaranteed permission to exchange places if their religious convictions did not agree with that of their princes.

True, Calvinists and separatists such as the Mennonites, the Amish and other sectarians did not acquire the same rights but the 1555 agreement did set the pattern for the succeeding centuries: Germans lived separately according to their religious affiliation and that separation was dual—by religion and by region. England, France, Norway, Sweden and other countries had national religions. Because separatists like the Mennonites were not included in this guarantee of freedom, they were the first to emigrate—more accurately they were asked to leave—resulting in the strong Mennonite settlements in rural Pennsylvania where William Penn bade them welcome.[11] Others, with interludes in East Prussia, exited to Russia where they established isolated German settlements on agricultural frontiers along the Black Sea and the Middle Volga River districts.

In addition to the "other worldly" separatist settlements in Pennsylvania, Ohio, Indiana, Iowa and other Midwest states, there are "separatistic" Catholic and Lutheran settlements in which German immigrants have been much less "other worldly" but in many respects no less "separatist" than the Mennonites and their subgroups, including the Amish and the Hutterites. Examples of traditionally isolated rural Catholic German settlements in the Midwest include the Stearns and Benson county region of Minnesota; DuBois, Franklin, Ripley and Dearborn counties in southern Indiana; Effingham, St. Clair, Madison and Clinton counties in south central Illinois; Fond du Lac, Calumet and Outagamie counties in Wisconsin; Dubuque, Shelby, Audubon and Carroll counties in Iowa; Cole and Osage counties in central Missouri; Auglaize, Mercer and Shelby counties in western Ohio; Logan county in Arkansas; Emmons county in south central North Dakota; Platte county in northeastern

Nebraska; Ellis county in Kansas and others such as Fayette and Colorado counties in Texas.

Examples of Lutheran-dominated rural German enclaves include Sibley, McLeod, and Carver counties in central Minnesota; Jefferson, Dodge, Ozaukee and Washington counties in southeastern Wisconsin; Allen and La Porte counties in northern Indiana; the Frankenmuth area of Saginaw, Tuscola and Bay counties in eastern Michigan; Madison and Sangamon counties in Illinois; St. Louis and St. Charles counties in eastern Missouri; and many counties on the eastern quarter of the three states of South Dakota, Nebraska and Kansas. German Protestant settlements were also strong in western Oregon.[12]

Germans in all of these rural enclaves have shown tenacity for their peasant way of life and its counterpart in the United States, the family farm. In 1880 nearly half of all German-born workers in the United States made their living from farming and they amounted to 10 percent of all the farmers in the traditional Midwest German belt. In some states the Germans greatly exceeded their expected average of the national population; for example, in Wisconsin where they comprised 27 percent of all farmers in 1880. In the same year they tallied 19, 16, and 14 percent in Minnesota, Kansas, and Nebraska, while amounting to the largest group of immigrant farmers in all but one [Michigan] of the 12 states of this region [Illinois, Indiana, Iowa, Kansas, Minnesota, Missouri, Nebraska, Ohio, North-South Dakota, and Wisconsin].[13]

As these data indicate and as scholars have been demonstrating recently, Germans have been outstanding for their persistence in remaining on family farms.[14] Three-quarters of a century later, according to the 1950 population census, Germans were 50 percent more dominant in agricultural occupations than their share would be based on an extrapolation of their nineteenth-century representation. By 1980, 27 percent of the rural farm population in the 12-state Midwest in 1980 identified themselves as of pure German ancestry with an added 22 percent of reported mixed German ancestry, amounting to nearly half the farming-core population in these agribusiness states. Some 36 percent of the national rural farm population report German ancestry.[15]

Therefore the Turner thesis about the frontier's power to amalgamate needs to be tempered with an appreciation of the concept of chain migration. Scholars must also factor in a realization that German-speaking villagers moved not just from Old World to New World but that a strong commitment to unmixed religions re-enforced the homogeneity of their New World settlements. This means that in the New World villagers and families tended to accept newcomers from out-region areas or "non-villagers" only if they were of like religion with the already established inhabitants. The question remains whether the Turner thesis was applicable for the assimilation of ethnic components on the American frontier. Given the fact that Germans have gained such prominence on the agricultural "frontier," has Turnerian assimilation been achieved?

Several micro-studies report that rural and farm Germans were considerably less rapid in assimilating than their metropolitan counterparts,[16] although enough studies have been completed to show that the urban Germans were not that much different.[17] Swedes and other Scandinavians generally were more rapid than the Germans in assuming the English language and thereby the culture of the American marketplace. Yet German customs and ethnic patterns did not yield more wealth or a better standard of living than those practiced by native Americans due solely to their delayed rate of integration. In the case of Illinois communities, for example, even though the Germans engaged in more thorough estate planning than the Yankees, German-owned farms ended up smaller than those held by Yankees.

Because German farms remained more limited, it became mandatory for members of the German ethnic group to supplement income from off-farm work. By giving higher priority to farm ownership continuity, often coupled with a tendency to have large families, these Illinois Germans ended up with fewer liquid assets. While they succeeded in keeping more of their heirs in agriculture, they ended up fragmenting their estates.

Due to somewhat reduced family size and a greater accommodation to outside entrepreneurial opportunities, the Yankee farmers witnessed greater outmigration of their members, resulting in larger portions left behind for their remaining heirs. Because the Germans were instinctively more concerned with an integrated, homogeneous community, they ironically created the antithesis—a bedroom community that lacks cohesion.[18] Parallel conclusions were reached in a study of rural German women in settlements on the Nebraska frontier.[19] Thus improved economic outcomes often did not result in ethnic maintenance.

Often rural German Catholics became the victims not only of Nativism from Yankees but of prejudice at the hands of their German Protestant neighbors, sometimes turning them into political conservatives [in the nineteenth century this meant Democrats] who perhaps earlier had gone along with their more liberal leaders in joining the Republican Party and its anti-slavery cause.[20] Sometimes rural German settlements began to assimilate in matters they considered unessential, especially if their size was too small to make their own agricultural markets viable and self-sufficient. In the communities of Perham and Freiberg in western Minnesota, for example, intermarriage of Germans with other ethnic groups remained well below the non-German rate but increasingly in the early twentieth century their economic well-being and diverse religious affiliation tended to weaken in "unessential" local German social structures.[21]

In other circumstances, because the local German community was perceived as too manipulative of elections during the late nineteenth and early twentieth centuries, non-Germans in the area seized upon the World War I opportunity to avenge themselves on the Germans when the persecution of Germans was winked at if not openly promoted by local authorities. In the community of Lowden, in Iowa's Cedar County, anti-German rhetoric reached such a high pitch that, while the defenseless Germans suffered the provocations as long as hostilities continued, they pursued matters with intense bitterness once the conflict had ended, resulting in lawsuits that dragged on into the 1920s.[22]

Frequently, rural Germans declined to participate in politics, not even voting, because they had been conditioned for such behavior by the lack of citizen involvement in a democracy in their native European villages. Office holding in the Old World was at best tolerated, but only at the local level.[23] Isolated

cases of the opposite situation derived when German rural settlements in Minnesota's Stearns county, for example, were so
homogeneous that no outsiders came forward and in such circumstances rural Germans quickly mastered the instruments of
community construction, development and defense by sitting on
petit juries, town boards, and as county commissioners.[24] Frequently the study of rural ethnic groups focused on the immigrants themselves and their hardships to the neglect of their
origins, cultural preconditioning and what they created out of
the land and the communities they founded in the New World.[25]

In many instances the Americanization of rural German
immigrants was greatly retarded by their lack of English language competency and the unwillingness of rural German religious leaders to foster English-language instruction. Pastors believed that the German language would isolate and protect their
members, thus preserving them in their faith.[26] A good example
is the Saginaw Valley in Michigan where Father Martin Kundig
established more than 40 churches and schools which for decades served the German-speaking clientele in the German language, a mission they continue today, though not in German.[27]

German-speaking immigrants from beyond the Reich's
borders, in particular those from the former Russian colonies on
the Volga and along the northern rim of the Black Sea, were
especially tenacious in retaining their ethnicity longer than
average American immigrants, even longer than those from Germany proper. Germans from Russia were conditioned to a life of
separateness by over a century of schools, churches, pastors,
books, and village administrations that were exclusively German. Consequently, when these immigrants came to the United
States, they exhibited a "stockade" mentality more vigorously
than did Germans from the Reich. Still, when the pressure was
on during World War I, the Germans from Russia at least
outwardly masked their Germanness enough to escape overt
censorship from non-German neighbors. In matters where economics and other considerations did not militate against their
being of German ethnicity, however, they tended to exhibit their
Germanness more casually or at least to mask it less well.[28]

On occasion efforts have been made to show that the assimilation of Germans hinged on the image the Fatherland en-

joyed in world opinion at any given time and that assimilation of
the Germans in America, especially in rural areas, depended on
whether the specter of being perceived as having German birth
or heritage was favorable or negative for the immigrant.[29]
Accordingly, the Germans in America took advantage of the
pride or shame that world opinion heaped on Imperial Germany
during the nineteenth and early twentieth centuries. Having
contributed beyond their proportion of the total population in
the Civil War, the Germans in America for the balance of the
nineteenth century could at least allege that they had played a
major moral role in ridding the nation of slavery and preserving
the Union. Never mind the fact that during the fray there was a
great deal of confusion in the minds of the Germans about their
duty and their allegiance to the "right side."[30]

Later, Germany under Chancellor Bismarck gained high
respect in the world for national prowess in science, industry,
technology, education, city planning and diplomacy. During his
long and skillful term as Chancellor, Bismarck often was called
upon to mediate world disputes. As evidence of this prestige
position for things German, German place names[31] sprouted all
across America: Over the Rhine, Little Saxony, Germantown,
Little Germany, at least 70 Humboldt renditions after scientist
Alexander, and hundreds of others, including at least 37 sites—
always small rural settings—that prided themselves on being
called by the name Berlin, united Imperial Germany's capital
city.

However, when the image of Germany became severely
tarnished by means of effective British propaganda referring to
Germans as Huns, Kaiserites, beer-swilling barbarians and
Belgian baby killers, the respectability Americans garnered by
being Germans also altered for the worse. German street and
place names—including the world-famous scientists, dramatists
and poets like Humboldt, Schiller and Goethe—suddenly vanished from the maps.

As writer Kurt Vonnegut puts it in his autobiographical
Palm Sunday, "The anti-Germanism in this country during the
First World War so shamed and dismayed my parents that they
resolved to raise me without acquainting me with the language
or the literature or the music or the oral family histories which

my ancestors had loved. They volunteered to make me ignorant and rootless as proof of their patriotism."[32]

During the Nazi period, of course, the German image shifted even further from that of enviable high technology, music, and sophisticated manufacture to that of least favored people on earth, ranking even below Stalinist Russia. The brutal Kaiser image of World War I led to the Hitler horror of World War II, which fostered accelerated German assimilation in America.

The reverse argument can also be made that following the German economic miracle of the 1950s and 1960s, as West Germany and after 1989 the whole of Germany again took its place in the European and world communities, that German Americans once again willingly avowed their German ancestry. The 1920 census immediately after World War I showed a dramatic decline of Americans willing to admit German birth or ancestry. In 1910, the reported German-born in the United States stood at 2,501,333. This figure on German birth declined ten years later in 1920 to just 1,686,108 even though the Germans in 1920 remained by far the largest foreign-born group in the United States population. Following the World War I negative propaganda against "Huns" and the like, those "officially" reporting German birth "declined" by 815,225 or by 33 percent despite the arrival over the same decade of 174,227 newcomers from Germany.

A similar pattern emerges when consideration is given to mother-tongue speakers in the United States. From a total of 9,187,000 mother-tongue German speakers in 1910 the figure dropped to 8,164,000 in 1920—a decrease of over one million, or about 11 percent.[33] These stark differences in the data suggest that it would not be reasonable to assume that the German-born or mother tongue speakers of German could possibly have declined in one decade by a 20–30 percent margin. It appears, rather, that in 1910 a person of German birth readily acknowledged German national origin to the census taker while in 1920 the stigma of being German caused Germans to deny their origins.

In addition, of all the statistics on non-English speakers in the United States for 1910 and 1920, the only one that showed a decline was German—by over a million despite the arrival of .7

million new speakers of German. Finally, the German language continued to be the most often reported non-English mother tongue for all succeeding censuses until 1980, when for the first time it was surpassed by Spanish. It must be concluded, therefore, that Americans of German birth, stock and language in 1920 simply under-reported their ethnicity, only to report more accurately in subsequent censuses. Interesting too is the fact that the sharpest 1920 declines took place in those states where oppression of the Germans was most acute. The reduction of German speakers was greatest in New York, Illinois, Ohio and Pennsylvania, while it remained more or less constant in Minnesota, increasing slightly in Michigan and California.[34]

Following this line of argument, the respectability Germany gained in the last forty years has brought back a willingness of Germans to acknowledge their ancestry. In the 1990 census nearly 58 million Americans report German ancestry [23.3 percent], far above the next largest ethnic group, the Irish, with 38.7 [15.6 percent] and the English with 32.7 million [13.1 percent]. This means that nearly a quarter of the American population today admits German ancestry. In states like Wisconsin, Minnesota, Iowa, Nebraska and the Dakotas, the ratio is close to half reporting German ancestry. The most German metropolitan region in the United States is Milwaukee-Racine, where 48 percent of the population have German ancestry.[35]

An American movement that always affected the Germans and their willingness to assimilate with their Yankee neighbors was Prohibition. Despite the desirability at times for Germans in America to stand together on issues of political or cultural discrimination, most scholars admit that they never did so except on the matter of freedom to consume alcoholic beverages, especially their right to do so in an open beer garden on Sunday afternoons.[36]

To this end the German-American Alliance [Deutsch-Amerikanischer Nationalbund] championed much that was in theory to the good of German Americans, e.g. physical education in the schools, conservation of America's forests, the need for all Germans in America to become citizens, and the furtherance of German in American public schools. But in reality the Alliance was most vigorous in promoting the right of Germans to drink beer at times and in places of their own choosing, which in turn garnered the Alliance lavish support from the American brewing industry which, in the early twentieth century, was almost exclusively owned by German Americans.

Thus, support for the Alliance grew in direct proportion as Prohibition waxed. And only when the Alliance waned to the point of finally being declared illegal by Congress in 1918 did Prohibition have clear sailing to become the law of the land in 1919.[37] Sometimes German-American leaders lamented: "Unfortunately the entire election debate again hinges on the tiresome old beer and schnapps cause. For this shabby issue, the Germans once more enter the fray united. When more important, higher-minded, more idealistic issues are at stake, they cower down in their familiar squabbling."[38]

There were also German-American leaders in rural regions who resisted the notion of a replicated Germany in America. Instead, they favored total assimilation. Gustav Körner addressing the Germans in his own Belleville, Illinois, put it succinctly in a speech declining to press for the admittance of German as an official Illinois courtroom language: "We are of the opinion that no array of immigrants from abroad has the right to continue to exist separately as an isolated breed if they arrive among a previously settled people who are not inferior in their cultural development. . . . We prefer our broadly based freedom over the meager continuation of an old way of life on foreign soil."[39]

In other words, special treatment on the plus side—language usage and other privileges could later lead to "special" treatment on the negative side—discrimination from the host society or even prejudice and bigotry in the regional courts. In a similar vein, H.L. Mencken, the son of German immigrants, was correct when he wrote in 1928: "The melting pot has swallowed up the German-Americans as no other group, not even the Irish."[40]

Despite the truth in the Mencken statement, most observers would concede that making out of a rural German first a German-American and then just an "American" required patience, tolerance and some trauma on the part of the newcomers. It also mandated openness and acceptance, particularly in rural areas, from members of the host society. The Turner

frontier was hardly the magic wand that made amalgamation
easy and automatic.

NOTES

1. Frederick Jackson Turner, *The Frontier in American History* (New
York, 1920), pp. 22–23.

2. See in general Kathleen Neils Conzen, *Making Their Own
America: Assimilation Theory and the Great Peasant Pioneer* (New York,
1990), commentary by Jörg Nagler, pp. 38–44.

3. Good examples are Russell Gerlach, *Immigrants in the Ozarks*
(Columbia, MO, 1977); Robert C. Ostergren, *A Community Transplanted:
The Trans-Atlantic Experience of a Swedish Immigrant Settlement in the
Upper Middle West 1835–1915* (Madison, WI, 1988); Walter D.
Kamphoefner, *The Westfalians: From Germany to Missouri* (Columbia,
MO, 1987); James M. Bergquist, "German Communities in American
Cities: An Interpretation of the Nineteenth-Century Experience," *Journal
of American Ethnic History* 4 (1984):9–30; Gary Foster, Richard Hummel
and Robert Whittenbarger, "Ethnic Echoes through 100 Years of
Midwestern Agriculture," *Rural Sociology* 52 (1987):365–78; Stanley
Nadel, *Little Germany: Ethnicity, Religion, and Class in New York City,
1845–1880* (Urbana, IL, 1990); Sonya Salamon, "Ethnic Communities and
the Structure of Agriculture," *Rural Sociology* 50 (1985):323–40 and
others. Maps showing rural ethnic groups in America help pinpoint the
settlements. For example, U.S. Bureau of the Census, *Statistical Atlas,
Twelfth Census of the United States, 1900* (Washington, DC, 1903), plates
55–75; Richard Hartshorne, "Racial Maps of the United States,"
Geographical Review 28 (1938):276–88; Neale Carman, *Foreign-Language
Units of Kansas*, Vol. 1, *Historical Atlas and Statistics* (Lawrence, KS, 1962);
Terry G. Jordan, *German Seed in Texas Soil: Immigrant Farmers in
Nineteenth Century Texas* (Austin, TX, 1966); La Vern J. Rippley, *The
Immigrant Experience in Wisconsin* (Boston, 1985), appendix maps; Karl B.
Raitz, "Ethnic Maps of North America," 68; *Geographical Review*
(1978):335–50. See also, James Paul Allen and Eugene James Turner, *We
the People: An Atlas of America's Ethnic Diversity* (New York, 1988), 51 ff.

4. The role of "chain migration" is explained by Walter
Kamphoefner, "Entwurzelt oder verpflanzt," in Klaus Bade, ed.,

Auswanderer—Wanderarbeiter—Gastarbeiter: Bevölkerung, Arbeitsmarkt und Wanderung in Deutschland seit der Mitte des 19. Jahrhunderts (Ostfildern, 1984), I:321–49.

5. Oscar Handlin, *The Uprooted*, rev. ed. (Boston, 1973), pp. 55–56, 95–97, 166–67.

6. See in general Jonathan Prude, "Town-Factory Conflicts in Antebellum Rural Massachusetts," in Steven Hahn and Jonathan Prude, eds., *The Countryside in the Age of Capitalist Transformation* (Chapel Hill, NC, 1985), pp. 71–102.

7. See James P. Shannon, *Catholic Colonization on the Western Frontier* (New Haven, CT, 1957), esp. Chapter 7: "The Poor Men Failed," 154 ff., quote 163, and Marvin R. O'Connell, *John Ireland and the American Catholic Church* (St. Paul, MN, 1988), pp. 149–152.

8. Edmund de S. Brunner, *Immigrant Farmers and Their Children* (Garden City, NY, 1929), p. xvi. Other early studies of the rural situation include Joseph Schafer, *Four Wisconsin Counties: Prairie and Forest* (Madison, WI, 1927), and his four part series "The Yankee and the Teuton in Wisconsin," *Wisconsin Magazine of History* 6 (1922–23):125–45, 261–79, 386–402; 7 (1923):3–19. See also Theodore Saloutos, "The Immigrant Contribution to American Agriculture," *Agricultural History* 50 (1976): 45-67.

9. Willi Paul Adams, *Deutsche im Schmelztiegel der USA: Erfahrungen im größten Einwanderungsland der Europäer* (Berlin, n.d.), Chapter 3: "Wohin? Deutsche zogen zu Deutschen," 11 ff. See also Heinz Kloss, *Atlas of 19th and 20th Century German-American Settlements* (Marburg, 1974), Peter Marschalck, *Deutsche Überseewanderung im 19. Jahrhundert: Ein Beitrag zur soziologischen Theorie der Bevölkerung* (Stuttgart, 1973), and Willi Paul Adams, "Die Assimilationsfrage der amerikanischen Einwanderungsdiskussion, 1890–1930," *American Studies* 27 (1982):275–291. See also in general Mack Walker, *Germany and the Emigration, 1816–1885* (Cambridge, MA, 1964).

10. The best general treatment of the German-American trauma during World War I is by Frederick C. Luebke, *Bonds of Loyalty: German Americans and World War I* (DeKalb, IL, 1974).

11. Among the many good sources, see Christine M. Totten, *Roots in the Rhineland: America's German Heritage in Three Hundred Years of Immigration 1683–1983*, rev. ed. (New York, 1988). Early histories of this rural immigration include Oswald Seidensticker, *Die erste deutsche Einwanderung in Amerika und die Gründung von Germantown 1683* (Philadelphia, 1883), Julius Friedrich Sachse, *The German Pietists of Provincial Pennsylvania* (Philadelphia, 1895), as well as more recent

publications like Hermann Wellenreuther, "Image and Counterimage, Tradition and Expectation: The German Immigrants in English Colonial Society in Pennsylvania, 1700–1765," and John A. Hostetler, "The Plain People: Historical and Modern Perspectives," in Frank Trommler and Joseph McVeigh, eds., *America and the Germans*, 2 vols. (Philadelphia, 1985), pp. 85–118.

12. Heinz Kloss, *Atlas*, Sections G, H, and F.

13. Conzen, *Making Their Own America*, p. 4.

14. A good study of this topic is Walter D. Kamphoefner, "The German Agricultural Frontier: Crucible or Cocoon," *Ethnic Forum* 4 (1984):21–35.

15. See *1890 Census of Population. General Social and Economic Characteristics, United States Summary*, Tables 76, 60, 238. Norwegians and Dutch were also uncharacteristically retentive of ethnicity in agricultural situations. Janel M. Curry-Roper and Carol Veldman Rudie, "Hollendale: The Evolution of a Dutch Farming Community [Minnesota]," *Focus* 40 (1990):13 ff.

16. Bradley H. Baltensperger, "Agricultural Change Among Nebraska's Immigrants 1880–1900," in Frederick C. Luebke, ed., *Ethnicity on the Great Plains* (Lincoln, NE, 1980), pp. 170–183. Swedes were much more rapid in their tendency to assimilate and to lose their cultural identity than were German-speakers.

17. For example, Stanley Nadel, *Little Germany* (Urbana, IL, 1990), and Hartmut Keil and John B. Jentz, eds., *German Workers in Chicago: A Documentary History of Working-Class Culture from 1850–World War I* (Urbana, IL, 1988). See also the case for Toronto in Sandra Felka, Paul Simpson-Housley and Anton de Man, "Locus of Control, Age, and Urban Residential Satisfaction in German Immigrants," *Psychological Reports* 64 (1989):1098, and the parallel study by M. Martinez and ibid., "Neighbourliness, Socializing and Residential Satisfaction in Urban Settings: Two Studies of German and Spanish Immigrants," *International Journal of Comparative Sociology* 32 (1991):310 ff. as well as George Helmuth Kellner, "The German Element on the Urban Frontier: St. Louis 1830–1860" (unpub. Ph.D. diss., University of Missouri-Columbia, 1973).

18. Edward V. Carroll and Sonya Salamon, "Share and Share Alike: Inheritance Patterns in Two Illinois Farm Communities," *Journal of Family History* 13 (1988):218–232.

19. Linda Schelbitzki, "Rural German-Speaking Women in Early Nebraska and Kansas: Ethnicity as a Factor in Frontier Adaptation," *Great Plains Quarterly* 9 (1989):239–251.

20. Bonnie J. Krause, "German Americans in the St. Louis Region, 1840–1860," *Missouri Historical Review* 83 (1988):233–310.

21. David Peterson, "'From Bone Depth': German-American Communities in Rural Minnesota Before the Great War," *Journal of American Ethnic History* 11 (Winter, 1992):27–55. See also broader studies, e.g. Allan Kulikoff, "The Transition to Capitalism in Rural America," *William and Mary Quarterly* 46 (1989):120–144, Mark Friedberger, *Farm Families and Change in Twentieth Century America* (Lexington, KY, 1988), and ibid., *Shake-Out: Iowa Farm Families in the 1980s* (Lexington, KY, 1989).

22. Nancy Barr, "Lowden: A Study of Intolerance in an Iowa Community During the Era of the First World War," *Annals of Iowa* 20 (1988):3–22.

23. William L. Jahraus, "The Relationship Between Ethnic Traditions and Officeholding of the Early German Russians of McIntosh County, North Dakota, 1883–1915," *Heritage Review* 12 (1982):20–35.

24. Conzen, *Making Their Own America*, p. 28.

25. See in this connection John Ibson, "Virgin Land or Virgin Mary? Studying the Ethnicity of White Americans," *American Quarterly* 33 (1981):284–307.

26. Susan Jean Kuyper, "The Americanization of German Immigrants: Language, Religion and Schools in Nineteenth Century Rural Wisconsin" (unpub. Ph.D. diss., University of Wisconsin Madison, 1980), *Dissertation Abstracts International* 42 (1981):111–12. See also Adams, *Schmelztiegel*, Chapter 6, "Deutsche Kirchen und Schulen: Behinderten sie die Integration?" 23 ff.

27. Timothy Pies, "Catholic Education Comes to the Saginaw Valley," *Michigan History* 74 (1980):32–60.

28. Among many sources, see Richard Sallet, *Russian-German Settlements in the United States* (Fargo, ND, 1974); Gordon Iseminger, "Are We Germans, or Russians, or Americans? The McIntosh County German-Russians During World War I," *North Dakota History* 59 (1992):2–16; and ibid., "The McIntosh County German Russians: The First Fifty Years," *North Dakota History* 51 (1984):4–23. See also Timothy J. Kloberdanz, "Volksdeutsche: The Eastern European Germans," in William C. Sherman and Playford V. Thorson, eds., *Plains Folk: North Dakota's Ethnic History* (Fargo, ND, 1988), William C. Sherman, "Assimilation in a North Dakota German Russian Community" (unpub. M.A. thesis, University of North Dakota, 1965), Hattie Plum Williams, *A Social Study of the Russian German*, University Series XVI (Lincoln, NE,

1916), and ibid., *The Czar's Germans With Particular Reference to the Volga Germans* (Lincoln, NE, 1975).

29. For examples, see La Vern J. Rippley, "German Assimilation: The Effect of the 1871 Victory on Americana-Germanica," in Hans L. Trefousse, ed., *Germany and America: Essays on Problems of International Relations and Immigration* (New York, 1980), pp. 122–136, ibid., "Ameliorated Americanization: The Effect of World War I on German-Americans in the 1920s," in Trommler and McVeigh, eds., *America and the Germans*, pp. 217–31, and Jonathan F. Wagner, "From German to American: The Image of Germany and Germans in North Dakota's German Language Press 1900–1930," *Heritage Review* 18 (1988):10–16.

30. Frederick C. Luebke, ed., *Ethnic Voters and the Election of Lincoln* (Lincoln, NE, 1971) and Wilhelm Kaufmann, *Die Deutschen im amerikanischen Bürgerkriege* (Munich, 1911).

31. For example, La Vern J. Rippley and Rainer Schmeissner, *German Place Names in Minnesota* (Northfield, MN, 1989).

32. Kurt Vonnegut, *Palm Sunday* (New York, 1981), p. 21.

33. Data from the 1910 Thirteenth and 1920 Fourteenth United States Censuses. See the breakdowns in Rippley, "Ameliorated Americanization," in Trommler and McVeigh, eds., *America and the Germans*, II:222 ff.

34. *Fourteenth Census of the United States*, 2:972.

35. Reported in many papers by the Associated Press, e.g. *Minneapolis Star Tribune* (December 17, 18, 1992) 1, and *USA Today* (August 4, 1992), as quoted in *Society for German-American Studies Newsletter* 13 (1992):30.

36. A succinct discussion of this issue appears in Adams, *Schmeltztiegel*, Chapter 8: "Ethnische Gruppen in der Politik: Deutschamerikaner als Wähler und Gewählte," pp. 29–34.

37. Clifton Child, *The German-Americans in Politics 1914–1917* (Madison, WI, 1939) discusses this development at length.

38. *Chicago Arbeiterzeitung* (1983) on a bill pending in the Illinois legislature, quoted by Adams, *Schmelztiegel*, 29.

39. Quoted by Heinz Kloss, *Um die Einigung des Deutsch-Amerikanertums* (Berlin, 1937), p. 200.

40. Quoted in Adams, *Schmelztiegel*, p. 39.

CHAPTER 12

Ethnic Elites and Their Organizations
The St. Louis Experience, 1900–1925

Margaret LoPiccolo Sullivan

Turn-of-the-century St. Louis provides unique opportunities for the study of ethnic elites and their organizations and associations. It is through the study of these relationships that we can come to understand how specific immigrant communities defined themselves in their new nation.

St. Louis was ethnically diverse almost from its establishment as a French trading post in 1764. As early as 1800, for example, St. Louis was a mix of Irish, French, German, and black migrants all seeking a better life.[1]

Situated at the juncture of the Mississippi and Missouri rivers, St. Louis became the transfer point for westward expansion and increased in size and population at an astounding rate in the decades before the Civil War. The number of residents increased from less than six thousand in 1830 to over 160,000 thirty years later.

Most of the newcomers came from Europe, which made St. Louis quite cosmopolitan. Nearly half the residents were foreign-born by 1850 and the percentage kept rising every year. By 1860, some 60 percent of the residents of St. Louis were foreign-born, making the city the most ethnic in the nation.

But an uncertain economy in the decades following the Civil War undermined the appeal of St. Louis as a magnet for the foreign-born. By 1900, the population of the Gateway City was second most native-born in the nation. To be sure, a small number of southern and eastern Europeans did settle in neighborhoods near the city's business district, but even as late as 1930, these groups made up only 7 percent of the population.

Such statistics obscure the ethnic ambience of St. Louis in the last half of the nineteenth century. During these years, St. Louis became a "second generation" city. Even though only 19 percent of St. Louis residents were foreign-born in 1900, well over 60 percent had foreign-born parents. German immigrants, their children and grandchildren constituted fully 56 percent of the city's population and the Irish-born and their descendants made up another 15 percent.[2]

This did not mean that ethnics were in charge; indeed, they were not. The majority of city fathers were native-born residents of English heritage. To be sure, both the Irish and the Germans prospered in St. Louis, but for the most part remained in middle-class occupations. In 1880, for example, 72 percent of the residents of German heritage held jobs as skilled laborers, merchants, white collar workers, or small business owners. The Irish moved up the occupational ladder a bit more slowly, but by 1900 most had entered the skilled trades and technical industries in large numbers.[3]

This is not to say that ethnics were second-class citizens in St. Louis.[4] The daily press, joined by the political establishment, frequently praised the contributions of the Germans and the Irish and encouraged the federal government to keep an open mind on immigration. A host of ethnic organizations provided a framework for the celebration of ethnic customs and values. Even though they had been born in America, the German Americans and Irish Americans of St. Louis were proud of their ethnic heritage and made efforts to sustain the culture of their forefathers in their new nation.

The fact that the second generation remained loyal to their roots undercut the popular assumption that immigrants and their children dissolved into a generational melting pot. That was not the case. Middle-class ethnics remained true to ethnic organizations because these organizations provided identity, social status, and leadership roles vis-a-vis the larger St. Louis community. It took several decades and another generation before the power of these organizations would diminish.[5]

St. Louis was a German-American city beginning in 1850, with the German residents outnumbering the Irish by a ratio of three to one.[6] Not surprisingly, the St. Louis Germans who achieved middle-class status and respectability by 1900 saw no need to abandon their ethnic roots. Audray Louise Olson's study of 284 German-born elites in St. Louis between 1850 and 1920 revealed that fully two-thirds were members of at least one German-American social organization. A second sample of one hundred second- and third-generation German Americans in the city at the turn of the century showed that fully half were members of at least one German organization.

These organizations spread across the socioeconomic classes.[7] Prosperous Germans, for example, sought membership in high status groups such as the "Leiderkranz." Founded in 1870, the Leiderkranz was the elite German American social club in St. Louis. In fact, fully 57 percent of its members owned their own companies and the remainder were doctors, lawyers and similar professionals. The growing prosperity of Germans in St. Louis was mirrored in the ever-increasing membership in the Leiderkranz. When membership reached 741 in 1914, the club considered setting a limit of 800 members.[8]

The Leiderkranz not only provided a beautiful place to entertain guests, it also helped to define the pinnacle of German-American prosperity in St. Louis. Leiderkranz was visible proof that in St. Louis, at least, a resident could be both German and American and still be a respected member of the community.

But Leiderkranz was only an aspiration for most Germans in St. Louis. With an ethnic community of such a large size, most Germans sought organizations that reflected their own socio-economic status and religious beliefs. There were clubs for German Catholics, German Lutherans, German Evangelicals and even clubs for German Freethinkers. Given this persistent ethnicity, it is not surprising that St. Louis had over 300 German-American organizations at the turn of the century.

Was there a common element to these 300 groups? A common ideology capable of bonding these increasingly diverse organizations had to be vaguely Teutonic yet still compatible with American values. The result of the search for order was cultural nationalism. German kultur was somehow superior to

Anglo-Saxon culture and enriched rather than conflicted with
American political, social, and economic values. This kultur was
so vague that it was used in a myriad of ways as a part of
various German-American festivities.[9]

The first and second generations had distinctly different
notions of ethnicity. The German-born in St. Louis embraced
language maintenance as the key to *kultur*. For this generation,
German books and newspapers as well as foreign language
instruction in the schools were vital to German-American well-
being. But the second and third generations, both largely educated in the United States, were proficient in English and saw
little need for the German language. For these later two generations, it was the *saengerbund* and the *turnverein* which mounted
massive and formal displays of German ethnic traditions that
were the heart of German *kultur*.[10]

As the only city-wide organization, the *turnverein* occasionally united the larger German-American community on
issues of concern. The prominence of the *turnverein* quickly gave
way to the German-American Alliance less than a decade later.
Founded in 1901, the Alliance was a nationwide federation of
German-American organizations. Although successful in many
cities, the Alliance struggled in St. Louis until 1907 when it
became the local lobby against the prohibition of beer and other
alcoholic drinks.

In organizing massive "German Day" celebrations where
kultur was praised and prohibition vilified, the Alliance came
very close to unifying the heterogeneous German-American
community in St. Louis. Even though Catholics and Lutherans
did not formally join the Alliance, Catholic organizations did
take part in some German Day celebrations such as the very
large centennial commemoration of the German Wars of Liberation in 1913.[11] When a united front was called for, it was the
local chapter of the Alliance that stepped forward.

Yet one group of German immigrants and their descendants rarely joined in the joint activities of the German-American
community. German Jews in St. Louis quickly abandoned the
German language and culture in the 1870s and 1880s and their
spokesmen insisted that Judaism was a religion without any
racial connotations. German Jews divorced themselves from the

old country and acculturated into American society as soon as they could.[12]

Yet the Jewish community in St. Louis did not disappear. Like the general German population, the German Jews of St. Louis established an elite social club to promote community relations. The Columbian Club was established in 1892 in an impressive building in the city's west end. Like the Liederkranz, the Columbian was highly visible in St. Louis society and all of its activities attracted the attention of the daily press. Rarely mentioning its ties to the Jewish community, the papers regularly reported on the Columbian Club's elaborate Christmas celebrations.

Also like the Liederkranz, the Columbian was a club for rich men and their families. A sample of its membership from the turn of the century revealed that 68 percent owned their own companies, 22 percent were doctors, lawyers or other professionals, 7 percent were in banking and another 2 percent were in real estate. Most of the Club's members also belonged to Reform congregations that minimized any sense of ethnicity. They emphatically denied that Jews were a race apart and portrayed themselves as thoroughly assimilated Americans with a religion that emphasized ethical principles rather than ancient rituals. According to one local rabbi, the difference between Jews and gentiles was "not so much a difference in tradition as a difference in customs and in inherited standards and ideals."[13] Other Jewish rabbis and secular leaders agreed with this assessment.[14]

The Reform Jewish community's desire to assimilate was challenged by a growing community of Eastern European Orthodox Jews who settled in the neighborhood north of downtown. The Reform community perceived the Orthodox community as foreign: "the outworn, outlived forms that limit, crush or hide the loveliness and loftiness of Jewish ideals."[15]

The Reform community in St. Louis also rejected Zionism with its emphasis on ethnic identity through political nationalism. One reform rabbi warned that petty concerns with once and future nation states would lead to charges of disloyalty to America. "The Jewish state is dead," intoned another Reform rabbi, "and the survivors speak the language of the people where he has his home."[16]

Yet the ethnicity and distinctive culture of these eastern European Jews remained in St. Louis. They were poor and the Reform community responded by establishing the Jewish Charitable and Educational Union. Its main project at the turn of the century was the Alliance Settlement House, which was opened in 1902 in the heart of the Jewish Italian ghetto on the north side of the city.

Leaders of the Charitable and Educational Union also were members of the Columbian Club, the site of Union meetings. Once again, the Union leadership mirrored that of the Columbian. A sample of turn-of-the-century Union leaders reveals that 76 percent owned their own companies, 19 percent were professional men, 3 percent were bankers, and 1 percent was real estate. The Club and the Union were the ties that bound Reform Jews to their ethnic roots.

Although the German community of St. Louis preserved its ethnic heritage through its social clubs, the Irish did not. A sample of St. Louis Irish elites taken from turn-of-the-century local histories indicates that less than 1 percent belonged to Irish-American organizations.

There are a number of reasons to account for this lack of Irish interest in ethnic organizations. First was the legacy of oppression in Ireland where such organizations were considered treasonous by the British government. Over a third of the sample, for example, did not belong to any social or political organization. Second was the close link between Irish nationalism and Roman Catholicism. Over two-thirds of the sample listed ties to parish and religious organizations. Thus, most Irish ethnic activities, from nationalist groups to St. Patrick's Day parades, were extensions of parish councils or committees.

This is not to say that the Irish were invisible. To be sure, they lacked the resources to establish a club like the Liederkranz. But like the Irish in virtually every city in the nation, the Irish of St. Louis celebrated St. Patrick's Day with banquets at the city's best hotels. These were generally informal gatherings not to be confused in any way with the impressive programs of Liederkranz.

By the turn of the century, two organizations had emerged as the sponsors of these banquets.[17] In 1900, for example, the so-called "Knights of St. Patrick" held the largest and most impressive St. Patrick's Day banquet. Of those attending that year, little more than a third were business executives, and about the same percentage were middle managers. A little less than a quarter were professionals and the rest were scattered among several occupational categories. The leadership of the Knights was far less impressive than that of Liederkranz.

A second Irish-American organization put a distinctive emphasis on being American as well as being Irish. The Irish American Society was very progressive for the times by excluding alcohol and including women among those attending the banquets. The occupational breakdown of those attending the IAS banquet was similar to the Knights: about a third were executives, 42 percent were middle managers, and 23 percent were professionals. The principal difference between the two groups was age and outlook. The IAS was dominated by the American-born Irish striving for upward mobility.

Not surprisingly, these two organizations were unstable. The Knights folded in 1907 and that same year saw the "American Sons of Erin" break away from the IAS. The two groups reunited in 1911 under the name "The Irish American Sons of Erin" and the group had a membership of nearly a thousand men a year later. But such forming, splintering and reforming, plus such a limited program, helps to explain why only a handful of Irish-American elites listed their affiliation in either organization.[18]

The explosive issue of Irish independence was the catalyst for a third Irish American organization in St. Louis. [27] Founded in 1902, the St. Louis branch of the United Irish Land League was part of an international effort to support John Redmond in his campaign to win home rule for Ireland. The organization was without much resolve, however, and the mere promise of home rule by 1914 was enough to end the local chapter of the Land League. A fourth organization, the United Irish Societies, emerged to replace the Land League.[19]

Not all Irish Americans in St. Louis were so confident of impending Irish independence. A small group of Irish nationalists, known collectively as "The Friends of Irish Freedom," organized 22 branches in the Irish Catholic parishes of St. Louis.

The failure of the British to grant home rule in 1914, followed two years later by the Easter Rising, galvanized Irish opinion in St. Louis and the nation. With ties to the radical organization *Sinn Fein*, the FOIF was a burst of Irish nationalism in St. Louis during the war years.

The occupational profile of the leaders of these organizations changed very little from that of the Knights and the Irish American Society. A sample of the leaders of the Irish Land League, for example, reveals that 43 percent were executives, 39 percent were professional men, and the remainder were middle managers and skilled tradesmen. A profile of the leaders of the Friends of Irish Freedom showed much the same statistics: 39 percent were businessmen, 43 percent were professionals and the remainder were middle managers. Even though their community was small by comparison with the Germans, the Irish in St. Louis did join together to celebrate St. Patrick's Day and work for Irish independence.[20]

Ethnic organizations occupied a comfortable and well-defined place in St. Louis society during the first 14 years of the twentieth century. But the beginning of world war in August of that year would utterly change the meaning and purpose of these organizations.

It was the German community in St. Louis that suffered through the greatest changes. Initially, with America on the sidelines, the war was a bond between German Americans and their ancestral homeland. Germans in St. Louis lobbied vociferously for the righteousness of the German cause and demanded that America stay neutral. In a burst of unity, the various German American organizations in the city held a mass meeting to protest the biased reporting on the war and urge cooperative action among the German American population of the city. In addition, local political and business leaders established a committee to raise money for the victims of war in the fatherland.

But the war relief committee was not enough for some St. Louis German Americans. This group met at the Liederkranz to organize the Citizen's War Relief Committee. The membership of this second committee overlapped with the first. A third committee, similar in purpose to the first two, was established by middle-class Germans in the city.[21]

Together these three relief committees cooperated in the last and largest German American event in the history of St. Louis—a six-day bazaar in October 1915 that attracted over 100,000 people and raised almost $100,000 for German relief. An analysis of the leadership of these committees reinforces the fact that these groups were controlled by business executives and professional men with a strong interest in German affairs.[22]

The success of these affairs added to the prestige and influence of German American leaders. But trouble was on the horizon. As long as these events raised money for widows and orphans, they were accepted by the general populace. But after the sinking of the Lusitania in the spring of 1915, German-American leaders found themselves caught up in controversy.

A few months after the war began in 1914, these German leaders had joined with Irish nationalists and a few isolationists in founding the St. Louis chapter of the Neutrality League. The League quickly divided, however, between pro-German elements and those who were truly neutral. The German American Alliance, once the champion of the repeal of prohibition, took up the cause of American neutrality. But even the Alliance had trouble building a united German front.[23]

Germany's use of submarine warfare and the United States entry into the war forced German American leaders and their organizations to choose between Germany and America. Both nationally and in St. Louis, few saw any real choice but America. The National German American Alliance contributed its entire treasury to the American Red Cross and disbanded. Other German organizations followed suit.

Not surprisingly, all things German—especially manifestations of cultural nationalism—came under attack. In the face of this hostility, the German American community of St. Louis began shedding the outward symbols of *kultur*. German groups anglicized their names and stopped the use of the German language. The German theater floundered and German language newspapers declined.[24]

The experience of the Leiderkranz was typical of what happened to these societies. Even though the membership purchased $184,000 in Liberty bonds, the Leiderkranz was suspect. The German language was abandoned for both speech and music and there was an effort to change the club's name. But nothing could be done to stem the loss in members from 781 in 1914 to 481 in 1918. By 1921, the organization could no longer afford its palatial clubhouse and was forced to move to smaller quarters. The once mighty Leiderkranz, the symbol of Germania in St. Louis, was on the decline.[25]

With a speed that must have shocked many, the German American elite of St. Louis found ethnicity to be a burden rather than a blessing. With *kultur* under attack, German social organizations declined and so did opportunities for leadership within the German American community. Post-war attempts to revive German American culture were unsuccessful.[26] American society no longer would accept large-scale ethnic enterprises.

In contrast to the tumult in the German Lutheran and Catholic communities during the war, the German Jewish community in St. Louis weathered the war with few changes. Having abandoned their German ethnicity before the war, German Jews were less vulnerable to attack. In fact, German Jewish leaders denounced the war as madness and folly and stood behind the government as 100 percent Americans. There was no decline in the membership of Jewish clubs or organizations.

However, the war did unite the Reform and Orthodox elements of the larger Jewish community in St. Louis. In 1914, the Reform community organized a local branch of American Jewish Relief for Sufferers from the War. The Orthodox Jews, as well as Jewish labor and socialist organizations, organized separate relief groups. But the larger cause of helping world Jewry pushed these separate efforts together. The Reform and Orthodox Jews began to hold joint meetings and came to recognize the contributions of one another.[27]

In short, these relief programs helped to change the attitude of Reform Jews toward the Orthodox. Even though they continued to oppose the Jewish political nationalism that was so popular among the Orthodox, Reform Jews did come to appreciate the need for "at least one spot on earth where the religion of the Jew can be restored to its former complete observance and holy influence."[28] When Rabbi Hillel Silver appealed for a Palestinian homeland at a Columbian Club banquet, the predominantly Reform Jewish membership contributed $40,000.[29]

Other, more subtle shifts also took place in the working relationship between the two Jewish communities in St. Louis. As the Orthodox community moved westward into better neighborhoods, the patronizing attitudes of the Reform community dissipated. The Alliance Settlement House joined the move west, changed its name to the Jewish Community Center and broadened its appeal to both Jewish communities. The Young Men's Hebrew Association, a predominantly Reform organization, became increasingly concerned about the "preservation of Jewish youth to Judaism."[30]

The war had a very different effect on the Irish American community of St. Louis. Unlike German American nationalists, Irish American nationalists were not in direct conflict with American foreign policy during the war. In fact, the call for Irish independence all but died out in St. Louis after the demise of the Neutrality League.

But as soon as the war was over, seventy-five local representatives of the Friends of Irish Freedom, the United Irish societies, and the Ancient Order of Hibernians met to plan a renewed drive for Irish independence. The FOIF quickly became the first among equals, only to die a natural death by 1920.[31]

Civil war broke out in Ireland in 1922, with the Irish parliament and Michael Collins on one side and Eamon de Valera and his rebels on the other; Irish Americans had to choose sides. National Association leaders, with strong ties to de Valera, pledged their support for the rebels. But the St. Louis Irish did not hear the call to arms and remained neutral on the civil war.[32]

The end of British rule and the outbreak of civil war in Ireland deprived the Irish in St. Louis of a common ethnic cause. Catholicism, that other Irish preoccupation, was also becoming more homogeneous and more American in the years after World War I.

The decline of Irish ethnicity is evident in the baptismal and marriage records of five so-called "Irish" parishes over the first two decades of the twentieth century. In 1900, the number of children with Irish surnames baptized in these parishes exceeded 50 percent; twenty years later the percentage was well under 50 percent and dropping fast.[33] In 1900, well over three-quarters of the marriages were between two people with Irish surnames; by

1920 the percentage had dropped to under 25 percent. As the Irish moved and assimilated, the Irish parish or ghetto vanished in all but memory.[34]

The decline of Irish ethnicity brought with it a correlated decline in the membership in Irish organizations such as the Ancient Order of Hibernians and the Knights of Father Matthew. The Knights of Columbus, which was founded for Catholics "of all races" seemed to gain in size and influence during those years.

A random sample of Irish American elites, as drawn from turn-of-the-century "mug books," underscores this trend. Only one individual listed membership in the AOH and that person was the head of the "Hibernian Investment Company." Twenty percent of the sample claimed membership in the Knights of St. Matthew and 30 percent were Knights of Columbus.[35] A membership sample 20 years later further documented the shift from Irish to Catholic social organizations. The Knights of Columbus were rising toward the peak of their power and influence in the years after World War I.[36] Irish nationalism was a distant memory in St. Louis by the middle of the 1920s.

Ethnic organizations and associations remained important vehicles for upwardly mobile ethnic elites well into the twentieth century. Economic advancement did not necessarily mean that these elites would abandon their roots. As long as these associations and organizations provided social status and a sense of pride, they were populated with the cream of the ethnic crop. But once ethnicity became "un-American" (as it did for the Germans) or unnecessary (as it did for the Irish), these organizations lost the reason for their existence and were quickly abandoned by their once loyal members.

NOTES

1. General histories of St. Louis published at the turn of the century paid little attention to immigration. More recent histories have

done a little better. See John Rothsteiner, *History of the Archdiocese of St. Louis* (St. Louis, 1928), William Faherty, *The Catholic Ancestry of St. Louis* (St. Louis, 1965), and James Neal Primm, *Lion in the Valley* (Boulder, 1981).

2. *12th United States Census, 1900: Statistics of Population*, pp. 80–81.

3. *11th United States Census, 1890: Population*, II:724–725; *12th U.S. Census, 1900: Occupations*, pp. 706–711.

4. Margaret Lo Piccolo Sullivan, *Hyphenism in St. Louis, 1900–1921* (New York, 1990), pp. 1–21.

5. For a general discussion of middle class immigrant communities, see John Bodnar, *The Transplanted: A History of Immigrants in Urban America* (Bloomington, IN, 1985).

6. Many of these statistics also appear in an essay by a former colleague, Martin G. Towey. See his "Kerry Patch Revisited: Irish Americans in St. Louis in the Turn of the Century Era," in Timothy J. Meagher, ed., *From Paddy to Studs: Irish American Communities in the Turn of the Century Era, 1880–1920* (Westport, CT, 1986). Towey's essay closely resembles the rough draft of a paper I shared with him over a decade ago. On the Germans in St. Louis, see Audray Louise Olson, "St. Louis Germans, 1850–1920: The Nature of an Immigrant Community and its Relation to the Assimilation Process" (Ph.D. diss., University of Kansas, 1970), pp. 267–269. The sample of second and third generation St. Louis Germans comes from Walter B. Stevens, *St. Louis, The Fourth City, 1764–1909*, 3 vols. (St. Louis, 1909), vols. 2 and 3.

7. Olson, "St. Louis Germans, 1850–1920," passim; Sullivan, *Hyphenism in St. Louis*, pp. 23–49; and David Detjen, *The Germans in Missouri, 1900–1918: Prohibition, Neutrality, and Assimilation* (Columbia, 1985).

8. Olson, "St. Louis Germans, 1850–1920," pp. 257–259; and Sullivan, *Hyphenism in St. Louis*, pp. 22–26.

9. There is a significant volume of literature on German American cultural nationalism. Among the most recent books are Frederick C. Luebke, *Bonds of Loyalty: German Americans and World War I* (DeKalb, IL, 1974), and Victor R. Greene, *American Immigrant Leaders, 1800–1910: Marginality and Identity* (Baltimore, 1987).

10. Olson, "St. Louis Germans, 1850–1920," pp. 251–257 provides statistical information on *saengerbund* and *turnverein* members. Sullivan, *Hyphenism in St. Louis*, pp. 23–34 describes their activities.

11. On the German American Alliance, see Clifton James Child, *The German-Americans in Politics, 1914–1917* (Madison, 1939). Detjen, *The*

Germans in Missouri, contains the most detailed account of the German-American Alliance in St. Louis.

12. On the German Jewish community in St. Louis at this time, see Sullivan, *Hyphenism in St. Louis*, pp. 144–196. On German Jews across the nation, see Naomi W. Cohen, *Encounter with Emancipation: The German Jews in the United States, 1830–1914* (Philadelphia, 1984), and Judith S. Goldstein, *The Politics of Ethnic Pressure: The American Jewish Committee Fight Against Immigration Restriction, 1906–1917* (New York, 1990).

13. *St. Louis Globe Democrat* (October 23, 1920).

14. *Jewish Voice* [St. Louis] (April 28, 1916); *Modern View* 26 (July 4, 1913):2.

15. *Modern View* 26 (June 20, 1913):2.

16. *Jewish Voice* [St. Louis] (February 14, 1902).

17. Lists of those attending these functions were published in the *St. Louis Post-Dispatch* (March 18, 1900). Of 184 men attending the banquets sponsored by the Knights of St. Patrick and the Irish American Society that year, 118 were located in *Gould's City Directory* (St. Louis, 1900). Multiple listings for individuals with the same names made it impossible to trace everyone.

18. On the celebration of St. Patrick's Day in St. Louis, see Sullivan, *Hyphenism in St. Louis*, pp. 83–96. Catholicism was a major part of these celebrations.

19. On Irish American nationalism in St. Louis, see Margaret Sullivan, "Constitution, Revolution and Culture: Irish-American Nationalism in St. Louis, 1902–1914," *Bulletin of the Missouri Historical Society* 28 (July 1972):234–245; and Sullivan, "Fighting for Irish Freedom: St. Louis Irish Americans, 1918–1922," *Missouri Historical Review* 65 (January 1971):184–206.

20. The sample of 56 individuals were the officers and committee chairmen listed in *The Western Watchman* (St. Louis) for the years from 1904–1921. These individuals were traced through *Gould's Directory* or local obituaries.

21. Olson, "St. Louis Germans, 1850–1920," pp. 185–188.

22. Ibid.

23. Ibid., pp. 191–202; Detjen, *The Germans in Missouri*, pp. 119–131; *St. Louis Globe Democrat* (December 17, 1914); *St. Louis Times* (January 1, 1915); and *St. Louis Star* (January 11, 1915).

24. On anti-German feelings in St. Louis during World War I, see Olson, "St. Louis Germans, 1850–1920," pp. 202–212; Sullivan,

Hyphenism in St. Louis, pp. 65–82; Detjen, *The Germans in Missouri*, pp. 138–176.

25. The Liederkranz did continue in the city after the war but in a much diminished capacity. See Olson, "St. Louis Germans, 1850–1920," pp. 237–238, and Sullivan, *Hyphenism in St. Louis*, pp. 81–82.

26. For a discussion of Germans in St. Louis in the 1920s with a particular emphasis on the impact of prohibition on the German-American social clubs, see Olson, "St. Louis Germans, 1850–1920," pp. 213–246.

27. *Modern View* 29 (November 27, 1914, December 18, 1914, and December 25, 1914).

28. *St. Louis Globe Democrat* (October 16, 1920).

29. *St. Louis Globe Democrat* (January 11, 1918, October 9, 1920, October 20, 1920, and November 20, 1920).

30. *Jewish Voice* (December 10, 1915), and Ruth Fishlowitz, *The "Y" Story: A Chronicle of the Jewish Center Movement in St. Louis* (St. Louis, 1964).

31. See ff. 28.

32. *Western Watchman*, (November 17, 1922).

33. Sample of baptismal records for the years 1900, 1910, and 1920 for St. Leo parish, St. Bridget parish, St. Theresa parish, St. Mark parish, and St. Matthew parish in St. Louis.

34. Sample of marriage records for the years 1900–01, 1910–11, and 1920–21 for the parishes noted above.

35. See ff. 24.

36. These samples were taken from a pool of 250 officers and committee chairmen who were listed in *The Western Watchman* for the years from 1904 through 1920 and linked to the occupational listings in *Gould's Directory* or in obituaries. For the broader role of political nationalism in the Irish American community, see Kerby Miller, *Emigrants and Exiles: Ireland and the Irish Exodus to North America* (New York, 1985), or a summary of his work, "Class, Culture, and Immigrant Group Identity in the United States: The Case of Irish American Ethnicity," in Virginia Yans-McLaughlin, ed., *Immigration Reconsidered: History, Sociology, and Politics* (New York, 1990).

Guide to Further Reading

Students and scholars of the history of European ethnicity in America know well of the large and growing volume of books and essays on the topic. It is not possible, therefore, to offer anything more than an introduction to the literature. Those interested in more specialized and detailed studies should consult the catalogs and databases at their local university libraries.

In general, this guide is limited to works published in the past thirty years. For the most part, the entries are books, but a few exceptions have been made for outstanding articles that have appeared in scholarly journals. The organization of the entries below follows the general organization of the book.

General and Group Studies

The serious study of the history of American immigration and ethnicity dates from about 1940 with the publication of pathbreaking books by Marcus Hansen and Oscar Handlin. Cited below is Hansen's dated but still useful collection of essays, The *Immigrant in American History.* Also of substantial value is Handlin's revised dissertation, *Boston's Immigrants,* an extraordinary study of immigrant life in one American community.

Several historians have added their voices to the scholarly debate over immigration and ethnicity since the 1940s. Of special note are the general histories by Thomas Archdeacon, John Bodnar, Roger Daniels, and, of course, Oscar Handlin. These books cover the sweep of the immigration experience with each one offering unique perspectives and points of emphasis. Also of substantial value are the works on specific immigrant groups, most particularly the essays that make up the monumental *Harvard Encyclopedia of American Ethnic Groups*. Edited by Stephan Thernstrom and others, *HEAEG* is the place to begin research on the history of European immigration and ethnicity.

Allen, James Paul, and Eugene James Turner, *We the People: An Atlas of America's Ethnic Diversity* (New York, 1988).

Anderson, Arlow W., *The Norwegian Americans* (Boston, 1975).

Appel, John J., ed., *The New Immigration* (New York, 1971).

Archdeacon, Thomas J., *Becoming American: An Ethnic History* (New York, 1983).

Baganha, Maria I.B., *Portuguese Emigration to the United States, 1820–1930* (New York, 1990).

Berthoff, Rowland T., *British Immigrants in Industrial America, 1790–1950* (Cambridge, MA, 1953).

Billigmeier, Robert H., *Americans from Germany: A Study in Cultural Diversity* (Belmont, CA, 1974).

Blegen, Theodore, ed., *Land of Their Choice: The Immigrants Write Home* (Minneapolis, MN, 1955).

Bodnar, John, *The Transplanted: A History of Immigrants in Urban America* (Bloomington, IN, 1983).

Buenker, John D., and Nicholas C. Burckel, eds., *Immigration and Ethnicity: A Guide to Information Sources* (Detroit, 1977).

Cordasco, Francesco M., ed., *Studies in Italian American Social History* (Totowa, NJ, 1975).

Debouzy, Marianne, ed., *In the Shadow of the Statue of Liberty: Immigrants, Workers, and Citizens in the American Republic, 1880–1920* (Urbana, IL, 1993).

DeConde, Alexander, *Half Bitter, Half Sweet: An Excursion into Italian American History* (New York, 1971).

DeJong, Gerald F., *The Dutch in America* (Boston, 1975).

Dinnerstein, Leonard, and Frederic C. Jaher, eds., *The Aliens: A History of Ethnic Minorities in America* (New York, 1970).

———, Roger L. Nichols, and David M. Reimers, *Natives and Strangers: Ethnic Groups and the Building of America* (New York, 1979).

———, and David M. Reimers, *Ethnic Americans: A History of Immigration and Assimilation* (New York, 1975).

Drudy, P.J., ed., *The Irish in America: Emigration, Assimilation, and Impact* (Cambridge, England, 1985).

Erickson, Charlotte J., *Invisible Immigrants: English and Scottish Emigrants in Nineteenth Century America* (Coral Gables, FL, 1972).

Feingold, Henry L., *Zion in America: The Jewish Experience from Colonial Times to the Present* (New York, 1974).

Fleming, Donald, and Bernard Bailyn, eds., *Dislocation and Emigration: The Social Background of American Immigration* (Cambridge, MA, 1974).

Fuchs, Lawrence H., *The American Kaleidoscope: Race, Ethnicity and the Civic Culture* (Middletown, CT, 1990).

Hale, Frederick, ed., *Danes in North America* (Seattle, WA, 1984).

Handlin, Oscar, *The American People in the Twentieth Century* (Cambridge, MA, 1966).

———, *The Uprooted: The Epic Story of the Great Migrations that Made the American People* (Boston, 1951).

Hansen, Marcus Lee, *The Immigrant in American History* (Cambridge, MA, 1940).

Higham, John, *Send These to Me: Jews and Other Immigrants in Urban America*, rev. ed. (New York, 1984).

Hoglund, A. William, *Finnish Immigrants in America, 1880–1920* (Madison, WI, 1960).

Horowitz, Donald L., and Gerard Noiriel, eds., *Immigrants in Two Democracies: French and American Experience* (New York, 1992).

Howe, Irving, *World of Our Fathers* (New York, 1976).

Iorizzo, Luciano, and Salvatore Mondello, *The Italian Americans* (Boston, 1971).

Jones, Maldwyn A., *American Immigration* (Chicago, 1960).

———, *Destination America* (New York, 1976).

Kraut, Alan M., *The Huddled Masses: The Immigrants in American Society* (Arlington Heights, IL, 1982).

Kunkelman, Gary A., *The Religion of Ethnicity: Belief and Belonging in a Greek American Community* (New York, 1990).

Kvisto, Peter, and Dag Blanck, eds., *American Immigrants and Their Generations: Studies and Commentaries on the Hansen Thesis after Fifty Years* (Urbana, IL, 1990).

Leyburn, James G., *The Scotch Irish: A Social History* (Chapel Hill, NC, 1962).

Lopreato, Joseph, *Italian Americans* (New York, 1970).

Luebke, Frederick C., *Germans in the New World: Essays in the History of Immigration* (Urbana, IL, 1990).

McCaffrey, Lawrence J., *The Irish Diaspora in America* (Bloomington, IN, 1976).

Mann, Arthur, *Immigrants in American Life: Selected Readings* (Boston, 1974).

Miller, Kerby P., *Emigrants and Exiles: Ireland and the Irish Exodus to North America* (New York, 1985).

Miller, Wayne C., and others, eds., *A Comprehensive Bibliography for the Study of American Minorities,* 2 vols. (New York, 1976).

Mooney, Peter J., *The Impact of Immigration on the Growth and Development of the U.S. Economy, 1880–1920* (New York, 1990).

Neidle, Cecyle S., *The New Americans* (New York, 1967).

Nugent, Walter, *Crossings: The Great Transatlantic Migrations, 1870–1914* (Bloomington, IN, 1992).

O'Grady, Joseph P., *How the Irish Became Americans* (Boston, 1973).

Olson, James Stuart, *The Ethnic Dimension in American History* (New York, 1979).

Polenberg, Richard, *One Nation Divisible: Class, Race, and Ethnicity Since 1938* (New York, 1980).

Prpic, George J., *South Slavic Immigration in America* (Boston, 1978).

Rippley, La Vern, *The German Americans* (Boston, 1976).

Rischin, Moses, ed., *Immigration and the American Tradition* (Indianapolis, 1976).

Rolle, Andrew, *The Italian Americans—Troubled Roots* (New York, 1980).

Runblom, Harold, and Hans Norman, eds., *From Sweden to America* (Minneapolis, 1976).

Sacher, Howard, *A History of Jews in America* (New York, 1992).

Saloutos, Theodore C., *The Greeks in the United States* (Cambridge, MA, 1964).

Seller, Maxine, *To Seek America: A History of Ethnic Life in the United States* (Englewood Cliffs, NJ, 1977).

Shannon, William V., *The American Irish* (New York, 1966).

Sowell, Thomas, *Ethnic America: A History* (New York, 1981).

Swierenga, Robert P., *The Dutch in America: Immigration, Settlement, and Cultural Change* (New Brunswick, NJ, 1985).

Taylor, Peter, *The Distant Magnet: European Immigration to the USA* (New York, 1971).

Thernstrom, Stephan, and others, eds., *Harvard Encyclopedia of American Ethnic Groups* (Cambridge, MA, 1980).

Tomasi, Silvano, and M.H. Engels, eds., *The Italian Experience in the United States* (New York, 1970).

Trefousse, Hans L., ed., *Germany and America: Essays on Problems of International Relations and Immigration* (New York, 1980).

Trommler, Frank, and Joseph McVeigh, eds., *America and the Germans*, 2 vols. (Philadelphia, 1985).

Vecoli, Rudolph, and Suzanne M. Sinke, eds., *A Century of European Migrations, 1830–1930* (Urbana, IL, 1991).

Walker, Mack, *Germany and the Emigration, 1816–1885* (Cambridge, MA, 1965).

Ward, Charles A., Philip Shashko, and Donald E. Pienkos, eds., *Studies in Ethnicity: The East European Experiences in America* (New York, 1980).

Wytrwal, Joseph A., *A Social History of the Poles in America* (Detroit, 1961).

Yans-McLaughlin, Virginia, ed., *Immigration Reconsidered: History, Sociology, Politics* (New York, 1990).

A Clash of Cultures

Strangers in the Land is the very apt title of John Higham's classic study of the conflict between native-born and immigrant cultures during the years from 1865 to 1925. Just as important, "strangers in the land" is an accurate description of the general feeling of tension between native-born Americans and the millions of immigrants who arrived in this country between 1830 and 1930.

In addition to Higham's outstanding book, students would do well to consult the works by Ray Allen Billington, Thomas Curran, Leonard Dinnerstein, Donald Kinzer, Seymour Martin Lipset, Robert K. Murray, Philip Perlmutter, and Barbara Solomon. All of these works chronicle the conflict, violence, and prejudice that permeated the European immigrant experience in the nineteenth and twentieth centuries.

Also of note are the works on the struggle of immigrants both individually and as a group to establish new identities in their adopted homeland. All students should consult the books by John Bukowczyk, Philip Gleason, Milton Gordon, Arthur Mann, and Werner Sollors. Also of particular value are the specialized books by Betty Boyd Caroli, Jules Chametzky, Dino Cinel, Charles Fanning, Victor Greene, Allen Guttmann, Edward Hartmann, and Jerre Mangione.

Adamic, Louis, *A Nation of Nations* (New York, 1945).

Alba, Richard, *Ethnic Identity: The Transformation of White America* (New Haven, 1990).

Altschuler, Glen C., *Race, Ethnicity, and Class in American Social Thought, 1865–1919* (Arlington Heights, IL, 1982).

Antin, Mary, *The Promised Land* (Boston, 1912).

Bennett, David H., *The Party of Fear: From Nativist Movements to the New Right in American History* (Chapel Hill, NC, 1988).

Billington, Ray Allen, *The Protestant Crusade, 1800–1860: A Study of the Origins of American Nativism* (New York, 1938).

Brown, Thomas N., *Irish American Nationalism, 1870–1890* (Philadelphia, 1966).

Bukowczyk, John J., *And My Children Did Not Know Me* (Bloomington, IN, 1987).

Burch, Betty Ann, *The Assimilation Experience of Five American White Ethnic Novelists of the Twentieth Century* (New York, 1988).

Chametzky, Jules, *From the Ghetto: The Fiction of Abraham Cahan* (Amherst, MA, 1977).

Cinel, Dino, *The National Integration of Italian Return Migration, 1870–1929* (New York, 1991).

Conzen, Kathleen Neils, *Making Their Own America: Assimilation Theory and the Great Peasant Pioneer* (New York, 1990).

Curran, Thomas J., *Xenophobia and Immigration, 1820–1930* (New York, 1975).

Diamond, Sander A., *The Nazi Movement in the United States, 1924–1941* (Ithaca, NY, 1974).

Dinnerstein, Leonard, *The Leo Frank Case* (New York, 1970).

————, ed., *Anti-Semitism in the United States* (New York, 1971).

Divine, Robert A., *American Immigration Policy, 1924–1952* (New Haven, 1957).

Eckstein, Neil T., *The Marginal Man as Novelist: The Norwegian American Writers H.H. Boyesen and O.E. Rolvaag as Critics of American Institutions* (New York, 1990).

Faderman, Lillian, and Barbara Bradshaw, *Speaking for Ourselves*, 2nd ed. (Glenview, IL, 1975).

Fanning, Charles, *The Irish Voice in America* (Lexington, KY, 1990).

Feldberg, Michael, *The Philadelphia Riots of 1844: A Study of Ethnic Conflict* (Westport, 1975).

Feldstein, Stanley, and Lawrence Costello, eds., *The Ordeal of Assimilation: A Documentary History of the White Working Class, 1830s to the 1970s* (Garden City, 1974).

Frederickson, George M., and Dale T. Knobel, "Policy Against Prejudice and Discrimination," in Stephan Thernstrom and others, eds., *Harvard Encyclopedia of American Ethnic Groups* (Cambridge, MA, 1980).

Gallo, Patrick, *Ethnic Alienation: The Italian Americans* (Rutherford, NJ, 1974).

Gerber, David A., ed., *Anti-Semitism and American History* (Urbana, IL, 1986).

Gambino, Richard, *Blood of My Blood: The Dilemma of the Italian Americans* (Garden City, NY, 1974).

————, *Vendetta* (New York, 1977).

Gleason, Philip, "American Identity and Americanization," in Stephen Thernstrom and others, eds., *Harvard Encyclopedia of American Ethnic Groups* (Cambridge, MA, 1980).

————, *Speaking of Diversity: Essays on the Language of Ethnicity* (Baltimore, MD, 1992).

Gordon, Milton, *Assimilation in American Life: The Role of Race, Religion, and National Origins* (New York, 1964).

Greene, Victor, *For God and Country: The Rise of Polish and Lithuanian Consciousness in America, 1860–1910* (Madison, WI, 1975).

Guttmann, Allen, *The Jewish Writer in America: Assimilation and the Crisis of Identity* (New York, 1971).

Hartmann, Edward G., *The Movement to Americanize the Immigrants* (New York, 1948).

Higham, John, *Strangers in the Land: Patterns of American Nativism, 1860–1925,* rev. ed. (New York, 1968).

Hutchinson, E.P., *The Legislative History of American Immigration Policy, 1798-1965* (Philadelphia, 1981).

Ibson, John Duffy, *Will the World Break Your Heart? Dimensions and Consequences of Irish American Assimilation* (New York, 1990).

Ifkovic, Edward, ed., *American Letter: Immigrant and Ethnic Writing* (Englewood Cliffs, NJ, 1975).

Inglehart, Babette F., and Anthony R. Mangione, *The Image of Pluralism in American Literature: An Annotated Bibliography on the American Experience of European Ethnic Groups* (New York, 1974).

Jackson, Kenneth T., *The Ku Klux Klan in the Cities, 1915–1930* (New York, 1967).

Kallen, Horace, *Cultural Pluralism and the American Idea* (Philadelphia, 1956).

———, *Culture and Democracy in the United States* (New York, 1924).

Keller, Phyllis, *States of Belonging: German-American Intellectuals and the First World War* (Cambridge, MA, 1979).

Kettner, James H., *The Development of American Citizenship, 1608–1870* (Chapel Hill, NC, 1978).

Kinzer, Donald L., *An Episode in Anti-Catholicism: The American Protective Association* (Seattle, WA, 1964).

Lerda, Valesia G., ed., *From "Melting Pot" to Multiculturalism: The Evolution of Ethnic Relations in the United States and Canada* (Rome, Italy, 1990).

Lipset, Seymour Martin, and Earl Raab, *The Politics of Unreason: Right Wing Extremism in America, 1790–1970* (New York, 1970).

Luebke, Frederick C., *Bonds of Loyalty: German Americans and World War I* (DeKalb, IL, 1974).

Mangione, Jerre, *Mount Allegro: A Memoir of Italian American Life* [1942] (New York, 1982).

———, *An Ethnic at Large: A Memoir of America in the Thirties and Forties* (New York, 1978).

Mann, Arthur, *The One and the Many: Reflections on the American Identity* (Chicago, 1979).

Marcuson, Lewis R., *The Stage Immigrant: The Irish, Italians, and Jews in American Drama, 1920–1960* (New York, 1990).

Miller, Sally, ed., *The Ethnic Press in the United States: A Historical Analysis and Handbook* (Westport, CT, 1987).

Miller, Wayne C., ed., *A Gathering of Ghetto Writers* (New York, 1972).

Molek, Ivan S., *Slovene Immigrant History, 1900–1950: Autobiographical Sketches* (Dover, DE, 1979).

Murray, Robert K., *Red Scare: A Study in National Hysteria, 1919–1920* (Minneapolis, MN, 1955).

Novak, Michael, *The Rise of the Unmeltable Ethnics: Politics and Culture in the Seventies* (New York, 1972).

Perlmutter, Philip, *Divided We Fall: A History of Ethnic, Religious, and Racial Prejudice in America* (Ames, IA, 1992).

Persons, Stow, *Ethnic Studies at Chicago, 1905–1945* (Urbana, IL, 1987).

Peterson, William, Michael Novak, and Philip Gleason, *Concepts of Ethnicity* (Cambridge, MA, 1980).

Pienkos, Donald, *For Your Freedom Through Ours: Polish American Efforts on Poland's Behalf, 1863–1991* (Boulder, CO, 1992).

Prichard, Nancy S., *A Selected Bibliography of American Ethnic Writing* (Urbana, IL, 1969).

Schenkman, Arnold, *Ambivalent Friends: Afro-Americans View the Immigrant* (Westport, CT, 1982).

Scholnick, Myron I., *The New Deal and Anti-Semitism in America* (New York, 1990).

Sollors, Werner, "Literature and Ethnicity," in Stephan Thernstrom and others, eds., *Harvard Encyclopedia of American Ethnic Groups* (Cambridge, MA, 1980).

———, *Beyond Ethnicity: Consent and Descent in American Culture* (New York, 1986).

———, ed., *The Invention of Ethnicity* (New York, 1989).

Solomon, Barbara M., *Ancestors and Immigrants: A Changing New England Tradition* (Cambridge, 1956).

Thatcher, Mary Anne, *Immigrants and the 1930s: Ethnicity and Alienage in the Depression and On-coming War* (New York, 1990).

Tischauser, Leslie V., *The Burden of Ethnicity: The German Question in Chicago, 1914–1941* (New York, 1990).

Tolzmann, Don H., *German Americana* (Metuchen, NJ, 1975).

———, *German American Literature* (Metuchen, NJ, 1975).

Wallace, Les, *The Rhetoric of Anti-Catholicism: The American Protective Association, 1887–1911* (New York, 1990).

Zake, Louis J., *The National Department and the Polish American Community, 1916–1923* (New York, 1990).

Zangwell, Israel, *The Melting Pot* [1909] (New York, 1925).

Haven in a Strange New Land

The historical literature on immigrant home ownership and family life is slim. As reflected in the limited number of books cited below, much work needs to be done just to tell the story of this influential and intimate aspect of European immigrant life in this country.

This is not to say that the literature is without value. In fact, there are a number of works that are first rate. Perhaps the best introduction to the topic is the essay on immigrant family patterns by Tamara Harevan and John Modell that appears in the *Harvard Encyclopedia of American Ethnic Groups*. Also of special note are the works of Samuel L. Bailey, James Benson, Hasia Diner, Donna Gabaccia, Gordon and Carolyn Kirk, and Virginia Yans-McLaughlin.

Baily, Samuel L., and Franco Ramella, eds., *One Family, Two Worlds: An Italian Family's Correspondence Across the Atlantic, 1901–1922* (New Brunswick, NJ, 1988).

Baum, Charlotte, Paula Hyman, and Sonya Michael, *The Jewish Woman in America* (New York, 1975).

Benson, James K., *Irish and German Families and the Economic Development of Midwestern Cities, 1860–1895* (New York, 1990).

Capozzoli, Mary Jane, *Three Generations of Italian American Women in Nassau County, 1925–1981* (New York, 1990).

Child, Irvin L., *Italian or American: The Second Generation in Conflict* (New York, 1943).

Cohen, Miriam, *Workshop to Office: Two Generations of Italian Women in New York City, 1900–1950* (Ithaca, NY, 1993).

Covello, Leonard, *The Social Background of the Italo-American School Child* (Leiden, Netherlands, 1967).

Diner, Hasia R., *Erin's Daughters in America* (Baltimore, MD, 1983).

Ehrlich, Richard L., ed., *Immigrants in Industrial America, 1850–1920* (Charlottesville, VA, 1977).

Evans, Sara M., *Born for Liberty: A History of Women in America* (New York, 1989).

Gabaccia, Donna R., *From Sicily to Elizabeth Street: Housing and Social Change Among Italian Immigrants, 1880–1930* (Albany, NY, 1984).

Glenn, Susan, *Daughters of the Shtetl: Life and Labor in the Immigrant Generation* (Ithaca, NY, 1990).

Harevan, Tamara, and John Modell, "Family Patterns," in Stephan Thernstrom and others, eds., *Harvard Encyclopedia of American Ethnic Groups* (Cambridge, MA, 1980).

Hutchinson, E.P., *Immigrants and Their Children* (New York, 1956).

Johnson, Colleen Leahy, *Growing Up and Growing Old in Italian-American Families* (New Brunswick, NJ, 1985).

Kennedy, Robert E., *The Irish: Emigration, Marriage, and Fertility* (Berkeley, CA, 1973).

Kirk, Gordon W., Jr., and Carolyn Tyirin Kirk, "The Impact of the City on Homeownership: A Comparison of Immigrants and Native Whites at the Turn of the Century," *Journal of Urban History* (August, 1981).

Lamphere, Louise, *From Working Daughters to Working Mothers: Immigrant Women in a New England Industrial Community* (Ithaca, NY, 1987).

McClymer, John, "Gender and the American Way of Life: Women in the Americanization Movement," *Journal of American Ethnic History* 10 (1991).

Moore, Deborah Dash, *At Home in America: Second Generation New York Jews* (New York, 1981).

Neidle, Cecyle, *America's Immigrant Women* (Boston, 1975).

Nolan, Janet A., *Ourselves Alone: Women's Emigration from Ireland, 1885–1920* (Lexington, KY, 1989).

Seller, Maxine, ed., *Immigrant Women* (Philadelphia, 1981).

Simons, Howard, *Jewish Times: Voices of the American Jewish Experience* (New York, 1988).

Tentler, Leslie Woodcock, *Wage Earning Women: Industrial Work and Family Life in the United States, 1900–1930* (New York, 1979).

Tomasi, Lydio F., *The Italian American Family* (New York, 1972).

Wrobel, Paul, *Our Way: Family, Parish, and Neighborhood in a Polish-American Community* (Notre Dame, IN, 1980).

Yans-McLaughlin, Virginia, *Family and Community: Italian Immigrants in Buffalo, 1880–1930* (Ithaca, NY, 1977).

Agents of Acculturation

The impact of both public and private social institutions on American immigrant life has been something of a preoccupation with historians. Both the quality and the quantity of studies on this sub-topic are excellent.

Even though ethnicity has not been a central subject of most histories of American religion, it has been an important theme. A first-rate overview of the topic is Timothy L. Smith's landmark essay, "Religion and Ethnicity in America," which is cited below. Also of particular value is the work of Laurence Moore and the collection of essays edited by Randall Miller and Thomas D. Marzik. Immigrant Catholic studies of special note are those by Harold Abramson, Jay Dolan, Richard Linkh, Dolores Liptak, James Olson, and Rudolph Vecoli. Studies of other religious groups include the work of June Alexander, Lawrence Davis, Dennis Engbrecht, and Ralph Janis.

The impact of education on immigrant assimilation has interested a wide range of social historians. An excellent introduction to this important topic is the essay by Michael Olneck and Marvin Lazerson that appears in the *Harvard Encyclopedia of American Ethnic Groups*. Other books of note are those by Carl F. Kaestle, Maris Vinovskis, Joel Perlmann, Selwyn Troen, Paula Fass, Robert A. Carlson, David B. Tyack, and Bernard J. Weiss.

Labor historians have produced a growing shelf of literature on immigrants in the workplace. Early work by David Brody and Gerd Korman has been supplemented by a host of young scholars including James Barrett, Lizabeth Cohen, Donna Gabaccia, and Ewa Morawska. Also of note are the studies of immigrants and small business by Laurence Lovell-Troy, the business of crime by Humbert Nelli, and leisure time by Roy Rosenzweig.

Abramson, Harold J., *Ethnic Diversity in Catholic America* (New York, 1973).

———, "Religion," in Stephan Thernstrom and others, eds., *Harvard Encyclopedia of American Ethnic Groups* (Cambridge, MA, 1980).

Alexander, June G., *The Immigrant Church and Community: Pittsburgh Slovak Catholics and Lutherans, 1880–1915* (Pittsburgh, PA, 1987).

Asher, Robert, and Charles Stephenson, eds., *Labor Divided: Race and Ethnicity in the United States Labor Struggles, 1835–1960* (Albany, NY, 1990).

Barrett, James R., "Americanization from the Bottom Up: Immigration and the Remaking of the Working Class in the United States, 1880–1930," *Journal of American History* 79 (1992).

———, *Work and Community in the Jungle: Chicago's Packinghouse Workers, 1894–1922* (Urbana, IL, 1987).

Bodnar, John, *Worker's World: Kinship Community and Protest in an Industrial Society, 1900–1940* (Baltimore, MD, 1982).

Brody, David, "Labor," in Stephan Thernstrom and others, eds., *Harvard Encyclopedia of American Ethnic Groups* (Cambridge, MA, 1980).

———, *Steelworkers in America: The Non-Union Era* (Cambridge, MA, 1960).

Broehl, Wayne G., Jr., *The Molly Maguires* (Cambridge, MA, 1965).

Carlson, Robert A., *The Quest for Conformity: Americanization Through Education* (New York, 1975).

Cohen, Lizabeth, *Making a New Deal: Industrial Workers in Chicago, 1919–1939* (New York, 1990).

Cross, Malcom, ed., *Ethnic Minorities and Industrial Change in Europe and North America* (New York, 1992).

Davis, Lawrence B., *Immigrants, Baptists and the Protestant Mind in America* (Urbana, IL, 1973).

Dolan, Jay P., *The Immigrant Church: New York's Irish and German Catholics, 1815–1865* (Baltimore, MD, 1975).

Dyrud, Keith P., Michael Novak, and Rudolph Vecoli, *The Other Catholics* (New York, 1978).

Engbrecht, Dennis D., *The Americanization of a Rural Immigrant Church: The General Conference Mennonites in Central Kansas, 1874–1939* (New York, 1990).

Erickson, Charlotte, *American Industry and the European Immigrant, 1860–1885* (Cambridge, MA, 1957).

Fass, Paula S., *Outside In: Minorities and the Transformation of American Education* (New York, 1989).

Fenton, Edwin, *Immigrants and Unions, A Case Study: Italians and American Labor, 1870–1920* (New York, 1975).

Gabaccia, Donna, *Militants and Migrants: Rural Sicilians Become American Workers* (New Brunswick, NJ, 1988).

Gerstle, Gary, *Working Class Americanism: The Politics of Labor in a Textile City, 1914–1960* (Cambridge, MA, 1989).

Gutman, Herbert, "Work, Culture, and Society in Industrializing America, 1815–1919," *American Historical Review* 78 (1973).

Greene, Victor, *The Slavic Community on Strike: Immigrant Labor in Pennsylvania Anthracite* (Notre Dame, IN, 1968).

Hoerder, Dirk, ed., *"Struggle a Hard Battle": Essays on Working Class Immigrants* (DeKalb, IL, 1986).

Janis, Ralph, *Church and City in Transition: The Social Composition of Religious Groups in Detroit, 1880–1940* (New York, 1990).

Kaestle, Carl F., *The Evolution of an Urban School System: New York City, 1750–1850* (Cambridge, MA, 1973).

———, and Maris Vinovskis, *Education and Social Change in Nineteenth Century Massachusetts* (New York, 1980).

Kopan, Andrew T., *Education and Greek Immigrants in Chicago, 1892–1973: A Study in Ethnic Survival* (New York, 1990).

Korman, Gerd, *Industrialization, Immigrants, and Americanizers: The View from Milwaukee, 1866–1921* (Madison, WI, 1967).

Kuzniewski, Anthony J., *Faith and Fatherland: The Polish Church War in Wisconsin, 1896–1918* (Notre Dame, IN, 1980).

Lane, A.T., *Solidarity or Survival: American Labor and European Immigrants, 1830–1924* (Westport, CT, 1987).

Lannie, Vincent P., *Public Money and Parochial Education: Bishop Hughes, Governor Seward, and the New York School Controversy* (Cleveland, OH, 1968).

Lazerson, Marvin, *Origins of the Urban School: Public Education in Massachusetts, 1870–1915* (Cambridge, MA, 1971).

Linkh, Richard M., *American Catholicism and European Immigrants, 1900–1924* (New York, 1975).

Liptak, Dolores, *European Immigrants and the Catholic Church in Connecticut* (New York, 1987).

———, *Immigrants and Their Church* (New York, 1989).

Lovell-Troy, Lawrence A., *The Social Basis of Ethnic Enterprise: Greeks in the Pizza Business* (New York, 1990).

Miller, Randall M., and Thomas D. Marzik, eds., *Immigrants and Religion in Urban America* (Philadelphia, 1977).

Moore, R. Laurence, *Religious Outsiders and the Making of Americans* (New York, 1986).

Morawska, Ewa, *For Bread and Butter: The Life Worlds of East Central Europeans in Johnstown, Pennsylvania, 1890–1940* (New York, 1985).

Nelli, Humbert S., *Business of Crime: Italian Syndicate Crime in the United States* (New York, 1976).

———, "The Padrone System in the United States," *Labor History* 5 (1964).

O'Connell, Marvin R., *John Ireland and the American Catholic Church* (St. Paul, MN, 1988).

Olneck, Michael, and Marvin Lazerson, "Education," in Stephan Thernstrom and others, eds., *Harvard Encyclopedia of American Ethnic Groups* (Cambridge, MA, 1980).

———, "The School Achievement of Immigrant Children," *History of Education Quarterly* 14 (1974).

Olson, James S., *Catholic Immigrants in America* (Chicago, 1987).

Parmet, Robert D., *Labor and Immigration in Industrial America* (Boston, 1981).

Perlmann, Joel, *Ethnic Differences: Schooling and Social Structure among the Irish, Italians, Jews, and Blacks in an American City, 1880–1935* (New York, 1988).

Pula, James, and Eugene E. Dziedzic, *United We Stand: The Role of Polish Workers in the New York Mills Textile Strikes, 1912 and 1916* (New York, 1990).

Rosenquist, Valerie, *The Iron Ore Eaters: A Portrait of the Mining Community of Moriah, New York* (New York, 1990).

Rosenzweig, Roy, *Eight Hours for What We Will: Workers and Leisure in an Industrial City, 1870–1920* (Cambridge, Engand, 1983).

Sanders, James W., *The Education of an Urban Minority: Catholics in Chicago, 1833–1965* (New York, 1977).

Smith, Timothy L., "Immigrant Social Aspirations and American Education," *American Quarterly* 21 (1969).

————, "Lay Initiative in the Religious Life of American Immigrants, 1880–1950," in Tamara Harevan, ed., *Anonymous Americans* (Englewood Cliffs, NJ, 1971).

————, "Protestant Schooling and American Nationality, 1800–1850," *Journal of American History* 53 (1967).

————, "Religion and Ethnicity in America," *American Historical Review* 83 (1978).

Tomasi, Silvano, *Piety and Power: The Role of the Italian Parishes in the New York Metropolitan Area, 1880–1930* (New York, 1975).

Troen, Selwyn K., *The Public and the Schools: Shaping the St. Louis System, 1838–1920* (Columbia, MO, 1975).

Tyack, David B., *The One Best System: A History of American Urban Education* (Cambridge, MA, 1974).

Vecoli, Rudolph, "Prelates and Peasants: Italian Immigrants and the Catholic Church," *Journal of Social History* 2 (1969).

Weiss, Bernard J., *American Education and the European Immigrant, 1840–1940* (Urbana, IL, 1982).

Weisz, Howard R., *Irish American and Italian American Educational Views, 1870–1900: A Comparison* (New York, 1976).

Zivich, Edward A., *From Zadruga to Oil Refinery: Croatian-Americans in Whiting, Indiana, 1890–1950* (New York, 1990).

Zunz, Olivier, *The Changing Face of Inequality: Urbanization, Industrial Development and Immigrants in Detroit, 1880–1920* (Chicago, 1982).

The Contours of Ethnic Community

The nature of ethnic community is amorphous, with each group offering its own definition, and the historical literature is just as diverse. Certainly all historians of ethnic communities owe a debt of gratitude to Oscar Handlin, whose 1941 book, *Boston's Immigrants*, was a model for all future studies of ethnic communities. Also of value are the studies by R.A. Birchell, Dennis Clark, Donald Cole, Kathleen Conzen, David Emmons, Humbert Nelli, Robert Orsi, Moses Rischin, and Stephan Thernstrom.

Among the comparative and rural studies worthy of special attention, students and scholars would do well to begin with the studies by John Baiamonte, Josef Barton, Ronald Bayor, John

Briggs, David Gerber, Thomas Kessner, Frederick Luebke, Clifford Nelson, and Jon Wefald.

In recent years, scholars have shown extensive interest in ethnic politics and leadership. Of note in these important areas are the studies by John Allswang, Judith Goldstein, Victor Greene, John Higham, Eric Hirsch, Richard Jensen, Edward Kantowicz, and Paul Kleppner.

Allswang, John M., *A House for All Peoples: Ethnic Politics in Chicago, 1890–1936* (Lexington, KY, 1971).

Appel, John J., *Immigrant Historical Societies in the United States, 1880–1950* (New York, 1980).

Baiamonte, John V., Jr., *Immigrants in Rural Society: A Study of the Italians of Tangipahoa Parish, Louisiana* (New York, 1990).

Barton, Josef J., *Peasants and Strangers: Italians, Romanians, and Slovaks in an American City* (Cambridge, MA, 1975).

Bayor, Ronald, *Neighbors in Conflict: The Irish, Germans, Jews, and Italians of New York City, 1929–1941* (Baltimore, MD, 1978).

Bender, Thomas, *Community and Social Change in America* (Baltimore, MD, 1982).

Birchall, R.A., *The San Francisco Irish, 1848–1880* (Berkeley, CA, 1980).

Bodnar, John E., ed., *The Ethnic Experience in Pennsylvania* (Lewisburg, PA, 1973).

———, Roger Simon, and Michael P. Weber, *Lives of Their Own: Blacks, Italians and Poles in Pittsburgh, 1900–1960* (Urbana, IL, 1982).

Briggs, John W., *An Italian Passage: Immigrants to Three American Cities, 1890–1930* (New Haven, CT, 1978).

Buenker, John D., *Urban Liberalism and Progressive Reform* (New York, 1973).

Cinel, Dino, *From Italy to San Francisco* (Stanford, CA, 1982).

Clark, Dennis, *The Irish in Philadelphia: Ten Generations of Urban Experience* (Philadelphia, 1974).

Cole, Donald B., *Immigrant City: Lawrence, Massachusetts, 1845–1921* (Chapel Hill, 1963).

Conzen, Kathleen N., *Immigrant Milwaukee, 1836–1860: Accommodation and Community in a Frontier City* (Cambridge, MA, 1976).

Emmons, David, *The Butte Irish: Class and Ethnicity in an American Mining Town, 1875–1925* (Urbana, IL, 1989).

Esslinger, Dean R., *Immigrants and the City: Ethnicity and Mobility in a Nineteenth Century Midwestern Community* (Port Washington, NY, 1975).

Gerber, Donald A., *The Making of an American Pluralism: Buffalo, New York, 1825–1860* (Urbana, IL, 1989).

Gerlach, Russell, *Immigrants in the Ozarks* (Columbia, MO, 1977).

Glazer, Nathan, and Daniel Patrick Moynihan, *Beyond the Melting Pot: The Negroes, Puerto Ricans, Jews, Italians and Irish of New York City* (Cambridge, MA, 1963).

Gleason, Philip, *The Conservative Reformers: German American Catholics and the Social Order* (Notre Dame, IN, 1968).

Golab, Caroline, *Immigrant Destinations* (Philadelphia, 1977).

Goldstein, Judith S., *The Politics of Ethnic Pressure: The American Jewish Committee Fight Against Immigration Restriction, 1906–1917* (New York, 1990).

Goren, Arthur J., *New York Jews and the Quest for Community* (New York, 1970).

Gottfried, Alex, *Boss Cermak of Chicago: A Study of Political Leadership* (Seattle, WA, 1962).

Greene, Victor R., *American Immigrant Leaders, 1800–1910* (Baltimore, MD, 1987).

Handlin, Oscar, *Boston's Immigrants, 1790–1865* (Cambridge, MA, 1941).

———, *Al Smith and His America* (Boston, 1958).

Higham, John, ed., *Ethnic Leadership in America* (Baltimore, MD, 1978).

Hirsch, Eric L., *Urban Revolt: Ethnic Politics in the Nineteenth Century Chicago Labor Movement* (Berkeley, CA, 1990).

Holloway, Thomas H., *Immigrants on the Land* (Chapel Hill, NC, 1980).

Jensen, Richard J., *The Winning of the Middle West: Social and Political Conflict, 1888–1896* (Chicago, 1972).

Jones, Peter D'A., and Melvin Holli, eds., *The Ethnic Frontier: Essays in the History of Group Survival in Chicago and the Midwest* (Grand Rapids, MI, 1977).

———, eds., *Ethnic Chicago*, rev. ed. (Grand Rapids, MI, 1983).

Jordan, Terry G., *German Seed in Texas Soil: Immigrant Farmers in Nineteenth Century Texas* (Austin, TX, 1966).

Kessner, Thomas, *The Golden Door: Italian Mobility in New York City, 1880–1915* (New York, 1977).

Kleppner, Paul, *The Cross of Culture: A Social Analysis of Midwestern Politics, 1850–1900* (New York, 1970).

Koepplin, Leslie W., *A Relationship of Reform: Immigrants and Progressives in the Far West* (New York, 1990).

Kroes, Rob, *The Persistence of Ethnicity: Dutch Calvinist Pioneers in Amsterdam, Montana* (Urbana, IL, 1992).

LaGumina, Salvatore, ed., *Ethnicity in American Political Life: The Italian American Experience* (New York, 1968).

Levine, Edward, *The Irish and Irish Politicians: A Study of Cultural and Social Alienation* (Notre Dame, IN, 1966).

Lichtman, Allen J., *Prejudice and the Old Politics: The Presidential Election of 1928* (Chapel Hill, NC, 1979).

Lieberson, Stanley, *Ethnic Patterns in American Cities* (Glencoe, IL, 1963).

Litt, Edgar, *Beyond Pluralism: Ethnic Politics in America* (Glenview, IL, 1970).

Lopata, Helen Z., *Polish Americans: Status Competition in an Ethnic Community* (Englewood Cliffs, NJ, 1976).

Luebke, Frederick, ed., *Ethnicity on the Great Plains* (Lincoln, NE, 1980).

———, ed., *Ethnic Voters and the Election of Lincoln* (Lincoln, NE, 1971).

———, *The Germans of Nebraska, 1800–1900* (Lincoln, 1969).

Mazur, Edward H., *Minyans for a Prairie City: The Politics of Chicago Jewry, 1850–1940* (New York, 1990).

Miller, Sally M., *The Radical Immigrant* (New York, 1974).

Miller, Thomas, *Immigrants and the American City* (New York, 1993).

Nadel, Stanley, *Little Germany: Ethnicity, Religion, and Class in New York City, 1845–1880* (Urbana, IL, 1990).

Nelli, Humbert, *The Italians of Chicago, 1880–1930* (New York, 1970).

Nelson, Clifford L., *German American Political Behavior in Nebraska and Wisconsin, 1916–1920* (Lincoln, 1972).

O'Grady, Joseph P., ed., *The Immigrants' Influence on Wilson's Peace Policies* (Lexington, KY, 1967).

Orsi, Robert, *The Madonna of 115th Street: Faith and Community in Italian Harlem, 1880–1950* (New Haven, CT, 1985).

Orton, Lawrence D., *Polish Detroit and the Kolasinski Affair* (Detroit, 1981).

Ostergren, Robert C., *A Community Transplanted: The Trans-Atlantic Experience of a Swedish Immigrant Settlement in the Upper Midwest, 1835–1915* (Madison, WI, 1988).

Pacyga, Dominic, *Polish Immigrants and Industrial Chicago: Workers on the South Side, 1880–1922* (Columbus, OH, 1991).

Parot, Joseph J., *Polish Catholics in Chicago, 1850–1920* (DeKalb, IL, 1982).

Pencak, William, Selma Berrol, and Randall M. Miller, eds., *Immigration to New York* (Philadelphia, 1991).

Phillips, Bruce A., *Brookline: The Evolution of a Jewish Suburb* (New York, 1990).

Plunkitt, George Washington, *Plunkitt of Tamanny Hall,* edited by William Riordan (New York, 1963).

Rippley, La Vern J., *The Immigrant Experience in Wisconsin* (Boston, 1985).

Rischin, Moses, *The Promised City: New York's Jews, 1870–1914* (Cambridge, MA, 1962).

Robin, Ron, *Signs of Change: Urban Iconographies in San Francisco, 1880–1915* (New York, 1990).

Roucek, Joseph S., and Bernard Eisenberg, eds., *America's Ethnic Politics* (Westport, CT, 1982).

Schrender, Yda, *Dutch Catholic Immigrant Settlements in Wisconsin, 1850–1905* (New York, 1990).

Shannon, James P., *Catholic Colonization on the Western Frontier* (New Haven, CT, 1967).

Shapiro, Yanathon, *Leadership of the American Zionist Organization, 1897–1930* (Urbana, IL, 1971).

Silva, Ruth, *Rum, Religion, and Votes: 1928 Reexamined* (University Park, PA, 1962).

Sullivan, Margaret LoPiccolo, *Hyphenism in St. Louis, 1900–1921: The View from the Outside* (New York, 1990).

Thernstrom, Stephan, *The Other Bostonians: Poverty and Progress in the American Metropolis, 1850–1970* (Cambridge, MA, 1973).

———, *Poverty and Progress: Social Mobility in a Nineteenth Century City* (Cambridge, MA, 1964).

Vecoli, Rudolph, "Contadini in Chicago: A Critique of The Uprooted," *Journal of American History* 51 (1963).

Ward, David, *Cities and Immigrants: A Geography of Change in Nineteenth Century America* (New York, 1973).

———, *Poverty, Ethnicity, and the American City, 1840–1925: Changing Conceptions of the Slum and the Ghetto* (New York, 1989).

Wefald, Jon, *A Voice of Protest: Norwegians in American Politics, 1890–1917* (Northfield, MN, 1971).

Contributors

Mary Elizabeth Brown teaches in the department of history at Kutztown University in Pennsylvania. Educated at the University of Virginia and Columbia University, Dr. Brown recently has completed a book on the Italian community in Greenwich Village to be published by the Center for Migration Studies. Her essays on Italian immigrants have appeared in a number of scholarly journals including *The Catholic Historical Review* and the *U.S. Catholic Historian.*

Betty Ann Burch has taught at liberal arts colleges in Indiana, Maine, and Wisconsin, at the University of Minnesota, and at Metropolitan State University in St. Paul. Dr. Burch is the former editor of *Spectrum*, the newsletter of the Immigration History Research Center and the author of *The Assimilation Experience of Five American White Ethnic Novelists of the Twentieth Century* (1990).

Mary Jane Capozzoli Ingui is on the faculties of Nassau Community College and Malloy College in New York. Educated at Adelphi University and Lehigh University, Dr. Ingui is the author of *Three Generations of Italian American Women in Nassau County, New York, 1925–1981* (1990), and co-editor of *Our American Sisters* (1987). She has recently completed a textbook on American history from 1877 to the present.

Edward R. Kantowicz is a freelance historian in Chicago and a former professor of history at Carleton University in Ottawa, Canada. Dr. Kantowicz has contributed essays on ethnicity and religion to a wide range of publications, including the *Journal of*

American History and the *Harvard Encyclopedia of American Ethnic Groups*. He is the author or editor of many books, including *Polish American Politics in Chicago* (1975), and co-editor of "The European Immigrant in American Society," a 28-volume collection published by Garland in 1990.

Carolyn Tyirin Kirk is a professor of sociology at Monmouth College in Illinois where she teaches courses on urban sociology and demography, political economy and stratification, and research methods. Dr. Kirk is the co-author of essays in the *Journal of Social History*, the *Journal of Economic History*, and the *Journal of Urban History*, among other publications.

Gordon W. Kirk, Jr., is a professor of history and chair of the department of history at Western Illinois University. Dr. Kirk is the author of *The Promise of American Life: Social Mobility in a Nineteenth Century Immigrant Community, Holland, Michigan, 1847–1894* (1978), and co-author of *Everyday Life of Working Americans: Textile Workers and their Families, 1888–1890* (1989).

Dale T. Knobel is an associate professor of history and executive director of the honors program at Texas A&M University. Dr. Knobel is the author of *Paddy and the Republic: Ethnicity and Nationality in Antebellum America* (1985). With George M. Fredrickson and others, he co-authored *Prejudice*, a collection of essays on the topic that first appeared in the *Harvard Encyclopedia of American Ethnic Groups*.

La Vern J. Rippley is a professor of German literature and culture at St. Olaf College in Minnesota where he has taught since 1971. Professor Rippley is the author or editor of eleven books, including a highly regarded survey, *The German Americans* (1976) and over 120 articles. A former Fulbright Fellow at the University of Munich, Dr. Rippley is the author of the essay on the Germans in the *Harvard Encyclopedia of American Ethnic Groups*.

David L. Salvaterra is an associate professor of history at Loras College in Iowa. Educated at Pennsylvania State University and the University of Notre Dame, Dr. Salvaterra is the author of *American Catholicism and the Intellectual Life, 1880–1950*, a volume in the series "The Heritage of American Catholicism" published by Garland in 1988.

Margaret LoPiccolo Sullivan has taught at St. Louis University and the University of Missouri at St. Louis and is currently chair of the social studies department at Parkway Central High School in Chesterfield, Missouri. Dr. Sullivan has contributed essays to many journals and is the author of *Hyphenism in St. Louis: The View from the Outside* (1990).

Robert P. Swierenga is a professor of history at Kent State University in Ohio. Professor Swierenga is the author or editor of ten books and more than 80 articles, including the essay on the Dutch in the *Harvard Encyclopedia of American Ethnic Groups*. Among his recent books are *The Forerunners: Dutch Jewry in the North American Diaspora* (1993), and *Belief and Behavior: Essays in the New Religious History* (1991). A former Fulbright Fellow, he is at work on a book on the processes and patterns of Dutch settlement in the United States.

Timothy Walch is an associate editor of the *U.S. Catholic Historian* and an administrator with the National Archives and Records Administration. Dr. Walch is the author or editor of a dozen books, including *Catholicism in America* (1989) and *The Diverse Origins of American Catholic Education* (1988). With Edward R. Kantowicz, he edited "The European Immigrant in American Society," a 28-volume series published by Garland in 1990.

Edward A. Zivich is a professor of history, industrial relations, and sociology at Calumet College of St. Joseph in Indiana. Dr. Zivich is the author of *From Zadruga to Oil Refinery: Croatian Immigrants and Croatian Americans in Whiting, Indiana, 1890–1950* (1990), and is currently at work on a book about the Congress of Industrial Organizations at Inland Steel.

Index

medicine, 96–97
"melting pot," 31, 35–36, 61, 209
Mencken, H.L., 209
Mennonites, 201
Mexican Americans. *See* Latinos
Michigan, 130, 132, 202, 205, 208
   Detroit, 72, 127, 150
   Grand Rapids, 127–128
middle class, 74, 78
Midwest. *See also* specific states
   Dutch Reformed congregations in, 120
   home ownership in, 74
   immigrant aid in, 120
   Irish and German Catholics in, 3–4
Miller, Kerby, 45
Miller, Randall, 242
Milwaukee, 72, 79, 127, 208
Minnesota, 20, 129, 199, 201–202, 204, 208
Missouri, 129, 201–202
   St. Louis, 127, 215–226
Modell, John, 63–64, 240
Monkkonnen, Eric, 70
Moore, Laurence, 242
Morawska, Ewa, 242
More, Louise Boland, 91
Moynihan, Daniel, 37–39
Murray, Robert K., 235

national identity, 122–123, 177. *See also* ethnicity
Native Americans, 17–19
nativists
   animosity of, 3–5, 61, 235
   conventions, 12
   ideology, 8–9, 13–25
   movements of, 4

   opposition to German Catholics, 204
   political power, 13–15
   societies, 7–28
naturalization
   delays in, 183
   nativist opposition to, 9, 14–16
Nebraska 202, 204, 208
neighborhoods, 175–177, 181–182. *See also* communities; ethnic enclaves
Nelli, Humbert, 242, 246
Nelson, Clifford, 246
The Netherlands, 119–134, 200
Neutrality League, 223, 225
New Jersey, 10, 92, 129
New York (state)
   Buffalo, 68, 92, 127
   Dutch in, 120, 129
   Germans in, 208
   Italians in, 92, 104–112
   labor in, 21
   Rochester, 127
New York City, 7, 10, 12, 21–22, 89–99
Noah, Mordecai, 12
Nolen, Janet, 92
North Dakota, 201–202, 208
Northeast 3–4, 74. *See also* specific states
Norwegians, 121
Novak, Michael, 35–36, 60

Odencrantz, Louise C., 91
Ohio, 201–202, 208
   Cincinnati, 127–128
   Cleveland, 98, 127
oil industry, 161–165, 161–171
Olneck, Michael, 242
Olson, James, 131, 242
Oregon, 5, 18, 20, 202